WORLD CONTRASTS

Brian Nixon

Bell & Hyman

Acknowledgements

The author and publisher would like to thank the following for permission to use photographs and illustrations.
Aerophoto Schiphol B.V. 6.51
Aerofilms 3.2, 4.81, 4.91, 6.31, 6.68 (Deane Dickason from Ewing Galloway, NY)
Airviews page 182
Aerocamera—Bart Hofmeester 4.87, 7.13, 7.14
J.Allan Cash 3.27, 3.31, 3.41, 4.21, page 74, page 137, 6.12, 6.14, 6.20, 6.24, 6.69, page 197, page 204, 7.28
Art Directors Photo Library 6.67
Axel Poignant 4.8
Barnaby's Picture Library 4.77
British Alcan 6.47
Camera Press 3.25, 3.28 (Sunil K. Dutt), page 49, 6.78
Camerapix-Hutchison 4.12
Canadian Department of Energy, Mines and Resources 4.49
CEGB 5.27
Earthscan 4.31, 4.78 (Peter Charlesworth)
Financial Times 5.16, 6.37
Richard and Sally Greenhill 4.65
Tom Hanley 6.75
Hoa-Qui 3.10
Information Canada Phototheque 4.50 (G. Hunter 1965)
Inter Nationes 5.7
Jamaica Information Service 6.44 (Garth Morgan)
Japan Information Centre, London 6.56
Journal of Geography 4.85
Massey Ferguson Training Centre page 51
Nippon Steel Corporation 6.40
Brian Nixon 5.6
Novosti Press 4.60, 6.8
Oxfam 4.13, 4.49 (Jeremy Hartley), 4.27, 5.36, 6.12
Royal Danish Ministry for Foreign Affairs 4.56 (© Sven Thoby)
Rubber Research Institute, Malaysia page 70, 4.38
Edward Talbot 7.5
Thai Airport Authorities 7.15
Travel Photo International 7.24
UK Atomic Energy Authority 5.31
USDA—Soil Conservation Service 4.92

First published in 1986 by
BELL & HYMAN
An imprint of Unwin Hyman Limited
Denmark House
37–39 Queen Elizabeth Street
London SE1 2QB

Reprinted 1987

© Brian Nixon 1986

British Library Cataloguing in Publication Data
Nixon, Brian
  World contrasts.
  1. Geography, Economic
  I. Title
  330.9   HF1025
ISBN 0-7135-2653-X

Cover photograph: Richard and Sally Greenhill
Cover design: Snap Graphics, London

Typeset, printed and bound in Great Britain by
The Alden Press, Oxford

Contents

Case studies

Preface

This book is designed to be used by students taking the new GCSE examinations.

In its organisation the book is thematic and great emphasis is placed on the contrasting patterns of land use, industry, trade and economic activity which have resulted from decades of rapid change. Particular attention is paid to one of the main themes in GCSE – the contrast between developed and less developed countries – and the importance of the links between the two is stressed, as is the fragility of some of those links. Whenever possible the dangers of using Developed World models as the basis for change in the Developing World is pointed out and attention is drawn to the appropriateness of the technologies used when this transfer takes place.

Most GCSE examining groups will expect teachers to select case studies to support their consideration of themes stated in the syllabus. With this in mind, a large number of case studies have been included in the book. Often several related studies are presented so that teachers can select examples which are most relevant to their needs. Furthermore, many of the case studies are extremely detailed with much of the information grouped and presented in visual form. This is to allow the material to be used in a variety of ways. Such flexibility will be necessary given the more complex methods of assessment suggested for GCSE. Exercises are also included, which will help develop basic geographical skills such as the interpretation of maps and diagrams, the analysis of statistics and the use of simple models as an aid to understanding the often overwhelming complexity of the real world.

1 A world of contrasts: an introduction

We live in a world of great contrasts – contrasts in landforms, contrasts in climate, and contrasts in development which to some extent reflect the physical differences.

Physical differences

The contrasts in relief (Fig. 1.1) are striking and in some cases they strongly influence the pattern of development. On high mountains the combination of steep slopes and altitude greatly restricts settlement and development. Such areas make up 15% of the earth's land surface. Elsewhere the effects of relief tend to be more localised – steep slopes may be a problem even in fairly low lying areas.

Of much greater significance, at least in terms of the area affected, are the climatic factors (Fig. 1.2) which restrict development. Two factors are particularly important:

1 In Antarctica and on the northern coasts of Europe, Asia and North America, development is severely restricted by low temperatures. If the high mountains of the tropics and the temperate latitudes are included, this area makes up about 15% of the earth's land surface.

2 An even greater area (23% of the land surface) is affected by lack of rainfall. These desert areas are widely scattered from the tropics to the poles.

Other climatic influences such as extreme heat or humidity are less important but they may have contributed to the low levels of development in equatorial regions.

Population

One indication of the extent of man's development of an area is the number of people living in that area. The map of population density (Fig. 1.3) shows the influence of negative factors such as high altitude, low temperatures and low rainfall (see Fig. 1.2). There is a striking concentration of population in the lowlands of the temperate latitudes (excluding the dry continental interiors) and in the tropics where parts of the highlands can also be settled.

Although population density is an indicator of the extent of development, it gives no indication of the *nature* of that development. This displays enormous contrasts – contrasts which are the result of the interaction of many and varied influences.

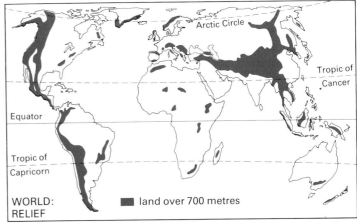

Fig. 1.1

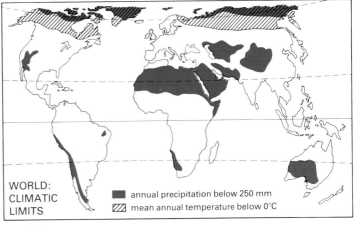

Fig. 1.2

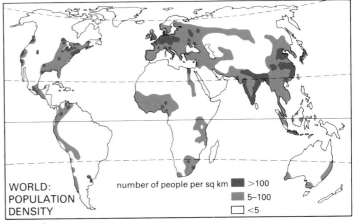

Fig. 1.3

Communism and the 'Free World'

In 1917 the first Communist government was established in Russia. Today there are more than 20 Communist states occupying 20% of the earth's land surface (Fig. 1.4) and the number is increasing. Politically and militarily these countries are opposed by alliances such as NATO (North Atlantic Treaty Organisation) drawn from the 'Free World' or the 'Western Democracies'. In terms of development, however, it is mainly the economic differences which are important. In Communist countries, markets for produce are generally controlled by the state and capital for investment in new economic activity is obtained from the state. In the Free World government controls are less strict but they do exist and are being extended for the formation of large economic groupings such as the European Economic Community (EEC).

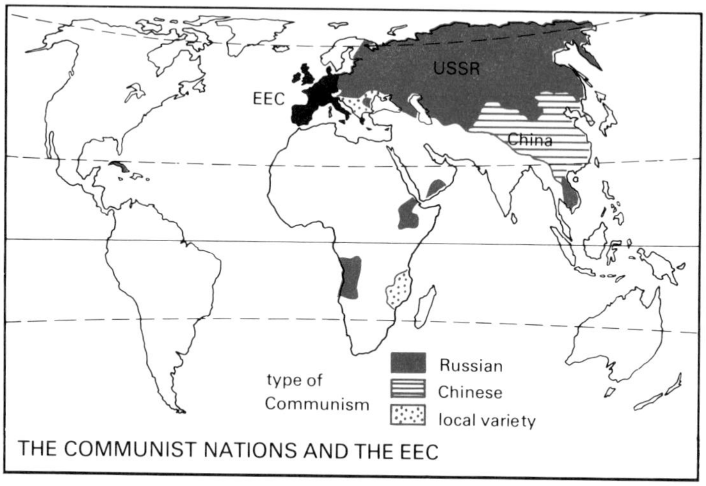

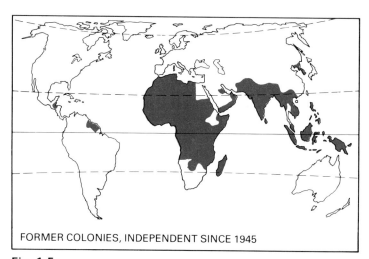

THE COMMUNIST NATIONS AND THE EEC

Fig. 1.4

The Colonial World

From the sixteenth century onwards people from European countries settled in lands far away from their homelands. The areas which they settled became colonies (Fig. 1.5) and the European settlers, who were often few in numbers, governed the native population and controlled the economic development of the new land. The mother countries benefited because the colonies produced cheap raw materials and provided a market for manufactured goods. Today almost all of these colonies are independent but many have gained independence only recently and the pattern of development strongly reflects their colonial past.

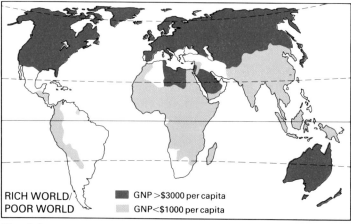

FORMER COLONIES, INDEPENDENT SINCE 1945

Fig. 1.5

Rich World/Poor World

Perhaps the most important contrast in the world today is that between the rich countries and the poor (Fig. 1.6). The rich countries include parts of North America, Europe and the USSR, Australasia and the oil producing countries of the Middle East.

The poor countries include parts of Central and South America, Africa and South East Asia. Here in many cases the share of the Gross National Product (GNP) per person is less than one tenth that in the richest countries. (GNP = the total value of all goods and services produced by a country in a given year.)

The contrast between rich and poor is made even greater by the fact that many of the poorest countries have been forced to borrow money from the rich countries. As a result they are now heavily

Fig. 1.6

in debt (Fig. 1.7), often with little prospect of paying even the interest on the money they have borrowed.

The economies of the poor countries are often weakened because they depend greatly upon one or two products (usually minerals or other raw materials) to earn money from trade with other countries (Fig. 1.8). They are, therefore, seriously affected if the price of those commodities fails to keep pace with the price of other goods. This has become very noticeable since 1973 when the price of oil began to increase rapidly. This has had serious consequences for the poor countries of the world.

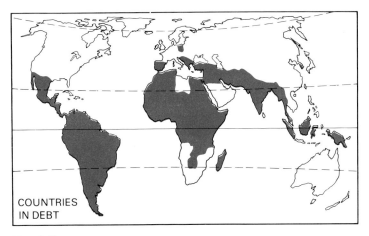

Fig. 1.7

A hungry world

It is estimated that 500 million people in the world today have an inadequate diet. In many countries the total amount of food eaten (measured in calories per day) falls below the level needed to maintain a healthy body (Fig. 1.9). In many more countries the diet is unbalanced, usually as a result of the lack of sufficient protein. Together this produces serious malnutrition and increased death rates, particularly among young children. It is, of course, the poor countries which make up this hungry world. Few of these countries have the resources to improve the situation – in spite of the fact that food production has generally increased threefold since 1945.

This increase in food production has been matched by an equally rapid increase in population. In most of the poor countries of the world population is increasing by more than 2% each year, compared with an increase of less than 1% among the rich countries. Such a difference may appear to be slight but it is perhaps the most significant difference in the world today – it underlies so many of the contrasts in development in the world.

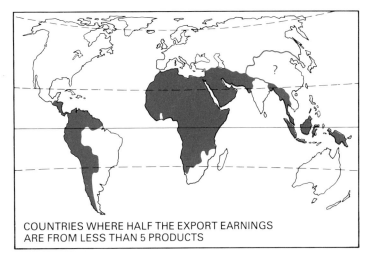

COUNTRIES WHERE HALF THE EXPORT EARNINGS ARE FROM LESS THAN 5 PRODUCTS

Fig. 1.8

The Developed and the Developing World

The divide between developed and developing countries is very important. It is a division which is referred to in a variety of ways:

1   the Developed World and the Developing World

2   the developed countries and the less developed countries

3   North and South

4   the Industrialised World and the Third World

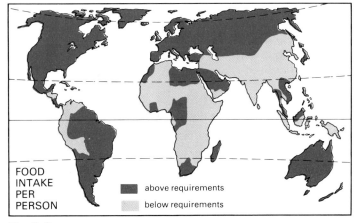

FOOD INTAKE PER PERSON

■ above requirements

▨ below requirements

Fig. 1.9

Whatever the terms used it is a division based on a number of indicators – the so called 'indices of development'. These include:

1   Wealth – developing countries are usually poorer than developed countries.

2   Resources – the less developed countries often lack basic resources, including food.

3   Population increase – less developed countries tend to have higher rates of population increase than developed countries (Fig. 1.10). As a result scarce resources are spread even more thinly among the people. This is reflected in higher levels of malnutrition and higher death rates.

4   Industrial development – less developed countries are generally much less heavily industrialised than developed countries. This is reflected in much lower levels of employment in industry, and a much greater dependence on employment in agriculture (Fig. 1.11).

5   Formal education – throughout the Developing World, levels of schooling (and in particular secondary schooling) are low. In Africa and most of South East Asia more than half of the adult population is unable to read or write (Fig. 1.12). This can slow down the rate of change. It may often hinder attempts to introduce industries and farming methods from the developed countries.

Using indicators such as these it is possible to make the divide between the Developed and the Developing Worlds. At the same time it is important to remember that these indicators have usually been devised in countries in the Developed World. As a result, there is a danger that the achievements of many less developed countries will not be recognised.

Obviously the division between the Developed and the Developing World (Fig. 1.13) is very striking, but it is far from complete. There are, for example, a number of countries, notably the oil producing countries, which are comparatively wealthy but which share many of the characteristics of the less developed countries. It is the study of the main features of this divide which occupies the remainder of this book.

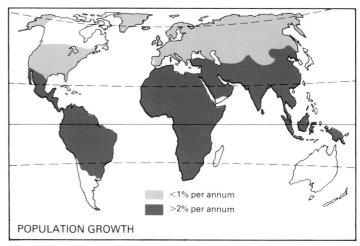

POPULATION GROWTH

<1% per annum
>2% per annum

Fig. 1.10

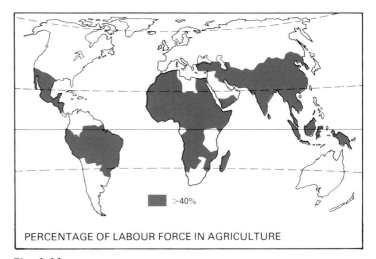

PERCENTAGE OF LABOUR FORCE IN AGRICULTURE

>40%

Fig. 1.11

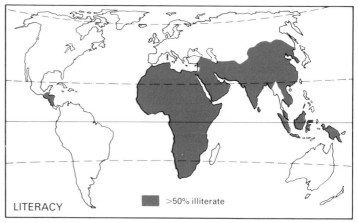

LITERACY

>50% illiterate

Fig. 1.12

	Developed countries	Less developed countries
1 Rate of population growth	LOW	HIGH
2 GNP (per head)	HIGH	LOW
3 Dependence upon raw materials for export earnings	LOW	HIGH
4 Dependence upon a small number of products	LOW	HIGH
5 Proportion of labour force employed in agriculture	LOW	HIGH
6 Levels of education	HIGH	LOW

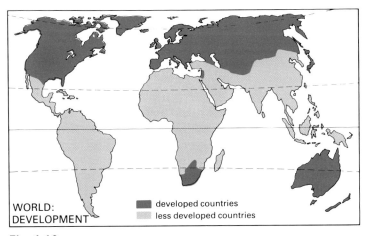

WORLD: DEVELOPMENT

Fig. 1.13

developed countries
less developed countries

Using information given in this chapter, complete the following exercise.

a i Make three lists under the following headings: developed countries; less developed countries; doubtful.
  ii Place each country in the above table under one of these headings.
b Study the three lists:
  i Describe the characteristics shared by the developed countries.
  ii Describe the characteristics shared by the less developed countries.
c Several countries are difficult to place in either of these categories.
  i What is the major difference between these countries and the less developed countries?
  ii How do they differ from the developed countries?

	Birth rate (per thousand)	Death rate (per thousand)	Life expectancy (years)	Infant mortality (per thousand live births)	Daily food intake* (kilocalories per person)	Energy consumption (KG of coal equivalent per person)	% of labour force in agriculture	Urban population (%)	% of adult population illiterate	Gross National Product ($ per capita)
Gambia	48	23	42	204	2261	121	78	18	80	370
Nigeria	50	17	49	133	2360	220	52	20	66	870
Brazil	30	8	64	75	2533	57	37	67	22	2220
Mexico	36	7	66	54	2796	1687	35	66	17	2250
USA	16	9	74	12	3670	10204	2	73	<1	12820
Peru	36	11	58	85	2185	595	39	65	27	1170
Bangladesh	47	18	47	135	1944	46	83	10	74	140
China	21	8	67	71	2500	578	59	13	15	300
India	35	13	52	121	1900	199	62	22	66	260
Japan	13	6	77	7	2900	3575	10	76	<1	10080
Saudi Arabia	45	13	55	111	2904	1680	60	25	75	12600
Spain	14	8	74	10	3345	2397	16	64	7	5640
Sweden	11	11	77	7	3201	5156	5	82	<1	14870
UK	13	12	74	11	3326	4651	2	75	<1	9110
USSR	19	10	72	28	3379	5738	16	63	<1	4750

* World average=2617

Some indices of development   (Note: These figures change over time and individual countries may change their status)

2 Population

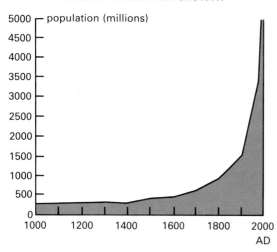

WORLD POPULATION GROWTH

Note: There has never been a census of the entire human population, therefore recent figures are no more than estimates and earlier figures are little more than informed guesses. This applies equally to the birth rates and death rates shown below.

Fig. 2.1 (a)

In a single decade the population of the world has increased by over 700 million. Within 500 years there could be one person for every square metre of the earth's surface. In little more than 1000 years the human population could weigh more than the earth itself. Both of these events would happen if the present rate of growth were to continue; neither will happen, because production of food and other natural resources could not possibly keep pace with such an increase, and a combination of famine and disease would eventually halt growth.

Are the alternatives quite so drastic? There is some evidence to suggest that they are not. Certainly rapid population growth is a recent development. For most of human history the population of the world grew at a very slow rate. This long period of stability came to an end only 300 years ago but since then the population has doubled twice to reach the present level of some 4000 million (Fig. 2.1). Is it possible, therefore, that there could be an equally dramatic change back to the earlier low growth rates? The evidence in some countries is that there could be, although it is not likely that the change would be rapid enough to prevent the world population doubling yet again – and this time within the space of 35 years! It is this prospect which is so astonishing and which makes it so important to understand the causes of the so called 'population explosion.'

Causes of the population explosion

World population increases when the number of births is greater than the number of deaths over a given period. The rate at which the population increases (the annual growth rate) is simply the difference between the annual birth rate and the annual death rate. Since the world population growth rate has obviously increased dramatically in recent years this suggests that the difference between the birth rate and death rate has increased. How and why this has happened is difficult to establish, largely because reliable statistics are so rarely available. One widely accepted theory is illustrated in Fig. 2.2.

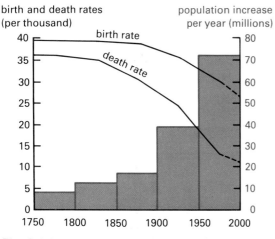

Fig. 2.1 (b)

Study the information given in Figs 2.1 and 2.2 and complete the following exercise.

a Describe the general trend of (i) the birth rate (ii) the death rate.
b Three distinct stages are shown in the diagram in Fig. 2.2. Describe the main characteristics of the birth rate and death rate in each of these periods.

THE DEMOGRAPHIC TRANSITION

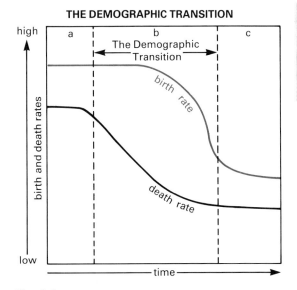

Fig. 2.2

FALLING DEATH RATE	FALLING BIRTH RATE
caused by:	caused by:
	decisions of parents to limit the size of the family
1 improved public health	
	encouraged by:
2 improved hygiene	1 more children surviving
	2 less need for child labour (particularly on the land)
3 improved diet	3 extension of schooling
	4 laws to control the employment of children
4 medical advances	
	together, 3 and 4 meant that parents had less to gain from having children
	5 old age pensions
	6 increased mobility of the population
	together, 5 and 6 meant that few old people were dependent upon their children
	helped by:
	recent medical advances eg contraception

According to this theory:

1   All countries start with high birth rates and high death rates. As a result population growth is generally slow.

2   Then the death rate begins to fall and within a short time this decline becomes rapid. In most areas it is obviously linked with improvements in the treatment of disease; improvements in public health, particularly in water supply and sewage disposal; more regular food production; and improved methods of transport which can be used to offset the effects of natural disasters such as famine.

3   The birth rate remains high and this, associated with the declining death rate, results in a rapid increase in population.

4   In some countries the birth rate begins to fall. The decline is slower than in the case of the death rate. The causes of the change are more difficult to understand as they depend on the decision of individual parents to limit the size of the family.

5   Eventually, however, the fall in the birth rate will match that already seen in the death rate. Then most areas will have low birth rates and low death rates and population growth will again be comparatively slow.

So far few countries have passed through all of these stages. As a result, the contrasts seen in different parts of the world are quite considerable.

Contrasting patterns of growth

The birth rate in Togo exceeds 50/1000; in Japan it is little more than 10/1000. The death rate in Guinea approaches 40/1000; in Sweden it is no more than 8/1000.

These figures alone are sufficient to give some indication of the scale of the contrasts which are to be found. However, as we have seen, population growth is the product of the relationship between birth and death rates, and a true impression can be obtained only by examining both together. This can be done most easily by plotting the rates for a number of countries on a simple scattergraph (Fig. 2.3).

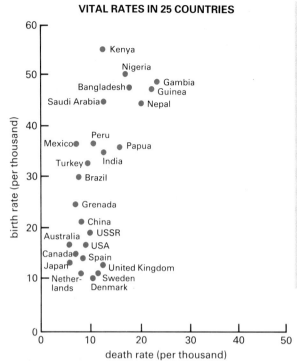

VITAL RATES IN 25 COUNTRIES

birth rate (per thousand) / death rate (per thousand)

Fig. 2.3

b   Which of these three groups is:
  i   likely to have the highest rate of increase?
  ii likely to have the lowest rate of increase?
  iii most obviously in the 'demographic transition'?
c   Nine countries can be easily distinguished from the rest.
  i   Draw a line around this group.
  ii Identify the main difference between these countries and the rest.
d   Using the table on page 11 draw your own scattergraphs to show the relationship between:
  i   birth rate and Gross National Product (GNP).
  ii death rate and GNP.
  iii infant mortality and GNP.
e i   Is a strong relationship apparent in any of these graphs? (This can be seen by drawing a straight line through the cluster of points so that the mean distance of the points from the line is as short as possible. If most points are near to the line the relationship is strong. If not it is weak.)
  ii If there is any relationship describe it.

These statistics suggest that population growth is closely linked to wealth. Rich countries tend to have low birth rates, low death rates and low population growth rates. Poor countries generally have rapidly rising populations.

In short, population growth is at the heart of the most important division in the world today – the divide between rich and poor; between developed and developing nations; between the Industrialised World and the Third World; between North and South. To understand these differences it is best to examine the situation in two contrasting countries – Sweden and India.

Population growth in India

India is one of the poorest countries in the world and industrial development is still in its infancy. For the past 50 years population growth has been extremely rapid and the population has more than trebled (Fig. 2.4(a)). Even more important, numbers have doubled in the last 20 years to reach the present level of 800 million and, if this trend continues, they will double again within the next 20 years.

This represents a true 'population explosion'. It was triggered by a rapid fall in the death rate which first became apparent during the 1920s (Fig. 2.4(b)). It is the speed with which the death rate fell which is most surprising – from 46/1000 in 1921 to less than one third of that figure today. Modern techniques in controlling and treating diseases such as malaria have played a part in this and the results have been dramatic. Today the same thing is happening in many other developing countries with similar consequences.

During the same period, however, there was virtually no change in the birth rate and it is this combination which has produced the present rise in population. It has also given rise to an age structure which is typical of all developing countries:

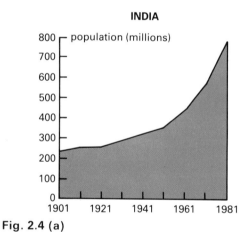

INDIA

population (millions)

Fig. 2.4 (a)

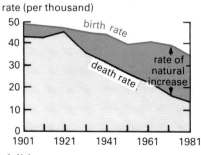

rate (per thousand)

birth rate
death rate
rate of natural increase

Fig. 2.4 (b)

14

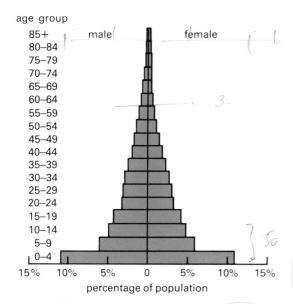

age group

Fig. 2.4 (c)

1 A large proportion of the population is under the age of five.

2 Deaths among children are frequent and the infant mortality rate is very high.

3 Half the population is under the age of 20.

4 Life expectancy is low.

This age structure (Fig. 2.4(c)) will have an important effect on future population growth. The presence of so many young people in the population means that a large proportion of women will be of child bearing age. In such circumstances it is hardly surprising that attempts by the government to introduce family planning have had little effect on the birth rate. Most families still tend to be large because parents regard children both as a source of labour and as an 'insurance policy' for the time when they can no longer work.

Population growth in Sweden

The situation in the Developed World is strikingly different. Sweden is one of the richest and most highly developed countries in the world. The population has been remarkably stable for more than 100 years and during that time the annual growth rate has rarely been higher than 1% (Fig. 2.5(a)). In fact recent figures suggest that the population may have started to fall.

This situation is the result of a death rate which has been declining for at least 200 years and a birth rate which began to fall rapidly at the beginning of the twentieth century (Fig. 2.5(b)). It is clear from these trends that Sweden's population explosion took place during the nineteenth century and that its effects were much less dramatic than those seen in India today. This is not really surprising since modern medicines and twentieth century technology have caused the death rate to fall at a rate which was never approached during the previous century.

Of greater importance for the poorer countries like India is what has happened to the birth rate. In 1880 the annual birth rate in Sweden was 30/1000, slightly lower than the level in India today. Sixty years later it had fallen to less than 20/1000 and the rate of national increase had once again become very low. These trends were also accompanied by an increasing life expectancy and this produced an age structure which is quite different from that seen in India. Instead of a clear pyramid, the graph (Fig. 2.5(c)) is almost straight sided up to the age of 65 when a pyramid shape at last appears. The proportion of old people in the population is obviously very large and is likely to increase further if the present low birth rate continues. The effects of this can be seen in the small size of the under five age group – the age group which dominates the population graph of India.

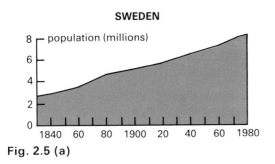

Fig. 2.5 (a)

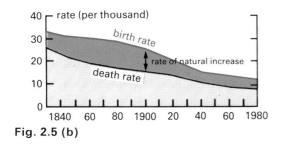

Fig. 2.5 (b)

Using information given in this section, complete the following exercise.

a Describe the main differences between Sweden and India in terms of (i) population growth (ii) trends in birth and death rates (iii) the age structure of the population.

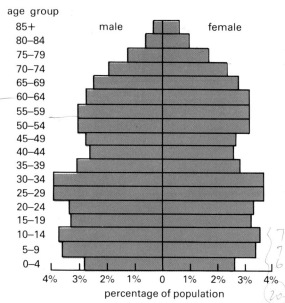

age group

male | female

85+
80–84
75–79
70–74
65–69
60–64
55–59
50–54
45–49
40–44
35–39
30–34
25–29
20–24
15–19
10–14
5–9
0–4

4% 3% 2% 1% 0 1% 2% 3% 4%
percentage of population

Note: the horizontal scale on this diagram differs from that used for the diagram showing the age structure of the population in India

Fig. 2.5 (c)

b Locate each country on the graph on page 13 which provides a model for population growth. Give reasons for your choice of position.
c Guinea is a country with a high birth rate and a high death rate.
  i   Where would you locate Guinea on the model?
  ii How does it differ from Sweden and India at a similar stage of development?
  iii According to the model what will happen to the population of Guinea in the future?

Sweden is obviously a country which has passed through the demographic transition and the most important question is whether developing countries like India will follow the same pattern. If they do the world population explosion could be halted. This can only happen if there is a dramatic fall in the birth rate. As we have seen, the reasons for changes in birth rate seem to be very complex and it is not certain that government attempts to encourage birth control and family planning in developing countries will have the desired effect. Indeed the birth rate in Sweden began to fall long before ideas about population control had been developed and the reasons for the fall included:

1   Infant mortality was reduced, more children survived and there was less obvious need for large families.

2   As industrial development gathered pace more families left the land and children were no longer needed to work the farm. This was accompanied by the introduction of compulsory schooling which meant that children could no longer work elsewhere.

3   The introduction of pensions meant that parents no longer needed children to look after them in old age.

Changes such as these take time, however, and it is quite clear that rapid population growth is likely to continue for some time in the developing countries and that the effects will be dramatic.

Some consequences of the population explosion

The changing balance between the Developed and Developing World

The population explosion is taking place only in developing countries which are still in the demographic transition. As a result population growth in these countries has been much more rapid than in the Developed World. This has reversed a trend which started when modern industry began in Europe.

At that time (about 1750) one quarter of the world's population lived in the countries which are now developed. Within 100 years, however, this balance had changed dramatically and by the end of the nineteenth century this proportion had

WORLD POPULATION: ANNUAL INCREASE (MILLIONS)

Year	Developed countries	Less developed countries	World
1750	0.9	2.8	3.7
1800	2.0	3.7	5.7
1850	4.5	3.2	7.7
1900	5.7	11.4	17.1
1950	10.2	67.8	78.0
1980	9.9	65.4	76.7
1950–2000 (est.)	8.6	97.5	106.1

ESTIMATED POPULATION GROWTH IN VARIOUS REGIONS OF THE WORLD

	Europe	SW Asia	India	China	Japan	SE Asia + Oceania	Africa	N&S America
1700	115	31	100	205	27	24	90	10
1750	140	32	130	270	32	28	90	11
1800	188	33	157	345	28	32	90	29
1850	266	34	190	430	33	37	95	59
1900	401	35	290	430	44	71	120	144
1950	548	74	439	503	82	158	198	321
1980	710	98	717	1027	117	364	470	612

risen to one third. This was the result of a rapidly falling death rate which produced a high rate of natural increase in these countries. There was little change in the balance until 1950 although it is obvious that many of the less developed countries were already entering the demographic transition.

Since 1950 the picture has changed out of all recognition and the population of the less developed countries has grown at a rate which is almost seven times greater than that of the developed countries. This means that, if present trends continue, the year 2000 will see an increase in the world population of more than 100 million. Of this increase, only eight million will live in the Developed World.

The effect of these changes on the world population map has been considerable (Fig. 2.6).

Compare the map, Fig. 2.6, with an atlas map of the world (a map based on equal area projection would be most suitable).

a   i   Name two continents which are larger on the population map.
    ii   Name two continents which are smaller on the population map.

WORLD POPULATION DISTRIBUTION: 1950 and 1983

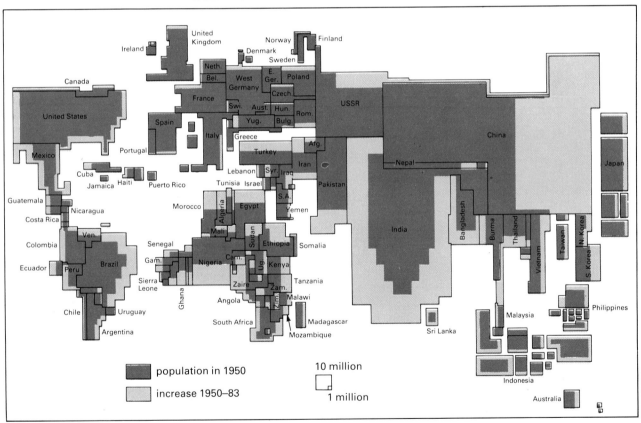

The darker shading shows the population in 1950, the lighter represents the increase between 1950 and 1980. This allows each region to be given an area proportional to the size of its population while retaining its familiar shape.

Fig. 2.6

WORLD POPULATION: BIRTH RATE/DEATH RATE AND NATURAL INCREASE (%)

Year	Developed countries	Less developed countries	Natural incr. DC	LDC
1750	38/34	41/37	4	4
1800	39/32	41/36	7	5
1850	37/27	41/36	10	5
1900	34/21	41/34	13	7
1950	23/10	41/21	13	20
1980	14/ 9	33/12	5	21

38/34 = birth rate 38/1000, death rate 34/1000
DC = developed countries   LDC = less developed countries

WORLD POPULATION (MILLIONS)

Year	Developed countries	Less developed countries	Total
1750	201 (25.4%)	590 (74.6%)	791
1800	248 (25.4%)	730 (74.6%)	978
1850	347 (27.5%)	915 (72.5%)	1262
1900	573 (34.7%)	1077 (65.3%)	1650
1950	858 (34.1%)	1658 (65.9%)	2516
1980	1131 (25.5%)	3301 (74.5%)	4432
2000 (est.)	1442 (23.5%)	4688 (76.5%)	6130

	Population density		GNP ($ per capita)	Food intake per capita (cals per day)
	1950	1982		
Australia	1	2	11080	3202
Brazil	6	15	2220	2517
China	48	106	300	2472
Gambia	24	56	370	2250
India	109	216	260	1998
Japan	223	318	10080	2883
Mexico	12	37	2250	2803
Nigeria	26	89	870	2337
Turkey	27	59	1340	2965
United Kingdom	206	228	9110	3315
USA	19	24	12820	3652
USSR	8	12	—	3389

b i Name two countries which are larger on the population map.
  ii Name two countries which are smaller.
c The table on page 17 gives the population of different countries and continents at various times.
  i In which areas was population concentrated in 1700?
  ii Name two areas which had small populations in 1700.
  iii How had this pattern of population distribution changed by 1980?
  iv Which areas experienced the most rapid rate of growth during the period 1700–1980?
d Population density is the number of people living in a standard area (usually one square kilometre).
  i Name three countries (choosing no more than one from each continent) which have high population densities.
  ii Name three countries which have low population densities.
  iii Explain how this can be deduced from the maps which you are using.

The concentration of population in Europe and South East Asia is quite clear, as is the high growth rate in areas like Latin America and parts of Africa. It is also obvious that population densities vary enormously and that while some countries appear to be bursting at the seams others are virtually empty. If variations in population density within countries are taken into account, the population problem in certain areas may be approaching crisis point.

Overpopulation

Expressed simply, this means that the population of an area is too large to be supported by the resources available and it results in a serious lowering of living standards among the people living there. Unfortunately it is not easy to establish when or where this is taking place. Population density alone cannot be taken as a guide. For example, the Netherlands with a population density of 349 per square kilometre would not generally be regarded as overpopulated, whereas Guinea (population density just over 20 per square kilometre) might come under consideration. The reasons for this are related to the natural resources available to support the population.

In a society with a relatively simple organisation the most important requirements will be food and shelter. These will usually be obtained from the fairly small area of land available to the individual family or tribe. As the population increases so more and more resources are taken from the land until a point is reached when the number of people outstrips the ability of the land to support them. Living standards will begin to fall and finally famine and disease will reduce the population to a level which can be supported.

In more advanced countries such as the Netherlands the situation is very different. Improved farming methods meant that for a long time food production could keep pace with population growth and, when this was no longer possible, food could be imported from other parts of the world. This was paid for using currency earned by the industries which had grown up in the country. As a result, the resources available to each person in the Netherlands and other developed countries continued to increase even when the population was growing rapidly.

This is perhaps the best way of identifying the problem. Overpopulation most clearly exists when the increase in numbers leads to a drastic lowering of living standards in the country concerned.

Food supply problems

It is the balance between population growth and food supply which is most important. For the past 20 years population growth, particularly in developing countries, has been rapid and severe food shortages might have been expected. In fact food production has more than kept pace with the increasing population and the average amount of food available to each person on the earth's surface has, if anything, increased. However, it has been the Developed World which has benifited most from this increased production and there has been little or no improvement in developing countries (Fig. 2.7). As a result it is in these countries that serious problems have arisen, including a number of major famines (Fig. 2.8).

POPULATION AND FOOD PRODUCTION

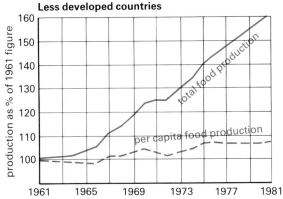

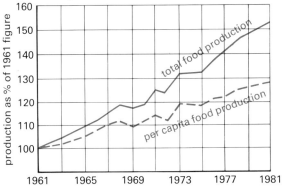

Fig. 2.7

Using information given in Figs 2.7 and 2.8, complete the following exercise.

a i What has been the percentage increase in world food production since 1961?
 ii What has been the percentage increase in per capita food production in the Developed World?
 iii What is the comparable figure for the Developing World?
b The map (Fig. 2.8) shows some of the major famines which have taken place in recent years.
 i Name three countries which have experienced famine but which have generally adequate food supplies (see Fig. 1.9).
 ii A major cause of famine has been drought in the areas bordering the Sahara Desert. Name four countries involved.
c In which general areas are the major famines located?

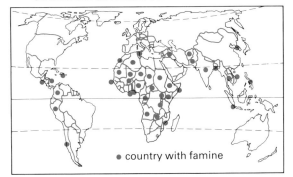

Fig. 2.8

The concentration of famine in developing countries in Africa, South East Asia and Latin America is very clear. These are all areas which have experienced very rapid population growth in recent years and in which food supplies are generally inadequate. But the relationship is not a simple one, and famine has often been the result of a dramatic change in circumstances. In countries like Vietnam and Kampuchea the change was the result of war while for the countries on the margins of the Sahara Desert it was climatic change and widespread drought which triggered a reduction in food production. In these circumstances help cannot always reach the areas concerned in time and many people die. More often, however, food can be brought into countries threatened by famine and the worst effects can be avoided. When famines occur it is often difficulty of distributing food which is the greatest problem rather than any general shortage of food.

However, the very fact that famines still occur suggests that the traditional checks to population growth are still important and that modern science has not yet freed the world from the threat of famine, war and disease.

MAIN MIGRATION ROUTES: 1850–1920

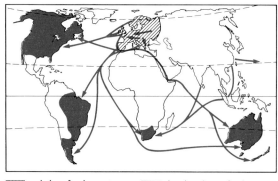

▨ origin of migrants   ■ destination of migrants

Fig. 2.9

Migration: a safety valve

Most of today's developed countries passed through the demographic transition during the nineteenth and early twentieth centuries and the problems experienced were very different from those seen today. In the first place the scale of the problem was much smaller. Populations in all parts of the world were generally low and, as we have seen in Sweden, the lowering of death rates produced a very small population explosion compared with that taking place in developing countries today. Not only this, in the nineteenth century there was a safety valve which is no longer available. At that time large areas of the world were developed and virtually unpopulated. These 'empty lands' – in the Americas, Australasia and Africa – could be settled by people from Europe. Within the space of 100 years it is estimated that no fewer than 30 million people crossed the Atlantic to North America alone (Fig. 2.9).

Why did so many people risk so much to leave their homes? It is tempting to believe that they were driven out by hardship, famine and war, and in certain countries such as Ireland this may have been true. In most cases, however, the emigrants chose to leave countries where industrial development was giving rise to improved living standards, and it must be that they moved because they hoped for a better life in a new country.

The causes of migration are complicated and the effects on the populations of the countries concerned are very striking. The effects of large scale *emigration* can be seen most clearly in the case of Ireland. Here the combination of general poverty and the failure of successive potato crops during the 1840s produced widespread famine which in time triggered off mass emigration to parts of Britain and North America. As a result the population actually began to fall (Fig. 2.10) and has never since regained the levels seen before emigration started. This slow rate of recovery is a result of the fact that it was the young adults who tended to emigrate and these were the people most likely to produce children. Those who remained behind tended to be older and the birth rate among this group was very low. Even with this low birth rate, it is estimated that without emigration the population of Ireland would today be approaching twelve million – four times the present population.

Countries which have experienced large scale *immigration* have very different population structures (Fig. 2.11).

POPULATION OF IRELAND: 1851–1981
(SHOWING THE EFFECTS OF EMIGRATION)

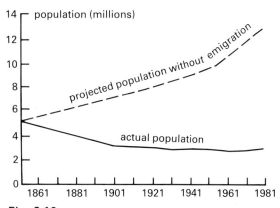

Fig. 2.10

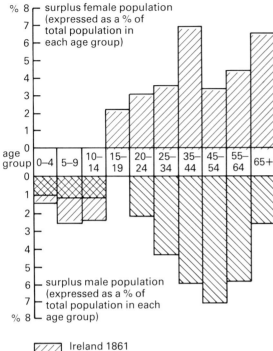

EFFECTS OF MIGRATION ON THE POPULATION OF TWO COUNTRIES

Ireland 1861 (a period of high emigration)

USA 1910 (a period of high immigration)

Fig. 2.11

Refer to Figs 2.10 and 2.11 and complete the following exercise.

a i Describe the differences in age structure between the population of Ireland in 1861 and the USA in 1910.
  ii Explain these differences, paying particular attention to the effects of migration.
b i What was the total population of Ireland in 1981?
  ii What is the population likely to have been if emigration had not taken place?
  iii Why is the difference so large?

Migration is continuing today although its nature has changed considerably. The main differences are given in the following table:

Nineteenth century migration	Recent migration
1 Usually a voluntary movement. 2 Main cause was the poor living standards in the countries of origin and better prospects abroad. 3 Main area of origin was Europe where falling death rates had caused a rapid increase in population. 4 Main destinations were to 'empty lands' in America and Australasia.	Two different types: 1 Voluntary migration a Causes similar to those in the nineteenth century. b Countries of origin are often the developing nations which are experiencing a 'population explosion' c Destinations are the developed countries where the rate of natural increase is now low and where until recently there was a demand for labour. 2 Forced migration, particularly following wars. This has become much more important and in some areas the refugee problem is very serious.

MAIN MIGRATION ROUTES: SINCE 1945

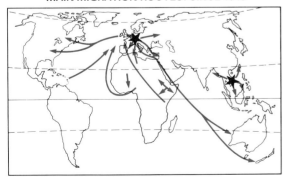

✦ caused by major wars

Fig. 2.12

The overall result of such changes is that the main movements in recent years have been from the developing countries to developed areas where work was available (Fig. 2.12). But these areas were already densely populated and the presence of large numbers of immigrants, many of them of a different race, has caused serious problems. As a result, in most of the developed countries immigration is now strictly controlled.

Although international migration (the movement of people between countries) is less important today, large scale movements are still taking place within countries. This is most clearly seen in the movement of people away from the countryside and the rapid growth of cities, particularly in less developed countries; and, in developed countries in the flight of people away from the cities to suburbs and to commuter settlements (see pages 42 and 43).

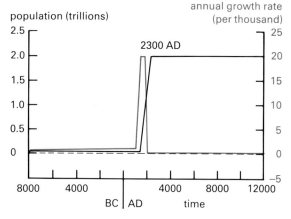

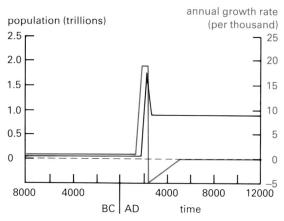

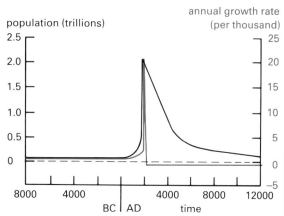

Fig. 2.13

Population growth in the future

The effects of the present population explosion are to be seen in every aspect of world geography. If it continues and the population does indeed double once again by the end of the century those effects will be even more striking. They may include:

1 The breakdown of traditional agricultural systems in a desperate attempt to increase food production.

2 The uncontrolled spread of industry in developing countries.

3 The unrestricted growth of cities.

4 The exhaustion of the natural resources needed to support the population.

5 The destruction of remaining natural environments, including the tropical rain forest.

6 Widespread soil erosion and environmental pollution.

So far an ever increasing rate of technological change has allowed many parts of the world to keep pace with population growth. In spite of this the effects of population pressure are to be seen almost everywhere. Indeed, for most of the Developing World it seems to have been a case of running desperately simply to stand still.

In the near future the problems are likely to become worse. Whether or not recent trends can be halted will depend on future population growth and this is uncertain.

The diagrams in Fig. 2.13 give three possible predictions of future population growth.

a The graphs indicate that population growth rates (the coloured lines) remained near zero for a long period.
  i Explain why growth rates were so low.
  ii What were the changes which gave rise to the population explosion?

b The graphs suggest that the present population explosion will last for a fairly short time. Why is this prediction likely to be true?

c The graphs suggest that growth rates will return to zero.
  i One graph is based on the immediate control of population growth. Which is it? What would happen to the world population in this case?
  ii One graph predicts disaster. Which is it? What would happen to the world population in this case? What could cause such a disaster?

3 Settlements

The large and rapidly growing population of the world is housed in a vast number of settlements most of which are also growing rapidly and in the process of changing. The present position, function and form of each of these settlements is the result of decisions taken in the past, often under conditions which no longer exist. This makes any understanding of the origin and growth of settlements difficult.

Settlements differ greatly in appearance in different parts of the world. Such differences often simply reflect differences in the building materials available and it is the similarities between settlements which are more important. There are a number of influences at work in all parts of the world. By concentrating on these similarities and on their underlying causes it is possible to describe and explain the most important features of settlements (Fig. 3.1) which may at first seem completely different.

A settlement is a dwelling place made up of one or more houses and other structures such as work places, roads and public open space.

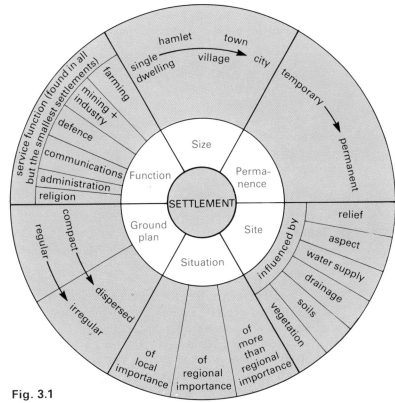

Fig. 3.1

Note: Many of these features change over time.

e.g. 1 Some settlements grow in size, others decline.
2 Early functions may disappear, as in the case of many defensive sites.
3 The original ground plan may be lost in later growth.

A settlement can range in size from a single house to a large city with thousands of houses and places of work. Many large towns and cities have grown to such an extent that they have engulfed smaller settlements which were once completely separate.

Today most settlements in the world are *permanent*, i.e. they are occupied throughout the year and for many years running. In some parts of the world, however, *temporary* settlements are common. These are often associated with comparatively simple methods of farming, e.g. nomadic herdsmen who have to move their stock in search of grazing (see page 55) and shifting cultivators who abandon land when the soil is exhausted (see page 52). In developed countries temporary settlements are rare, although there may be barns and farmsteads in mountainous areas which are occupied only during the summer when high pastures are used. A more recent development has been the building of special holiday resorts which may also be occupied for only part of the year, e.g. ski resorts.

Origins of settlements

Settlements do not grow up by chance. In almost every case the *position* is chosen with specific purposes in mind. At its simplest this might be the growing of food, but in many instances other factors such as defence or communications may be important.

More obviously, the actual *site* chosen for a settlement is strongly influenced by physical factors. The site is the land on which the settlement is built and it is chosen in preference to other possible sites in the surrounding area. Many factors can influence this choice but the most important are:

1 **Relief**
For example, a on gently sloping or level land
           b on a ridge or spur
           c on a hill top
           d on a river terrace above the flood plain.

2 **Climate, soil and vegetation**
For example, a on warmer south facing slopes
           b positions which are sheltered from the wind
           c at high altitudes in the tropics
           d on lowland in colder areas
           e on the margins of forests, deserts, etc.

3 **Water**
For example, a access to water by building near rivers, streams, springs or wells
           b avoiding badly drained land
           c making use of waterways for transport.

The site can also have a strong influence on the *ground plan* of the settlement. In some cases the influence is obvious. Valley sites often produce elongated settlements while on a hill top the buildings tend to cluster around the highest and most easily defended point. In most cases, however, the relationship is more complicated.

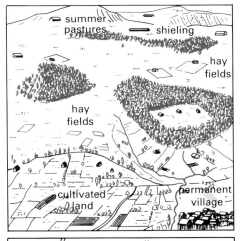

Alpine Village: Vosges Mountains, Alsace

1 Permanent village on lower valley sides
2 Main activity is farming, mainly dairying
3 Flat land near village cultivated or laid down to grass
4 Animals kept here or fed indoors during the winter
5 Animals moved to pastures high up on the mountain side during the summer (transhumance)
6 Small farmsteads built on these pastures since village too far away to allow daily journey (shieling)
7 Small fields used to grow hay on the lower mountain sides. Barns have been built here to store the hay
8 This entire system is breaking down but the village remains

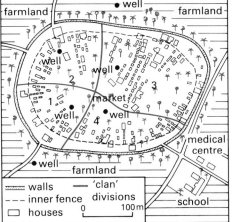

Walled Town: Eastern Nigeria

1 Permanent settlement
2 Population over 3000
3 Water available from shallow wells
4 Walled for defence
5 Compact shape
6 Layout within walls regular
7 Houses in lines
8 Extended family groups live in each compound
9 The entire town is divided into four areas and each area is occupied by a group of related families (a clan)
10 The market is at the centre of the town
11 Building has spread beyond the inner fence and has now extended beyond the walls

Farming village: Ganges Delta, Bangladesh

1 Permanent settlement
2 Each village made up of scattered groups of houses
3 Each group of houses is built on a mound
4 This raises the houses above the level of all but the most severe floods
5 Land is available near to each group of houses
6 The village is small and is of local importance

Fig. 3.2

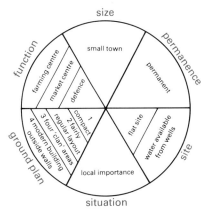

The three settlements shown in Fig. 3.2 are located in very different parts of the world. A summary diagram has been completed for each of the settlements.

Write a description of the ground plan of each of the settlements and of the factors which influenced both the site and form of the settlements.

Growth of settlements

The origin of many individual settlements can often be explained in terms of fairly simple influences such as position or the physical characteristics of the site. More difficult to understand, however, is the pattern of later growth. Why, for example, have some settlements become large while others have grown little or even declined?

To explain this it is necessary to look at the *function* of settlements. As we have seen, all settlements are established with specific purposes in mind – for example, to gain easy access to food and water or to gain protection against possible enemies. After a while some of these settlements gained another important function – they began to supply goods and services to people living in the surrounding area. Some of these settlements were better situated to take advantage of this development than others – for example, settlements located at crossing points on rivers or at the convergence of routeways. It is not therefore surprising that many such settlements have become important service centres and have often grown into large towns and cities.

Settlements vary enormously both in size and in the range of services offered; and there appears to be a definite order or 'hierarchy' of service centres. Many attempts have been made to describe this hierarchy. The simplest are based on population. For example:

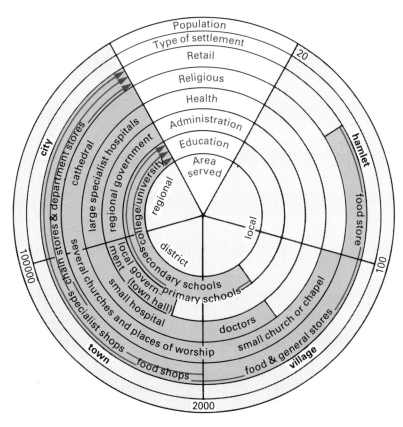

THE HIERARCHY OF SETTLEMENT, ACCORDING TO FUNCTION

Fig. 3.3

RANK SIZE RULE APPLIED TO THE 15 LARGEST CITIES IN THE USA IN 1981

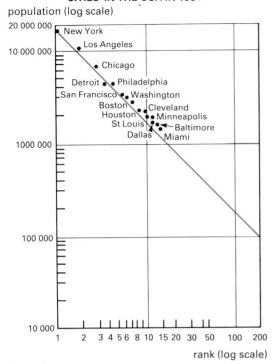

Fig. 3.4

1 As settlements increase in size so they become fewer in number. This is easy to test and the statistics given in Fig. 3.7 confirm this pattern for settlements throughout the world. A similar pattern would emerge for any country or region on the earth's surface.

2 In some parts of the world there seems to be a relationship between the size of the settlements in an area and the size of the largest settlement in that area. This relationship has been expressed in the Rank Size Rule. This states that if the settlements of a region or country are arranged in rank order of size, the second settlement will be half the size of the largest; the third, one third of the size; the fourth, one quarter; the fifth, one fifth; etc.

The graph, Fig. 3.4, illustrates the Rank Size Rule using the fifteen largest cities in the United States in 1980.

a i Describe how the actual rank size distribution differs from the predicted one (the coloured line).

ii On a copy of the graph draw a second line (parallel to the one shown on the graph) which provides a better fit for the actual distribution.

iii With this new line would New York have to be larger or smaller?

b i Using the same axes and scales, plot the figures for the cities of the United States in 1950.

ii Draw the predicted rank size relationship for these figures. To do this, locate the largest or primary city – New York – on the vertical axis. From this point draw a line at an angle of 45° from the axis. This expresses the rank size relationship.

iii How does the pattern of distribution differ from that shown on the previous graph?

c Which of the following statements are supported by evidence contained in the two graphs?

i In 1950 New York was too large when compared with the major cities of the United States.

ii By 1980 this situation had been reversed and New York was too small when compared with the other cities.

iii The primary city (the largest city) was growing less rapidly than the other cities in the United States between 1950 and 1980.

d Either by drawing graphs or by the multiplication method described below, apply the Rank Size Rule to the population statistics for Brazil in 1950 and 1980.

i Describe the distribution pattern in 1980, paying particular attention to the size of the primary city.

ii Has this pattern changed markedly since 1950?

iii Does the relationship more closely resemble that seen in the United States in 1950 or 1980?

iv How has the pattern of growth differed in the two countries between 1950 and 1980?

POPULATION OF MAJOR CITIES IN THE USA AND BRAZIL

USA	1950	BRAZIL	1950	1980
New York	12.3	Sao Paulo	2.4	8.7
Chicago	4.9	Rio de Janeiro	2.8	5.5
Los Angeles	4.0	Recife	0.6	1.4
Philadelphia	2.9	Porto Alegre	0.4	1.2
Detroit	2.7	Salvador	0.39	1.5
Boston	2.2	Belo Horizonte	0.37	1.9
San Francisco	2.0	Fortaleza	0.26	1.3
Pittsburgh	1.5	Santos	0.24	0.45
St Louis	1.4	Belem	0.23	0.93
Cleveland	1.3	Curitiba	0.14	0.94

Note: According to the Rank Size Rule, the population of the second city multiplied by 2 should equal that of the largest or primary city. The population of the third city multiplied by 3 should also equal that of the primary city, etc.

This provides a quick method of applying the rule without drawing the graph.

The application of the Rank Size Rule illustrates an important difference between the developed countries and less developed countries. In less developed countries the primary city often dwarfs the other cities, giving a very poor relationship with the line of prediction. Furthermore, primary cities are also tending to

SETTLEMENT STUDY: ZIMBABWE

Predicted pattern: Christaller's model

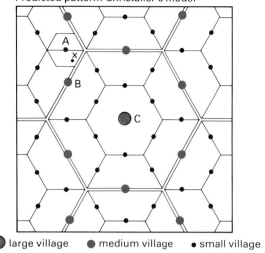

● large village   ● medium village   • small village

Actual pattern: Belingwe, Zimbabwe

0   10   20 km

● large village   ● medium village   • small village

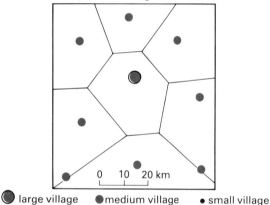

	Size of village		
	Small	Medium	Large
Number of centres	79	16	5
Average number of activities	11	17	18
Number of:			
general dealers	8	9	16
grinding mills	3	3	3
eating houses	2	3	7
butchers	2	2	4
bottle stores	1	1	1
petrol stations	x	1	1
beer halls	x	x	x
carpenters		1	1
greengrocers		1	1
hotels			1
clinics			x
sports fields			x
shoe repairers			x

x = service occurs in more than half the centres of this size

Fig. 3.5

grow at a more rapid rate. In the Developed World, on the other hand, the relationship between the primary city and the smaller cities is usually much closer to that predicted by the Rank Size Rule and the pattern of recent growth (the smaller cities have grown more rapidly than the primary city) has improved the accuracy of prediction.

Size is only one part of the study of settlements and it produces little understanding of any hierarchy which may exist. For this it is necessary to look at the function of settlements as service centres and in particular at the different types of services offered by different settlements (Fig. 3.3).

Generally speaking, the larger the settlement, the greater the range of services provided. For example, in a small village there will be few shops and those which do exist are likely to be general stores selling everyday items such as food. In a town there will be many such shops but, in addition, there are likely to be shops which sell specialised goods such as furniture, clothes or agricultural machinery. These goods are bought less frequently and this means that the shops depend upon people travelling in to the town from the surrounding areas. In other words the service area of a town will be larger than that of a village, which in turn will be larger than the area served by a hamlet.

This has an obvious effect on the spacing and distribution of settlements. We have already seen that small settlements are more numerous than large settlements. This means that the distance between them will be less than the distance between large settlements. Actual distances will vary in different parts of the world but this relationship can be seen everywhere. In addition there appears to be a degree of order in the distribution of settlements and, in particular, in the relationship between settlements of different sizes. Many attempts have been made to describe and explain this pattern and one of the simplest is shown in Fig. 3.5.

In Christaller's model, village A is shown at the centre of its service area for which it provides very basic amenities (the service area is shown as a hexagon because hexagons fit together most efficiently with no gaps or areas of overlap). The village itself comes under the influence of a larger settlement – B – which provides a much wider range of services to village A and five other villages similar in size to A. In the same way B itself comes under the influence of an even larger centre – C – which also has a hexagonal service area and which provides an even wider range of services. (Notice that in each case the area served by the smaller settlement is divided into three and each part is allocated to a different higher order of settlement.)

Study Fig. 3.5 and complete the following exercise.

a   Imagine that you are a member of a family living at location x near village A, in Christaller's model. Using information given in Fig. 3.3, answer the following questions.

   i   In which centre (A, B or C) are you likely to find the nearest church, primary school, hospital, secondary school?

ii   From which centre are you most likely to obtain the following goods or services: instant coffee, a dentist, a piece of furniture, fashionable clothes, a medical consultant, a hammer?

b   The map shows the actual pattern of settlement in the Belingwe Tribal Trust Lands, Zimbabwe.

i   Trace the pattern of settlement predicted by the Christaller theory.

ii   Place the tracing over the map of Zimbabwe and try to match the two patterns (this can best be done by placing settlement C over the large village).

iii   Now try to draw service areas around the settlements in Zimbabwe (one hexagon is shown).

iv   Plot the predicted location of small villages around one of the medium size villages.

v   What is the average distance between (a) medium size villages, and (b) small villages? Why are they so close together?

c   Using the map of Zimbabwe repeat exercise a ii. Assume that you are living in a village located in a similar position. (In some cases the service may not be available.)

In developing countries the pattern of settlement is more likely to resemble the predicted pattern and the main differences tend to be caused by physical factors such as relief and drainage. In developed countries, however, the situation is different. Here improvements in transport have made the larger centres more accessible and, as a result, the smaller service centres (hamlets and villages) have declined in importance. This has been one of the factors which has given rise to the rapid growth of cities in the world during the twentieth century.

The growth of cities

In 1950 the number of people living in cities (i.e. settlements with a population of more than 100 000) was approaching 400 million; by 1980 that figure had reached 1150 million (Fig. 3.6). A large increase is to be expected at a time when world population is increasing rapidly but these figures suggest that the population living in cities (the urban population) is growing at a more rapid rate than the population as a whole. This is confirmed by the fact that in 1950 the proportion of the world's population living in cities was 16%, while in 1980 it had risen to 27%.

This growth in urban population has been accompanied by a dramatic increase in the number and size of cities (Fig. 3.7). Within the space of 30 years the number of cities with a population greater than 100 000 has more than doubled. Growth has been greatest among the largest settlements and the number of 'million cities' has increased from 23 in 1950 to 187 in 1982. The effects of this can be seen in the graph showing the combined population of all the cities of a given size. This shows that, although the number of million cities is still comparatively small (note the pyramid shape of the right hand graph), the

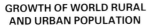

GROWTH OF WORLD RURAL AND URBAN POPULATION

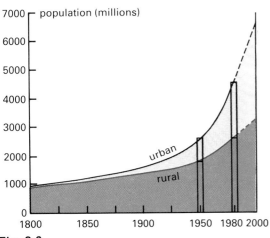

Fig. 3.6

29

WORLD CITIES BY SIZE AND POPULATION

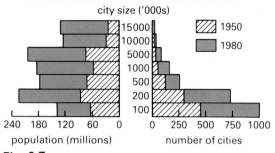

Fig. 3.7

combined population of these cities is now much larger than that of the smaller cities. In fact, if growth continues on this scale, by the end of the century 40% of the world's population will live in large cities and there will be one city with a population of more than 100 million! Of course this may not happen because of the physical problems of maintaining a city of that size.

The growth of cities varies enormously from place to place.

Study the map, Fig. 3.8.

a i   In which areas were the majority of million cities located in 1950?
  ii   Which areas have experienced the greatest growth in the number of million cities since 1950?
b Referring to the maps on pages 7–11:
  i   Describe the type of country in which million cities were likely to be located in 1950.
  ii   Describe the type of country in which the new million cities are to be found.
c Using the statistics for Gross National Product and size of urban population (see table on page 11):
  i   Draw a scattergraph with GNP on the horizontal axis and percentage urban population on the vertical. Plot the data for each of the countries in the list.
  ii   Describe the relationship shown and say whether it is weak or strong.
  iii   A more accurate measure can be obtained by calculating the correlation coefficient.

Before 1950 most of the large cities of the world were located in the developed countries. In these countries urbanisation had followed the growth of industry. Cities had expanded rapidly during the nineteenth century when the Industrial Revolution was at its height. This was particularly true in Europe and North America. Since 1950 the cities in the Developed World have continued to grow but their growth has been overshadowed by urbanisation in the less developed countries (Figs 3.8 and 3.9).

To a great extent the growth of cities is a reflection of the population explosion which has taken place in less developed countries. However, the urban population is increasing more

URBANISATION IN THE DEVELOPED AND LESS DEVELOPED COUNTRIES

	Developed countries		Less developed countries	
	1950	1980	1950	1980
Urban population (millions)	457	849	247	949
Urban population (% of total)	53	71	15	29
Population in million cities	128	303	45	327
Average growth rate (total pop.)	1.3	0.8	2.0	2.3
Average growth rate (urban pop.)	2.5	1.5	4.9	4.1

GROWTH OF MILLION CITIES

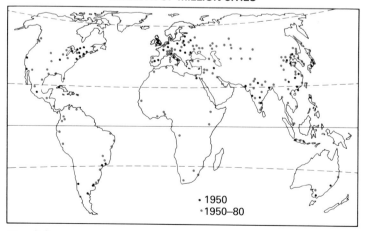

• 1950
• 1950–80

Fig. 3.8

GROWTH OF URBAN POPULATION: BY AREA

(the use of a logarithmic scale means that the lines indicate *rates* of growth)

urban population (millions)

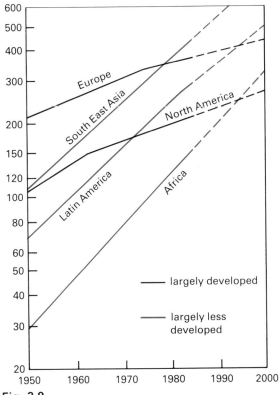

Fig. 3.9

Fig. 3.10 *The twentieth century city: Sao Paulo, Brazil*

rapidly than the population in rural areas. In spite of this rapid growth, the proportion of the population living in cities is still much lower in the less developed countries. It is possible, therefore, that the period of rapid growth will last for many years, slackening only when the level of urbanisation approaches that found in the Developed World today. On the other hand, if the period of rapid population growth in the less developed countries is comparatively short, the growth of cities may also be limited. At the moment, however, there is little sign of this.

Why have cities grown so rapidly? There are two obvious causes:

1 People have moved into the city from the surrounding countryside either to find work or because the city offers the prospect of a better life.

2 The natural increase in population is higher in cities than in other areas. To some extent this is the result of many of the immigrants being young and, therefore, more likely to have children. Even more important, however, is the fact that death rates are generally lower in cities, even in cities in the less developed countries. This is perhaps surprising, since living conditions in many of these cities appear to be very poor.

The cities which have developed during this period of rapid growth are very complex. At the same time, they have certain features in common.

1 The size of the city will be limited by the transport available. The time needed to travel from the outskirts to the centre is unlikely to be more than one hour.

2 The land use (Fig. 3.11) will include houses, industrial buildings, roads and footpaths, institutions such as schools and hospitals and public open space.

3 The use of land within the city will display clear patterns.

4 These patterns will be determined by the behaviour of the people living in the city. For this reason they are often very complicated, as can be seen in the following case studies.

LAND USE IN A TYPICAL CITY

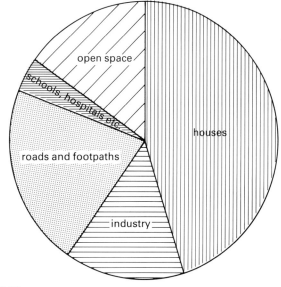

Fig. 3.11

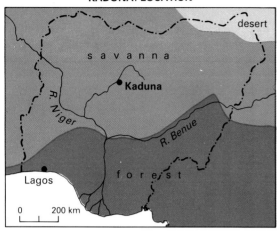

KADUNA: LOCATION

Fig. 3.12

A city in the Developing World: Kaduna, Northern Nigeria

The second half of the nineteenth century saw increasing British influence in the area which today forms the state of Nigeria. The coastlands had been acquired as early as 1861 and in 1900 British rule was extended far inland. It was at this time that a railway was planned to link the interior to the coast. By 1911 the railway from Lagos had reached the Kaduna River and it was decided to build a new administrative centre for the Northern Territories at the point where the railway crossed the river. This marked the beginning of the city of Kaduna (Fig. 3.12) and its origins and pattern of growth (Fig. 3.13) can be traced from this time.

Origins and early growth

Using the model, Fig. 3.1, on page 23 this can be summarised as follows:

a Site
1 A major bridging point where the Kaduna River narrows.
2 Water supply available from the river.
3 A surrounding area which was fertile.

b Situation
1 The settlement was of regional importance.
2 Its importance increased as the railway network developed.
3 It occupied a central position in the Northern Territories.

c Function
1 Military – Kaduna was built to house a large garrison and to provide support for the troops in the field.
2 Administrative – the town housed the main government buildings for the Northern Territories.
3 Communications – Kaduna was an important railway centre.

d Ground Plan
1 The first town was planned.
2 The street pattern was a regular grid iron.
3 Three separate areas were planned – military, administrative and residential.

It is around this original planned town that later growth has taken place.

Later growth

KADUNA: FEATURES OF GROWTH

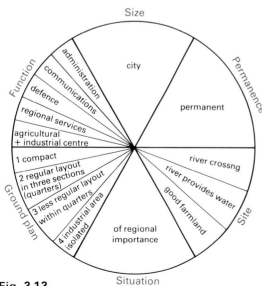

Fig. 3.13

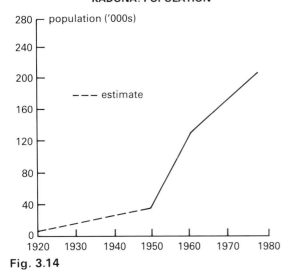

Fig. 3.14

iv Which of the following factors may have influenced the large number of immigrants from the Eastern Region: *the population of the region is large/the roads between the two areas are good/living standards in the Eastern Region are low/ the Eastern Region is near to Kaduna?*

c   Name the industries which provide jobs for the population.

The pattern of growth shown in Fig. 3.14 is typical of that found in most of the less developed countries. A long period of stability ended with the Second World War and from 1950 onwards a period of rapid population growth occurred. To a great extent this growth was closely linked to a general increase in population. As we have seen, however, the growth of major cities has been even more rapid, indicating a high rate of migration to the city. The causes of this in the case of Kaduna, and in most cities of the Developing World, are very complicated.

1   The rapid increase in population led to a reduction in living standards in rural areas.

2   The cities appeared to offer better prospects of employment, particularly since industrialisation was taking place there. In Kaduna it was the cotton industry (using cotton grown in the surrounding areas) which was the main attraction.

3   Improvements in transport made migration easier, even when the distances were large (Fig. 3.15).

As a result migration to the city increased rapidly. Most of the immigrants were young; the men moving to obtain work, the women to join husbands or to marry. Because they were young, they were more likely to have children and this, in turn, added to the growth of the city.

The structure of the city

The origins of the settlement can still be traced in the city today (Figs. 3.16 and 3.17).

1   At the centre of the city is the government quarter with its regular pattern of wide tree-lined streets and areas of public open space.

2   To the north is an area still controlled by the military.

3   South of the Kaduna River is the industrial quarter, with several large textile mills.

It is in these areas that the main work places are found (Fig. 3.18) and they are served by a number of residential districts. These house the bulk of the population and it is here that the main problems of city growth are to be found.

While population growth was slow the residential areas could be planned and development was controlled. Many of these were laid out in the form of compounds, rather than as individual houses (Figs 3.19 and 3.21). This meant that immigrants could live in large or extended family groups as they had done in the country villages from which they moved. Furthermore, new arrivals could often move into a compound occupied by people from the same area, or even the same village. As a result the problems caused by the change to urban life were much less serious.

REASONS FOR MOVING TO KADUNA

	(% of immigrant population)	
	Male	Female
Job available	17.7	1.1
Job probably available	6.4	0.7
Seeking work	49.8	5.0
Family reasons	25.0	93.0
Other reasons	1.1	0.2

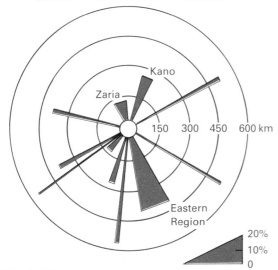

Fig. 3.15

PHYSICAL LIMITS TO THE SPREAD OF KADUNA

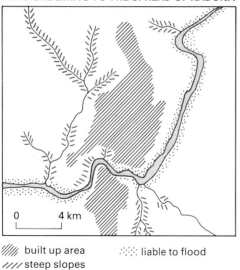

///// built up area
//// steep slopes

:::::: liable to flood

Fig. 3.16

KADUNA: GROWTH

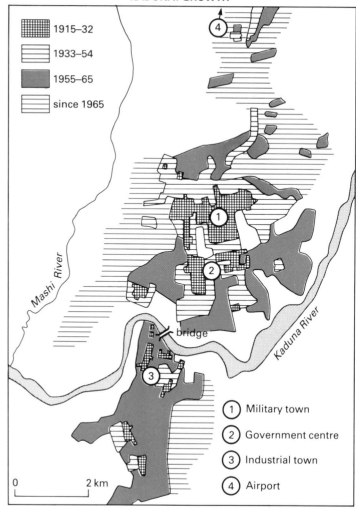

1915–32
1933–54
1955–65
since 1965

Mashi River

Kaduna River

bridge

1 Military town
2 Government centre
3 Industrial town
4 Airport

0   2 km

Fig. 3.17

Since 1950, however, this pattern of development has changed dramatically. Population began to grow rapidly, and to house the increased numbers new residential areas were built. Most of these were unplanned and lacked even basic amenities such as running water or drains (Fig. 3.20).

KADUNA: MAIN WORK PLACES AND JOURNEYS TO WORK

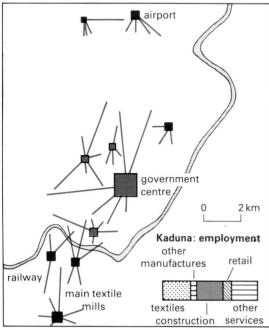

airport

government centre

0   2 km

railway

main textile mills

Kaduna: employment

other manufactures

retail

textiles   construction   other services

■ main industrial centres
■ main centres of service industries
— main journeys to work

Fig. 3.18

Using information given in Figs 3.16–21, complete the following exercise.

a   Where is the main source of water?
b   i   What proportion of the houses have flush toilets (water closets)?
    ii What is the main form of toilet available in the city?
c   i   Name two physical influences which limit the growth of the city.
    ii What influence has this had on the present shape of the city?
    iii What evidence is there that transport facilities are poor?
    iv What influence is this likely to have on the spread of the city?

A traditional compound in Kaduna

1 Built of mud bricks.
2 Few windows.
3 Buildings face into a central courtyard.
4 The compound is surrounded by mud brick walls.

The design gives:
1 Cool living quarters.
2 Protection from the strong winds, particularly those from the desert.

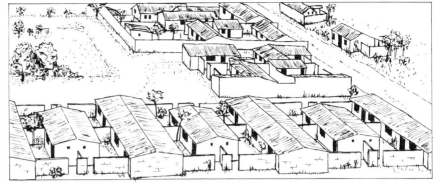

Fig. 3.21

At present, even in the unplanned residential areas which have grown up in recent years, the density of housing remains low and the problems of water supply, sanitation and refuse collection are not serious. Because transport facilities are poor, however, it is unlikely that building will be able to spread far away from the main places of work and this suggests that population densities will increase rapidly in the existing residential areas and that the city may suffer severe overcrowding.

Function and influence

As we have seen, most settlements supply goods and services to the people who live in them and in the surrounding areas. Most cities provide a wide range of services to a very large area.

Kaduna, for example, was established as the administrative centre for the Northern Territories of Nigeria – provinces which at the time covered an area of more than 600 000 square kilometres. It was also the main military centre for the same vast area and housed a large garrison. Both of these functions depended upon Kaduna's position at the centre of the railway network. Since 1911, however, other centres have grown up in the region and the area served by the city has been greatly reduced. Such functions are typical of cities in the developing countries which were until recently colonies of European powers.

As a service centre Kaduna also shares many features with other cities of the Developing World.

1 Food is generally bought at outdoor markets. The main market in the city centre serves the entire city and some of the surrounding villages, but most families use smaller neighbourhood markets which are within easy walking distance of their homes.

2 Other articles are bought from large company warehouses while shops of the kind found in cities in developed countries are mainly in the city centre.

3 This pattern of services is produced by the lack of an efficient transport system.

4 There are, however, certain services which can only be obtained from the city centre and for these, people are prepared to travel great distances. Such services include hospital treatment, legal services and even some forms of entertainment. There is also a tendency for large companies, including banks and insurance companies, to establish offices in the city centre.

This is a characteristic of all cities. They grow because

KADUNA: NUMBER OF PERSONS PER COMPOUND

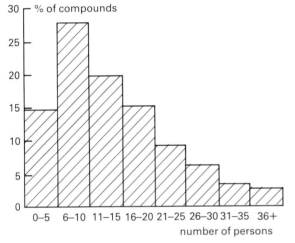

KADUNA: COMPOUND SIZE

Average number of:

persons per compound	14.6
households per compound	4.3
persons per household	3.4

Fig. 3.19

KADUNA: SANITATION
(% of houses with facilities)

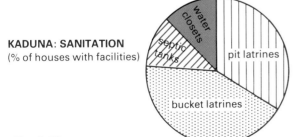

Fig. 3.20

communications both within the city and with the surrounding region are better than elsewhere. The city centre develops many distinctive features because it is the most accessible part of the city. In the case of Kaduna this process is still in its early stages. In other cities in the Developing World, however, the process is more advanced – where growth has been particularly rapid, the structure of the city can be dramatically different.

CALCUTTA: LOCATION

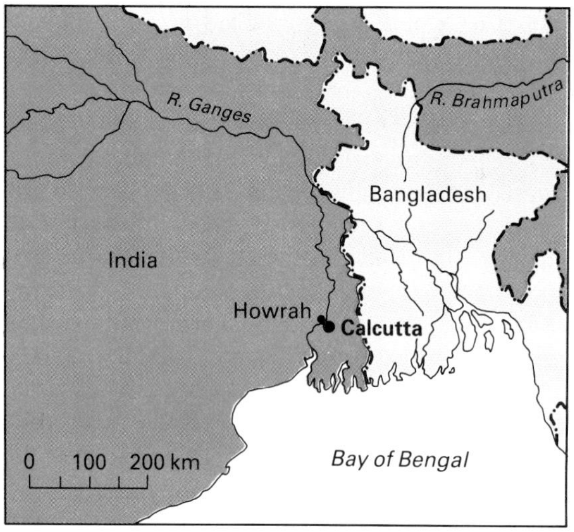

Fig. 3.22

Calcutta: a city under pressure

Calcutta (Fig. 3.22) is the largest city in India. Its built up area exceeds 1000 square kilometres and the population is now more than nine million. In spite of its great size, however, the city displays many features similar to those already seen in Kaduna.

1   It was a colonial city, founded by the British East India Company in 1690 as the centre of its trading activities in the Indian sub-continent.

2   As British influence spread Calcutta became the centre of British government in India, a position it kept until 1912 when it was replaced by Delhi. Like Kaduna, therefore, the city had important administrative and military functions and the effects of this can be seen in the structure of the city today (Fig. 3.23). At the centre of the city, for example, is Fort William, a military base built in 1757; and surrounding this is the Maidan, an area of parkland which houses many government buildings.

3   Because Calcutta was the administrative centre for the whole of India, as well as the main port and centre of economic activity, many Europeans lived there. Their houses were in a special high class residential quarter which bordered the parkland of the Maidan. To the north and south, and completely separated from it, were the native quarters. Here living conditions were very much poorer.

4   Employment was provided in the port and in the industrial areas which began to develop along the Hooghly River and, in particular, in Howrah on the west bank of the river.

5   This early city, which grew steadily during the nineteenth and early twentieth centuries has been engulfed in a mass of unplanned tenements built to house a population which within the space of 60 years has grown by more than six million. It is this pattern of growth, seen to a greater or lesser degree in cities throughout the Developing World, which is of particular interest.

The causes of growth

	India		Indian cities		Calcutta	
	Population (millions)	Growth rate (%)	Population (millions)	Growth rate (%)	Population (millions)	Growth rate (%)
1901	238	—	25	—	1.107	—
1911	252	5.8	25	0	1.222	10.4
1921	251	−0.3	28	8.2	1.328	8.7
1931	278	10.7	33	19.1	1.486	11.9
1941	318	14.4	44	31.9	3.534	37.8
1951	360	13.2	62	41.4	4.578	29.5
1961	439	21.9	78	26.4	5.405	18.1
1971	547	24.6	109	38.2	7.031	30.1
1981	694	26.8	160	39.0	9.510	35.2

Using information given in the adjacent table, complete the following exercise.

a   Draw graphs to show the growth of population (i) in all Indian cities and (ii) in Calcutta.
b   i   What is the population of Calcutta today?
    ii   During which period did the population of Calcutta grow most rapidly?
c   i   Compare the pattern of growth for Calcutta with that for all Indian cities.

CALCUTTA: GROWTH

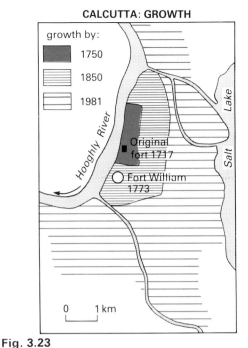

growth by:
- 1750
- 1850
- 1981

Hooghly River

Salt Lake

Original fort 1717

Fort William 1773

0   1 km

Fig. 3.23

CALCUTTA: ORIGIN OF IMMIGRANTS

Rural	62%
Urban	38%

CALCUTTA: EDUCATION LEVELS OF IMMIGRANTS

Secondary & Higher	25%
Primary	14%
Illiterate	47%

ORIGIN OF RECENT IMMIGRANTS TO THE CITY OF CALCUTTA (by state)

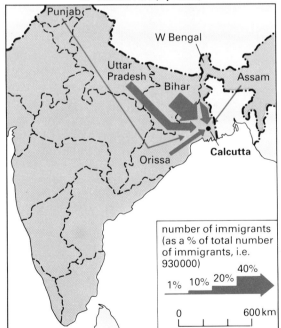

Punjab

W Bengal

Uttar Pradesh

Bihar

Assam

Orissa

Calcutta

number of immigrants (as a % of total number of immigrants, i.e. 930000)

1% 10% 20% 40%

0   600 km

Fig. 3.24

ii Is Calcutta growing *more slowly/more rapidly* than most other Indian cities today?

d i Throughout the twentieth century, has the urban population of India (i.e. the population living in cities) grown *more slowly/more rapidly* than the population as a whole?

ii When did the urban population grow most rapidly?

iii When did the Indian population as a whole grow most rapidly?

e Using this information suggest one factor which led to the rapid growth in the urban population.

The recent rapid growth of Calcutta and the other major industrial cities has taken place against a background of massive population increase in the country as a whole. As we have already seen, this has been the result of a reduction in death rates while birth rates have tended to remain high (see page 14).

Most of this growing population was – and still is – to be found in small rural villages. The scale of the population increase here has, however, driven more people to seek work in the cities. For the past 50 years Calcutta has been one of the main destinations for migrants (Fig. 3.24) and this has led to a growth rate which is more rapid than that for India as a whole. This, in turn, is reflected in the structure of the population of cities like Calcutta.

1 Men usually greatly outnumber women, suggesting that men seek work in the city and that, if they are successful, they are joined by wives and families.

2 The proportion of young children is very high, partly as a result of the fact that infant mortality rates are lower in the city than in the villages of the countryside.

3 The population is generally more youthful than in the country as a whole. This means that a large proportion of the female population is of child bearing age and this has led to very high rates of natural increase in the city. In fact it is the number of children born in the city which is the main cause of the continued growth of Calcutta, for there is strong evidence that the city is no longer attracting immigrants in such large numbers. This may be the result of the problems which rapid growth has produced, particularly in the slum areas.

The problems of growth

It is estimated that one quarter of the population of Calcutta lives in slums and that for a large proportion of the remainder the quality of life is very low. This is because the growth of population has completely outstripped the resources of the city.

For those newcomers to the city who have little or no money and are looking for work there are three alternatives.

1 They may move into parts of the old city (Figs 3.25 and 3.26) which offer poor but cheap housing, often in single rooms in tenement blocks or compounds. Such housing is available in the old native quarter, particularly now that the wealthier occupants have moved out into the old European city (Fig. 3.27) which remains a high class residential area.

2 Alternatively, they may move into the squatter settlements or 'bustees' (Fig. 3.28) which have grown up on the margins of the built up area or on waste land within the city. These are usually clusters of huts made of mud and scraps of wood and

Fig. 3.25 *The former native quarter of Calcutta*

Hooghly River

station

industry

HOWRAH

③

① Salt Lake and marshes

industry

station

Fort William

Maidan

industry

②

docks

0   1   2 km

① Business + Commercial District

② Former European Quarter

③ Former Native Quarter

≣ slums (bustees)

— city boundary

■■ railways and station

Fig. 3.26

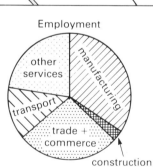

Employment

other services

manufacturing

transport

trade + commerce

construction

Fig. 3.27 *The high class residential area of Calcutta*

metal. Such houses are obviously cheap – although a rent is usually paid both for the land and for the hut. Against this, however, they are usually far from the main places of work, particularly for people too poor to pay the cost of travel.

3   It is the need to find work more than anything else which has led to the rapid increase in the numbers of people living on the pavements near the city centre. These people appear to be the poorest of the poor but many of them choose to live in this way because they can find work more easily near the city centre.

Although different in appearance, many of the slum areas share certain characteristics.

Fig. 3.28 *Bustees in Calcutta*

CALCUTTA: ENVIRONMENTAL PROBLEMS

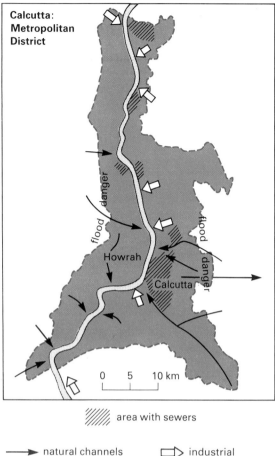

Calcutta: Metropolitan District

Howrah

Calcutta

flood danger

flood danger

0 5 10 km

///// area with sewers

→ natural channels used as sewers

⇨ industrial pollution

Fig. 3.29

The following statements refer to the slums of Calcutta. Copy those which you think are correct.

The slums of Calcutta: (1) are generally located in the old city (2) are more densely populated (3) are located on the outskirts of the city (4) house 25% of the city's population (5) have no regular water supply (6) have no regular supply of treated water (7) have a majority of houses with private water supplies (8) depend mainly upon water points located in the street (9) have inadequate sewers and drains (10) have no regular system of refuse collection (11) are occupied mainly by young couples with large families (12) have a population in which men greatly outnumber women (13) have infant mortality rates which are much higher than those in rural villages (14) are located near to major centres of employment (15) have high unemployment rates (16) are growing more rapidly than the slums in other Indian cities.

As in Nigeria there is a tendency for immigrants from the same area to move into the same neighbourhood in the city. Even more important, in Calcutta, as in most Indian cities, there are strong social divisions and people from the same class or 'caste' tend to live in the same areas.

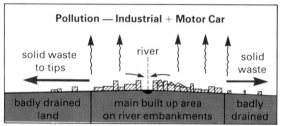

Pollution — Industrial + Motor Car

solid waste to tips

river

solid waste

badly drained land

main built up area on river embankments

badly drained

Fig. 3.30

Fig. 3.31 *Traffic congestion in Calcutta*

Poor housing is only one of the problems faced by Calcutta and other large cities in the Developing World (Fig. 3.30).

1 Industries have also failed to keep pace with population growth, particularly the old established industries such as textiles. As a result, levels of unemployment are often high. Since the main reason for people moving to the city is to find work, this makes cities like Calcutta less and less attractive. In recent years many immigrants have left the city and returned to their home villages.

2 The number of people has put a great strain on the system of transport. Traffic congestion (Fig. 3.31) is now so severe that it actually restricts growth and this together with the poverty of many of the people has limited the development of the city as a service centre.

Such problems have combined to make Calcutta less attractive and today, after a long period of supremacy, Calcutta is growing less quickly than other large cities in India – a feature it shares with many of the great cities of the Developed World.

Chicago: a city in the Developed World

Although cities throughout the world have many features in common, those in developed countries show a different pattern of growth and have very different functions. This, in turn, has led to the shape and form of the city being different. Many of these differences can be seen in Chicago (Fig. 3.32), the second largest city in the United States.

The first settlement was built on the site of present day Chicago in the 1770s when a small trading post was established. In 1803 a fort was built to protect settlers from attacks by Indians and to control the overland route between the Great Lakes and the Mississippi. It was the importance of this route between two major waterways which gave rise to the early growth of the town, particularly after 1836 when work began on a canal link (Fig. 3.33). Later development also owed much to the position of Chicago in relation to the communications network of North America.

CHICAGO: LOCATION

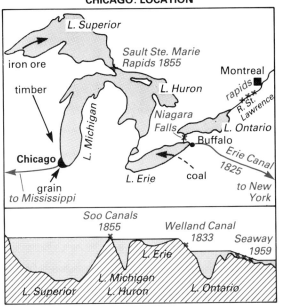

Fig. 3.32

Using information given in Figs 3.32 and 3.33, complete the following exercise.

a i   When did it become possible to transport goods by water between Chicago and the Atlantic Ocean?
   ii Which engineering project made this possible?
   iii When were the canals linking Lake Superior to Lake Michigan built?
   iv To which raw materials did this give access?
   v   How is this reflected in the industrial development of Chicago?
   vi Describe the obstacles to navigation between Lake Superior and Montreal.
   vii Describe how these obstacles were overcome.
b i   When did Chicago begin to grow rapidly?
   ii Name the main industries of the city at that time.
   iii Give one reason for the location of these industries in the Chicago area.

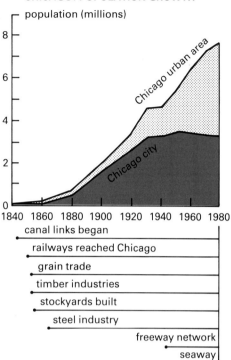

CHICAGO: POPULATION GROWTH

population (millions)

Fig. 3.33

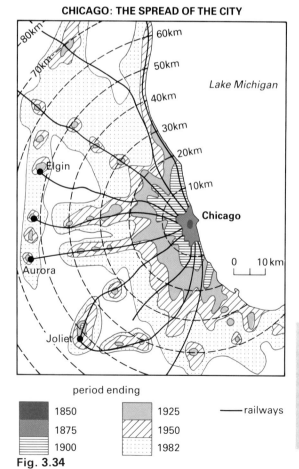

CHICAGO: THE SPREAD OF THE CITY

period ending

1850	1925	——— railways
1875	1950	
1900	1982	

Fig. 3.34

The completion of the canals at Sault Ste Marie, at the Niagara Falls and around the rapids on the St Lawrence made Chicago into a port for ocean going vessels. For almost a century, however, the size of these vessels was restricted by the smallness of the canals on the St Lawrence – a problem which was only overcome when the Seaway was opened in 1959. Even more important for the growth of the city was the coming of the railways. This gave access both to the raw materials of the surrounding region and to markets in the industrial cities on the Atlantic coast.

Less obviously, the development of the transport system, and in particular of the railway network, had an important influence on the physical growth of Chicago (Fig. 3.34) and on the location of activity within the city. In fact, in common with most cities in the Developed World, it is changes in the pattern of communications which have produced many of the most striking changes in the city itself.

Growth

1 The city grew up near the point where the Chicago River enters Lake Michigan and the early port facilities were built there. Throughout this period, when dependence upon water transport was almost complete, Chicago remained compact and the area near the river mouth was the centre of activity.

2 The building of the railways, and in particular commuter railways, led to a rapid increase in the built up area of the city. Towns and villages were built on or near the railways and these were gradually engulfed as ribbons of growth spread from the city along the lines. This gave the city an irregular shape with long narrow 'fingers' of housing and industry radiating from a heavily built up central area.

3 This shape, characteristic of many cities built during the railway age, became less clear with the coming of the motor car and the development of road transport. Initially the building of major roads, especially freeways, produced a pattern of growth which closely resembled that which followed the building of the railways, with housing built along the lines of communication. With the private motor car, however, access to the roads which linked the city to the surrounding area was easy. This led to the spread of building onto the land between the main roads. As a result the built up area of Chicago expanded rapidly and the shape of the city became more regular. At the same time the increased use of the motor car produced congestion in the city centre and this in itself was to have important consequences.

Refer to the map, Fig. 3.34

a   Draw a rough outline of the city of Chicago in 1875 and try to account for this shape.
b   Draw a rough outline of the city in 1950. Describe its form and explain how it has been influenced by the development of communications.
c   Repeat this exercise for the city in 1980.

CHICAGO: INDUSTRIAL AREAS

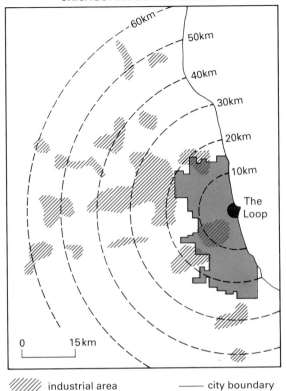

///// industrial area　　——— city boundary

Fig. 3.35

Industry: location and growth

From the early nineteenth century onwards Chicago developed as a major industrial centre. At first it was the area along the lakeshore, near to the port, which attracted industry. This is because most of these early industries depended upon bulky raw materials which were carried by water. The building of the railways did little to change this pattern and the stockyards and flour mills, although mainly served by rail, were located near to the old city centre.

By the late nineteenth century, however, sites near the city centre were already becoming congested and new sites were favoured by industrialists. The steel industry, for example, had special requirements (see page 162) and was already finding space beyond the city limits near Calumet Harbor in the south and as far north as Gary. Both locations provided large open sites near the shores of Lake Michigan which offered easy access to the coal and ores ships using the waterways. Such sites were attractive to other industries and it was here that the heavy industries of the region clustered.

For some industries the railways offered the chance of breaking away from city centre locations and from 1870 onwards industry, like population, spread outwards along the railway lines. The effects of this change can be seen in the distribution of industry in the city today (Fig. 3.35) – in spite of the fact that during the past 30 years the movement of freight by rail has declined in comparison with freight movements by road and water (Fig. 3.36). It produced a pattern of industrial centres which radiate from the city centre. This is a pattern which is found in many cities throughout the world.

Since 1950 road transport has become more important and new industrial centres have been established near to the main freeways. Many of these locations are planned industrial estates which have attracted a large range of industries, including some from sites near the city centre. Most have been new industries and these have helped to change the industrial structure of the city.

Chicago displays features seen in many other cities. The industries which led to much of the early growth – usually heavy industries such as steel making, flour milling, meat packing and timber processing – have moved to new, less crowded, locations. They have been replaced within the city by other industries such as light engineering and electronics which need less space.

All industries depend upon people to work in them and the industrial development of Chicago was accompanied by the building of houses for the labour force. Until quite recently most of this housing was clustered around the main centres of employment so that the journey to work was kept to a minimum. Since 1950, however, the availability of the motor car has caused this simple pattern to break down and the city now draws its workforce from a vast area (Fig. 3.37). As a result the old city has become surrounded by an ever-increasing suburban area, linked to the centre by commuter railways and freeways. This has produced striking changes in the city.

MOVEMENT OF FREIGHT IN THE CHICAGO AREA

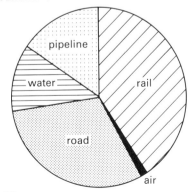

Fig. 3.36

43

PEOPLE TRAVELLING TO WORK IN THE CITY

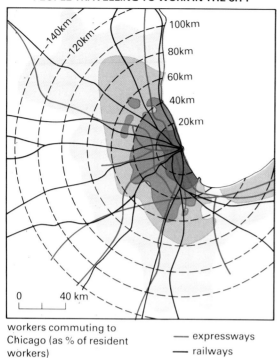

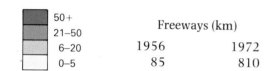

workers commuting to Chicago (as % of resident workers)

—— expressways
—— railways

	50+
	21–50
	6–20
	0–5

Freeways (km)	
1956	1972
85	810

Fig. 3.37

CHICAGO: POPULATION CHANGE

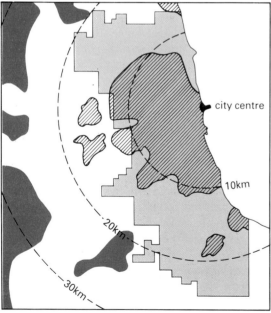

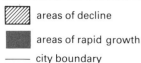

areas of decline

areas of rapid growth

—— city boundary

Fig. 3.38

Refer to the maps on this page.

a   i   What is the greatest distance travelled by workers in the city of Chicago? Compare this with the pattern for Kaduna (see page 34).
    ii   From which directions are the longest journeys made?
    iii   Why are such long journeys possible from these areas?
    iv   What evidence is there that it is road rather than rail transport which is the most important influence on this pattern?
b   Describe the type of people who live in the outer suburbs.
c   Describe the type of people who live in the areas near the city centre.
d   Refer to the population graph on page 42 and describe the effects of these changes on the growth of population in the city and in its surrounding area since 1950.

It is in the inner city that the changes have been most dramatic (Fig. 3.38). Here the old residential areas, built during the nineteenth and early twentieth centuries to house the people who worked in the nearby industries, have begun to decay. The movement of the wealthier members of this work force into the suburbs began with the building of the first commuter railways. It has become increasingly rapid with the opening of the freeway network and the relocation of many industries away from the city centre. As a result, both population and employment have declined in the central area of Chicago. Furthermore, it tends to be the poor who remain in the inner city (Fig. 3.39) and this speeds up the decline of once prospering neighbourhoods.

Another feature of the inner city has been the tendency for people of the same class and of similar origins to live in the same neighbourhood. This has led to the formation of ghettos, and in Chicago today the two largest ghettos are those occupied by the Negroes and the Spanish speaking population (Fig. 3.40). Other groups once lived in these ghetto areas but they moved as they became more prosperous. This is a process which has taken place in cities throughout the Developed World and even in some less developed countries.

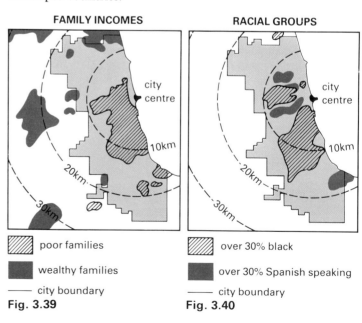

FAMILY INCOMES

poor families

wealthy families

—— city boundary

Fig. 3.39

RACIAL GROUPS

over 30% black

over 30% Spanish speaking

—— city boundary

Fig. 3.40

The city centre

Within the inner city, with its poor housing, run-down industries, wasteland and general deprivation, stands the city centre itself. This is usually the most striking and most distinctive part of any city. In Chicago, as in most cities in the Developed World, the city centre can be identified simply by the height of the buildings (Fig. 3.41). Here the entire area (known as the Loop because of its position within a loop of the now disused elevated railway) contains some of the tallest buildings in the world. This is the result of the enormous demand for land in the city centre – a demand which has produced some of the highest land values in the world. Because land is so valuable maximum use is made of it by building upwards.

Why are land values so high in central Chicago? The simple answer is that the central area is the most accessible part of the city. This means that it is the part of the city which can be reached most easily by people from all parts of the surrounding region. As a result, it is the best location for industries which serve the people in that region. Service industries dominate employment in the city centre. The main hospitals, medical consulting rooms, law firms, government buildings and law courts are all found there. Equally important, the city centre has for a long time been the focus of the retail trade and most of the main shops have branches there (Fig. 3.42). The central area has a special function as a shopping centre. Because it is accessible to a large number of people from the surrounding region, it is the obvious location for specialist shops which will be used infrequently or by only a small proportion of the population.

Fig. 3.41 *Central Chicago showing the Central Business District and its immediate surrounds.*

CHICAGO: SHOPPING CENTRES

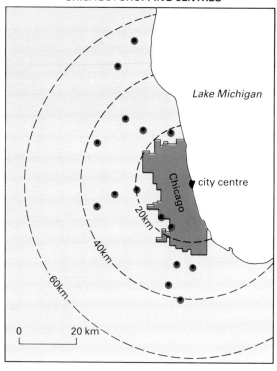

● shopping centres   —— city boundary

Fig. 3.42

In Chicago, as in most American cities, there is a tendency for the central area to break up into separate districts, each with its own special characteristics. The most distinctive of these is the Central Business District (CBD). Here, within a very small area, are found the major banks and insurance companies, along with the regional offices of some of the largest industrial and commercial companies in the world. They occupy the most valuable sites in the city and their buildings are the largest and most impressive.

Government agencies, both local and national, also have offices in the city centre and they are clustered together with the law courts to form a clearly defined administrative district. The shopping area is less clearly defined, although even here there is a strong tendency for the largest stores to cluster together in a single street – State Street.

All of these functions depend upon easy access and all have been affected by the congestion which threatens to strangle the city centre. The commuter railways and improved bus services helped to create the problem. The freeways and the private motor car have made it almost unmanageable. Large areas of the inner city were cleared and left as parking lots but still the congestion increased. As a result, the city centre has become less attractive and many companies have found cheaper and equally accessible sites in the suburbs. This can be seen most clearly in the pattern of shopping. City centre shopping has declined and been to a great extent replaced by shopping at large out-of-town centres, located near to the freeways. Such sites are much cheaper than those in the city centre and they can be reached by so many people that even specialist shops are attracted to them.

The effect on the city centre has been striking. As activities have moved out into the suburbs, so the number of people travelling to the centre has declined – another feature shared by most of the great cities of the world.

Understanding the city

The three case studies – Kaduna, Calcutta and Chicago – give some impression of the complexity of the modern city. Many attempts have been made to understand this complexity and to produce models which can be applied to a large number of cities in different parts of the world. Two of these models are given in Fig. 3.43.

CHICAGO: THE USE OF THE CBD

	1950	1975
Number employed ('000)	59	29
Shoppers ('000)	323	256

BURGESS: CONCENTRIC RING MODEL

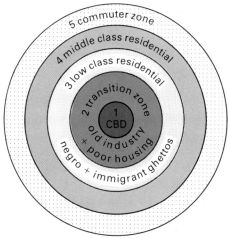

Fig. 3.43 (a)

Refer to the maps and diagrams in this section.

a   Burgess's model was based on Chicago in the 1920s. Can it still be applied to the city today?
   i   Draw the coastline of Lake Michigan, locate the centre of Chicago on it, and draw the concentric zones of the Burgess model, leaving the outer zone without limit.
   ii Locate the area known as the Loop. Describe its appearance and how it differs from the surrounding city. List the special functions of this area.

46

HOYT: SECTOR MODEL

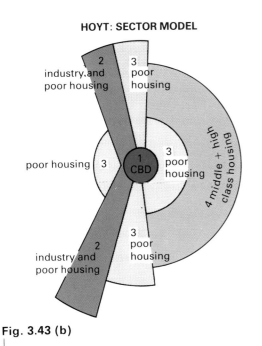

Fig. 3.43 (b)

iii Study the map Fig. 3.35. Is there a zone of industry near the city centre? Why is it declining?

iv Study the maps Figs 3.38–40. Locate the Negro and Spanish speaking ghettos on the model. Does their position agree with that suggested by Burgess?

v Again using these maps, locate the high class residential areas of Chicago. Are they in the areas suggested by the model?

vi Try to apply the model to Kaduna.

b The Sector Model provides an alternative view of the structure and growth of cities.

i Which of the following features of city growth are most likely to encourage the development of sectors: *the decline of the city centre/a radial pattern of communications/the movement of population to the outskirts of the city/the presence of port facilities in the city?*

ii Make a tracing of the Sector Model. Extend the sectors to enlarge it if necessary.

iii Place the tracing on the map showing industrial location in Chicago (Fig. 3.35). Centre the CBD on the Loop area and rotate the tracing. Is there any evidence that sectors have developed in Chicago?

iv Repeat the exercise for the map (Fig. 3.39) showing family incomes.

MAIN FEATURES OF A COLONIAL CITY IN THE DEVELOPING WORLD

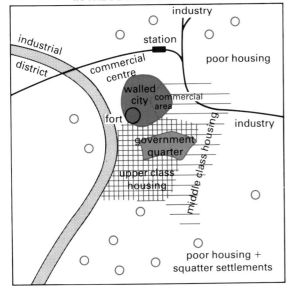

○ squatter settlements

━■ railway and station

Fig. 3.44

It is obvious that no single model can be used to describe and explain the full complexity of the modern city. Indeed many cities show signs of both concentric zones and radial sectors and these can change markedly with time. Furthermore, many cities have become so large that neighbouring settlements have been absorbed into the built up area. As a result the overall structure of the modern city is likely to be even more complex and it is probable that there will be several smaller, but important, centres around the Central Business District.

It is also clear that it is difficult to apply such models to cities in developing countries. There are of course certain features shared with cities in the Developed World, e.g. industrial development along lines of communication, but the original structure was often very different. In many parts of the world, for example, the cities grew as colonial centres and this led to the establishment of clearly defined quarters for government and administration, European housing, industry and commerce and 'native' housing (Fig. 3.44). Traces of these divisions are still to be found in such cities. Even more important, the population explosion in the Developing World has produced city growth on a scale seen nowhere else and the main features of this growth have been the areas of poor housing and shanty towns which have encircled the city. These features are now found in virtually no city in the Developed World.

4 Agriculture

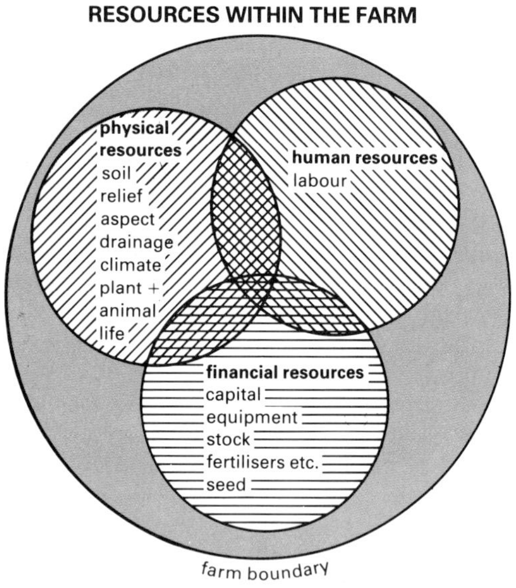

RESOURCES WITHIN THE FARM

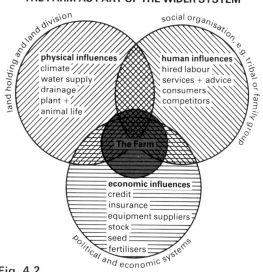

Fig. 4.1

THE FARM AS PART OF THE WIDER SYSTEM

Fig. 4.2

In 1950 there were 2500 million people living on the earth's surface. Thirty years later this number had almost doubled. All of these people have to be fed and it is not surprising both that the pattern of world food production is complicated and that it has changed dramatically in recent years.

Food is produced on farms. In most areas farms are small and easy to recognise but in some parts of the world they are vast and appear to have no clear boundaries. Whatever their size, however, all farms have certain things in common. For example, they make use of similar resources. Some of these are shown in the diagram (Fig. 4.1) where they are grouped under three main headings.

1   **Physical resources**
a   the land, including its relief, slope and aspect
b   the soil
c   the climate and in particular the rainfall, seasonal temperature and hours of sunshine
d   the natural vegetation
e   the wildlife which occupied the area before farming began. Physical factors tend to be most important where relatively simple farming methods are used, but they influence all types of farming.

2   **Human resources**
The most important of which is labour – either hired labour or the labour provided by the family or village group which works the land.

3   **Economic and financial resources**
These can be very complicated but they include the capital available to the farmer and the equipment of the farm. The latter includes not only machines and tools but also the stock (the farm animals), the seed for the next crop and even the crops standing in the fields.

On any single farm these resources are very closely connected and, as the diagram shows, there are large areas of overlap between the physical, human and economic influences at work. This means that the operation of a single farm is bound to be very complicated.

In addition, however, each farm forms part of a much broader pattern of farming and the influences of this more general agricultural system can extend far beyond the boundaries of the individual farm (Fig. 4.2). For example, among the physical influences, the natural drainage of the land may depend upon a river system which has its sources hundreds or even thousands of kilometres away; while, at a more local level, plant and animal life may enter the farm, introducing pests and diseases. The same is true of human and economic resources. Farmers may make use of hired labour; farm output may be influenced by the demands of consumers who may live in other parts of the world; money may be borrowed from banks and other financial institutions; and the government may control the prices paid for the produce. As a result, the operation of the individual farm can be influenced by decisions taken far away by large companies, by central government, and by even larger organisations such as the European Economic Community.

It is clear from the diagram that these influences are closely connected and that a change in one part of the farm system is likely to cause other changes. Furthermore, some of these changes will be completely unexpected. It is important to remember this, particularly at a time when change is taking place at an ever increasing rate in the world. Three developments are of particular interest.

1   The population explosion which has increased the demand for food to such an extent that in some countries farming systems are placed under great strain.

2   Technological change which has enabled overall food production to keep pace with population growth. The most obvious example of this has been the 'Green Revolution' which has increased crop yields throughout the world.

3   Political change which, although less obvious, has been very important. This is perhaps most clearly seen in the Communist countries where change in the political system led to a total reorganisation of agriculture. In the USSR, for example, the Communist government introduced a system of collective farms, while in China the traditional system of farming was replaced by a system of communes. Such changes followed revolutions but almost every government in the world today has taken some control of food production, usually by fixing prices or controlling food imports.

A farm is an area of land or water devoted to the growing or rearing of crops or animals. Any farm, therefore, can be studied in terms of:

1   the resources needed for farming (the inputs)

2   the layout, organisation and operation of the farm (the processes)

3   the products of the farm, including waste products, information etc. (the outputs).

Terracing allows intensive cultivation of rice in the Philippines

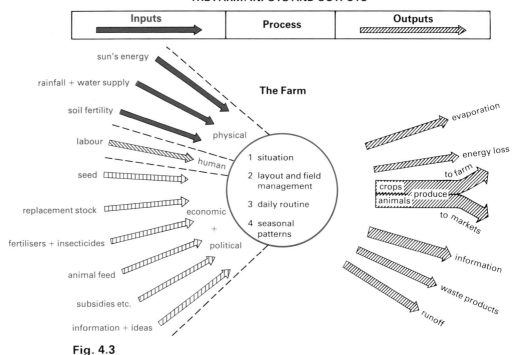

THE FARM: INPUTS AND OUTPUTS

Fig. 4.3

Compare the diagram, Fig. 4.3, with Figs 4.1 and 4.2 and complete the following questions:

a What are the three major influences on the farm system?
b Describe the factors which influence the development of farming.
c Both sets of diagrams show the farm as a system and as part of much larger systems. Describe how the two representations differ.

Although the diagram, Fig. 4.3, fails to show the relationships which exist between the various influences, it can be used to identify major contrasts in world agricultural systems. General differences emerge from an examination of the various inputs and outputs.

Classification by type of output

1 If the main output of the farm comprises crops the farm is an *arable* farm.

2 If the main output of the farm is obtained from animals the farm is a *pastoral* farm.

In some cases both crops and animals appear among the output of the farm – a proportion of the crops being used to feed stock of various kinds. This is called a *mixed* farming system. Such systems are often very complicated, particularly those found in the highly developed industrial countries of the world.

Commercial arable farming in Britain

Classification by destination of output

1   When the produce of the farm is retained to feed the farmer and his family the farming system is described as *subsistence* farming. This type of farming is found mainly in less developed countries.

2   If the bulk of the produce is sold in markets, whether they be nearby or in another country, the system is said to be a *commercial* farming system. Most farming in the Developed World is of this type.

Classification by scale of inputs and outputs

This raises more difficult problems. There are, however, two major types of farming which ought to be mentioned:

1   On some farms yields (i.e. the amount of food produced per hectare) are very high. Such high yields are usually obtained because inputs, particularly of labour, machinery or fertiliser, are high. This type of farming is called intensive farming.

2   Other farms may have low yields per hectare. Often this is the result of physical factors such as poor soils or low rainfall. It is, however, sometimes associated with the small scale of the inputs of labour and capital. This type of farming is called *extensive* farming.

Classification by land holding and farm organisation

The analysis of farm types according to inputs and outputs produces relatively few major types. If the organisation of the farm is taken into account, however, the number of types increases enormously. This is best studied by examining a number of case studies. But first we will look briefly at the main contrasts in farm organisation.

A classification of some of the main agricultural systems in the world with examples

	ARABLE (i.e. a concentration on the production of crops)		PASTORAL (i.e. a concentration on the rearing of animals)		MIXED (i.e. farm output shared between crops and animal products)	
	TROPICAL	TEMPERATE	TROPICAL	TEMPERATE	TROPICAL	TEMPERATE
EXTENSIVE (i.e. low yields per hectare)	SUBSISTENCE Shifting cultivation of ground nuts & rice in the Gambia	COMMERCIAL Cereal production on the Great Plains	SUBSISTENCE Nomadic cattle rearing in in East & West Africa	COMMERCIAL Cattle ranching on the Great Plains	SUBSISTENCE Shifting garden production of taro, sweet potato & pork in the Solomon Islands	COMMERCIAL Wheat/sheep farming in South Australia
INTENSIVE (i.e. high yields per hectare usually resulting from high inputs of labour, capital fertiliser, etc.)	SUBSISTENCE Rice cultivation in SE Asia COMMERCIAL Rubber production in Malaysia	COMMERCIAL Vegetable production in the Netherlands	COMMERCIAL Dairy farming in the Kenyan Highlands	COMMERCIAL Dairy farming in Eire	SUBSISTENCE/ COMMERCIAL Communes in SE China	COMMERCIAL Dairy farming in Denmark COMMERCIAL Pig and beef farming in the Corn Belt of the USA

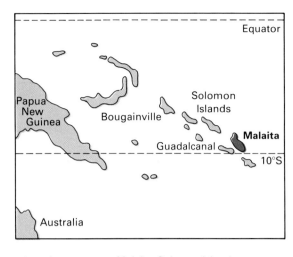

Location:	Malaita, Solomon Islands
Climate:	Equatorial High temperatures, heavy rainfall
Growing season:	365 days
Farming System:	Subsistence Shifting, garden cultivation
Produce:	Sweet potatoes Taro Pig meat

Fig. 4.4

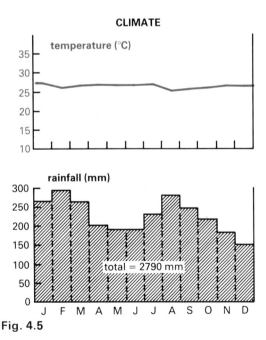

Fig. 4.5

Subsistence farming systems

1   In some areas land is held by an entire village or a tribe and individual families are allowed to make use of it. This is *communal* land holding and it is most common in less developed countries, although it has been introduced in a modified form in some Communist countries. Elsewhere individual land holding is usual, with the farmers either owning or renting the land.

2   In many less developed societies communal land holding is associated with the practice of cultivating small areas of land which are abandoned when the fertility of the soil begins to decline. A new area of land is then cleared for cultivation and the original plots are left to recover. This type of farming is called *shifting cultivation*. Closely related to this are the *nomadic* practices of pastoral farmers. In this case herds of animals are moved from place to place so as to allow grazed land to recover. Such methods are obviously wasteful of land and over much of the world today *sedentary* farming is normal, with family groups remaining in the same place, farming the same plots of land.

Shifting garden cultivation: Solomon Islands

Shifting cultivation is a system under which food crops are produced from an area of land which is then abandoned so that the natural vegetation can recover. During this period another piece of land is cultivated. This enables land to recover its fertility and reduces the risk of soil exhaustion and soil erosion. Such systems are wasteful of land and are practised in few areas of the world today. The remote inland areas of the Solomon Islands (Fig. 4.4) are one region where a very simple form of shifting cultivation is found.

Characteristics of the system

1   The land is held communally by the members of a village and small areas are allocated to individual family groups.

2   This land is usually taken in the form of two very small garden plots, chosen to give a variety of soil types, drainage and relief. For example, in mountainous areas a household often chooses to cultivate an upland and a lowland (valley) garden, growing different crops in each.

3   Cultivation rarely continues beyond a third crop – this usually takes less than three years since there is no break in the growing season and new crops can be planted immediately after the harvest.

4   Several considerations lead to the decision to abandon a garden:

a   Most important by far is the fact that yields decline with each crop. After three crops, they may be less than half the levels obtained when cultivation began. No fertilisers are used to maintain soil fertility and minerals are quickly washed out of the soil by the heavy rains.

b   It also seems likely that diseases begin to affect the crops more seriously after the first planting.

c Weeding becomes more difficult as the natural vegetation spreads into the clearing and suckers grow from the tree stumps.

5 Eventually, as more and more clearings are abandoned, the distance between the garden plots and the village becomes too great. Then the entire village is moved. Until this happens individual families build temporary houses on the garden plots.

Shifting cultivation (Solomon Islands)

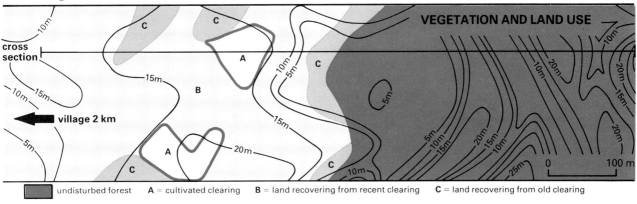

VEGETATION AND LAND USE

cross section

village 2 km

0   100 m

undisturbed forest   A = cultivated clearing   B = land recovering from recent clearing   C = land recovering from old clearing

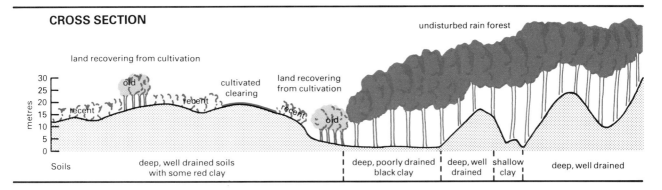

CROSS SECTION

undisturbed rain forest

land recovering from cultivation

land recovering from cultivation

cultivated clearing

Soils   deep, well drained soils with some red clay | deep, poorly drained black clay | deep, well drained | shallow clay | deep, well drained

YEAR'S WORK IN THE TWO GARDENS (0.25 ha)

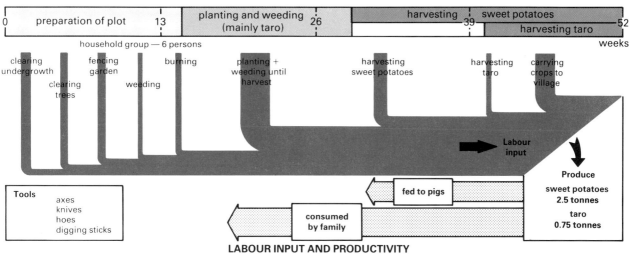

| 0 | preparation of plot | 13 | planting and weeding (mainly taro) | 26 | harvesting | 39 | sweet potatoes | 52 |
| harvesting taro |

household group — 6 persons

weeks

clearing undergrowth | clearing trees | fencing garden | weeding | burning | planting + weeding until harvest | harvesting sweet potatoes | harvesting taro | carrying crops to village

Labour input

Tools
axes
knives
hoes
digging sticks

fed to pigs

consumed by family

Produce
sweet potatoes
2.5 tonnes
taro
0.75 tonnes

LABOUR INPUT AND PRODUCTIVITY

Fig. 4.6

53

Length of fallow	Yield of sweet potatoes (tonnes per hectare)
Over 15 years	10.0
10 years	8.0
5–9 years	6.0
0–4 years	4.8
successive crops	3.5

PLAN OF CULTIVATED CLEARING (0.1 ha)

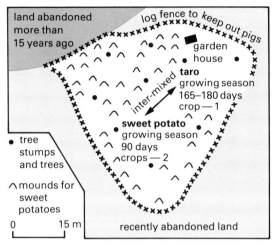

Crop	Area		Number of crops	Total yield (tonnes per ha)
taro	⅓	} of total land	1	9
sweet potato	⅔		2	15

Fig. 4.7

Fig. 4.8 *Shifting cultivation: cultivating sweet potatoes on a garden plot*

Methods of farming

Once the site of a new garden plot (Fig. 4.7) has been chosen, whether it is in undisturbed forest or on previously cleared land, a great deal of heavy manual labour is needed to prepare the land (study Fig. 4.6). Undergrowth and small trees are cleared and branches are lopped from larger trees. This litter is allowed to dry and is then piled around the larger trees where it is burned. This kills the trees and they are either felled or left standing in the garden plot. Some useful trees are spared, in particular the sago palm which provides thatch for house-building.

To protect the clearing from pigs, the felled trees are used to build a strong fence. Planting takes place between the dead trees and the tree stumps and no attempt is made to separate the crops. Instead, sweet potatoes are planted on mounds made by digging up the soil with a hoe or stick and taro is planted at intervals between the mounds. This method of inter-cropping is common under shifting cultivation systems, since it increases yields and reduces the need for weeding. Both are root crops and both require high temperatures and heavy rainfall. Given these conditions the crops grow rapidly. The sweet potato quickly shades out weeds and this saves a great deal of labour. Harvesting can begin after three months and a second crop of sweet potatoes can be planted before the taro is ready for harvesting. This means that productivity is very high and the garden produces a surplus of food. This is fed to pigs which provide the protein in the diet.

Refer to Figs 4.5–7 and complete the following exercise.

a   i   What evidence is there to suggest that the climate is equatorial?
   ii   There are two rainfall maxima. When do they occur? What causes them?
   iii   What effect do these maxima have on mean temperatures?
b   i   What is the size of the household; the area of the clearing shown in the map; the total area worked by the family?
   ii   Why is it necessary to build a garden house?
c   i   Briefly describe the main activities on the farm during the year and explain why there is no clear seasonal pattern.
   ii   List the activities in order, according to the amount of labour required.
d   i   Name the two crops grown.
   ii   'Intercultivation' takes place. Explain what this means.
   iii   Name two advantages of cultivating sweet potatoes rather than taro.

Work is divided among the family. The men clear the land, often calling upon other villagers to help with the felling of large trees. The women are then responsible for growing the crops and weeding the clearing while the men hunt wild pigs and look after the domesticated pigs which feed in the forest.

MODEL OF THE FARMING SYSTEM IN THE SOLOMON ISLANDS

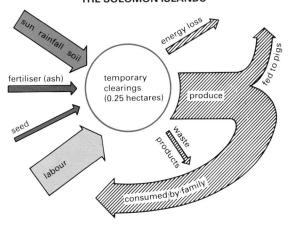

(Compare this with the general model on page 00.)
Note: 1 high natural energy input
      2 very high labour input
      3 high output
      4 low energy and waste loss

Fig. 4.9

After the first crop, yields decline and, within two years, the clearing will be abandoned. This is because the only fertiliser used is the ash produced by the burning of the undergrowth. In addition the soils are poor and, like most soils in the tropics, are quickly leached by the heavy rainfall.

Although each clearing is in itself highly productive, this system of farming (Fig. 4.9) requires a large area of land to ensure its success. After use at least 15 years fallow is needed for the forest to recolonise the land and for the fertility of the soil to be restored. If this amount of time is not available yields begin to suffer (see Table on page 54). Unfortunately, such long periods of fallow can no longer be guaranteed. In recent years, as in most of the Developing World, the death rate has been reduced and the population has increased rapidly. This has made it necessary to clear more land and this, in turn, has reduced the periods of fallow. In addition, commercial farming in the form of coconut plantations is spreading rapidly and this too is reducing the amount of land available to the shifting cultivators. Modern methods of farming have taken over on the coastal lowlands and true shifting cultivation is now practised only in the more remote highlands.

At the same time it must be remembered that this traditional farming can produce very high returns with little damage to the land. This is not always true of the new methods of farming which have been introduced.

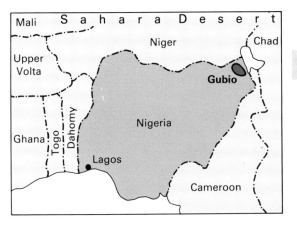

Location:	Gubio, North Eastern Nigeria
Climate:	Semi-arid High temperatures throughout the year Low, irregular rainfall (average 250 mm a year)
Vegetation:	Poor savanna grassland and scrub
Farming system:	Subsistence Nomadic stock rearing
Stock:	Cattle, goats

Fig. 4.10

Nomadic stock rearing: North Eastern Nigeria

Shifting cultivation is designed to maintain crop yields and to ensure that the farmland recovers after cropping. It is for similar reasons that many stock rearers move their herds from one area of pasture to another since this reduces the danger of overgrazing. Nomadic stock rearing was once widespread but with rapidly growing populations and increasing pressure on the land it is now becoming much more restricted. The savanna grasslands to the south of the Sahara Desert are typical in this respect. For centuries the area was occupied by the Fulani – a nomadic people who moved their cattle along well defined routes in search of pasture. Gradually, however, the best pastures were occupied by farmers, leaving only the poorest and driest areas open to the herdsmen. As a result many of the Fulani were forced to settle down while those who retained their herds moved eastward into the area near Lake Chad. One of the main centres today is near the town of Gubio (Fig. 4.10).

Farming and the environment

Surrounding Gubio is a vast area of lowland. For the most part this lowland is covered by small sand dunes (Fig. 4.11). These reach 20 metres in height and form long ridges, running from north west to south east. Conditions on the dune ridges are very different from those in the hollows and this has an important effect on farming. A more important influence is the seasonal pattern of rainfall and it is this which largely determines the movement of animals.

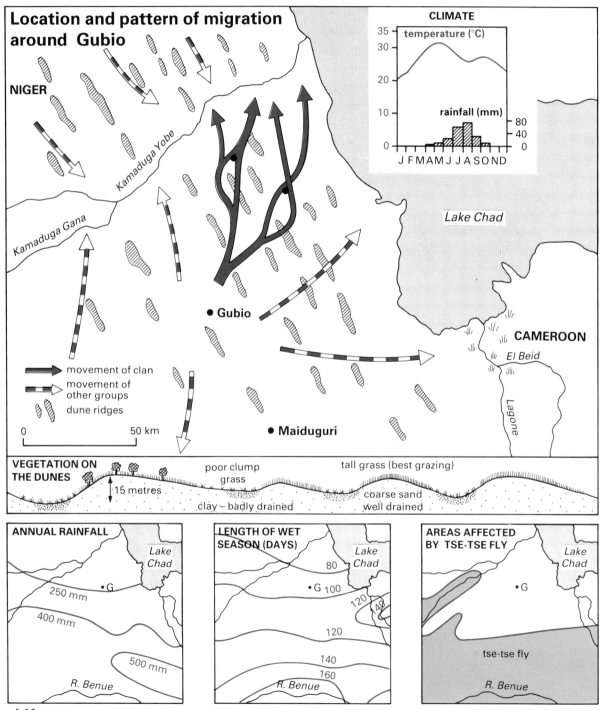

Location and pattern of migration around Gubio

NIGER

Kamaduga Yobe

Kamaduga Gana

Lake Chad

● Gubio

CAMEROON

El Beid

Lagone

● Maiduguri

→ movement of clan
→ movement of other groups
⬭ dune ridges

0   50 km

CLIMATE

temperature (°C)

rainfall (mm)

J F M A M J J A S O N D

VEGETATION ON THE DUNES

poor clump grass

tall grass (best grazing)

15 metres

coarse sand well drained

clay – badly drained

ANNUAL RAINFALL

Lake Chad

●G

250 mm

400 mm

500 mm

R. Benue

LENGTH OF WET SEASON (DAYS)

Lake Chad

80

●G 100

120

140

160

120

R. Benue

AREAS AFFECTED BY TSE-TSE FLY

Lake Chad

●G

tse-tse fly

R. Benue

Fig. 4.11

Study the maps in Fig. 4.11 and complete the following exercise.

a i What is the approximate total annual rainfall at Gubio?

    ii During which months does most rain fall?

    iii Which season can be called the wet season?

    iv Describe the general pattern of rainfall in North Eastern Nigeria, concentrating on the pattern of distribution and the length of the wet season.

b i During which season are the grasslands around Gubio used for grazing?

    ii In the dune fields where is the best pasture found?

    iii Describe the vegetation in the troughs between the dunes and explain why it is poor.

c During the dry season animals are moved from the Gubio region.

    i Name the four areas used for dry season grazing.

    ii In each case explain why the pasture is likely to be better there during the dry season.

d i Which animals are reared in the Gubio district?

    ii What is the density of stock per square kilometre?

    iii Why are few animals reared near the Kamaduga Gana?

Fig. 4.12 *Grassland with acacia in North Eastern Nigeria*

The influence of physical conditions on the pattern of farming is striking.

1 Grazing is generally poor (Fig. 4.12) and large areas are needed to feed one animal.

2 During the long dry season the quality of the pasture declines even further. A large number of animals are moved either to pastures in the river valleys and on the shore of Lake Chad (where some water remains) or to the south which is generally wetter.

3 Free movement is not always possible. Many of the wetter areas are now occupied by farmers who do not welcome the animals of the nomadic herdsman. Others are infested by the tse-tse fly which transmits serious diseases to cattle. During the wet season the tse-tse fly is widespread on the savanna. During the dry season it is restricted to the wetter areas, particularly the river valleys. It is these areas which could provide dry season pasture.

Fig. 4.13 *Cattle grazing at a waterhole in North Eastern Nigeria*

The organisation of farming

The Fulani live in family groups which are often large and contain a number of relatives. Each of these extended family groups lives in a compound (Fig. 4.14) and a number of compounds are grouped together, to form a clan.

Every family owns a number of cattle which are grazed communally with those of the rest of the clan (Fig. 4.13). The animals are milked and the milk is either used to feed the family or is bartered for other foodstuffs such as grain. Little meat is eaten because the Fulani regard cattle as wealth and are reluctant to kill the animals.

Decisions concerning the movement of stock are taken by the heads of the families which make up the clan. Towards the end of November a major decision is taken to leave the pastures around Gubio. The entire clan then begins a slow journey across the dunefields towards the pastures on the lowlands near Lake Chad. At the same time other clans will begin moving towards pastures in other areas. For a time the movement is slow as the animals are allowed to graze the stubble on neighbouring farmland. In return they provide manure for next year's crop in the fields. As the grass dries, however, grazing becomes poor and the need to move to fresh pastures becomes more pressing. This lack of grazing may force the clans to split up and individual family groups will find their own way to the dry season pastures near the lake. Lack of rain causes the lake itself to shrink and this exposes areas of marshland which can be grazed. Eventually even these pastures are exhausted and the onset of the rains in April sees the beginning of a rapid journey back to the lowlands around Gubio. Here large areas of grassland are then burnt so as to remove dead grass and to encourage new growth.

COMPOUND OF FULANI FAMILY GROUP
(24 cattle graze within 6 km of compound)

shelters for
wives and children of head
thorn fence
○ hearth
shelter for old people
calves tethered on line
corral for animals
● fire
shelter for young men
shelter for girls

PATTERN OF MIGRATION

May–September (wet season)	— Lowlands near Gubio
October–November	— Farmland near Gubio (animals graze on stubble)
December–February	— Journey to Lake Chad
February–April	— Lowlands near Lake Chad
May	— Return to Gubio

Fig. 4.14

THE RESULTS OF OVERGRAZING

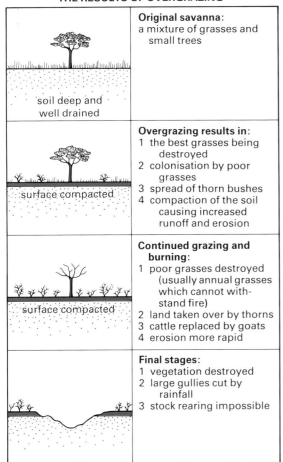

	Original savanna: a mixture of grasses and small trees
soil deep and well drained	
	Overgrazing results in: 1 the best grasses being destroyed 2 colonisation by poor grasses 3 spread of thorn bushes 4 compaction of the soil causing increased runoff and erosion
surface compacted	
	Continued grazing and burning: 1 poor grasses destroyed (usually annual grasses which cannot withstand fire) 2 land taken over by thorns 3 cattle replaced by goats 4 erosion more rapid
surface compacted	
	Final stages: 1 vegetation destroyed 2 large gullies cut by rainfall 3 stock rearing impossible

Fig. 4.15

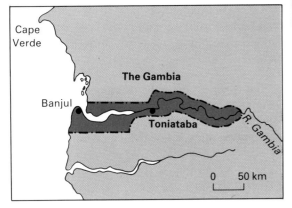

Location:	Toniataba, the Gambia
Climate:	High temperatures 1000 mm rainfall; long dry season
Growing season:	Less than 150 days Limited by drought
Farm system:	Sedentary cultivation with some shifting cultivation Part subsistence, part commerical
Produce:	Groundnuts Rice Cattle

Fig. 4.16

Even during the wet season the movement of stock must continue so that grazed areas are allowed to recover. This means that villages must be moved too, since animals are usually grazed near to the settlements and the risk of overgrazing is most serious here.

The future

This type of farming is not the most productive in terms of land use and in many areas it has given way to other types of farming. As a result the area of pasture available has been reduced, with the best land being taken over for crop production. This has led to overgrazing (Fig. 4.15) which can eventually completely destroy the land. The stages in this process are as follows.

1   Most animals select the best grasses and if the land is not allowed to recover these will eventually disappear.

2   Regular burning encourages this process.

3   Poor grass and thorn scrub then take over the land.

4   Soil erosion increases until the vegetation cover is completely destroyed.

The rate at which this destruction is taking place has increased with the rapid growth of population in recent years and as a result of the effects of drought.

Attempts to improve the situation have not always been successful. For example, wells have been sunk to provide a regular water supply for the people and their stock. The main result of this has been to encourage grazing around the wells until the vegetation there has been destroyed.

Groundnut and rice cultivation: The Gambia

The pressures which are for the first time affecting the shifting cultivators of the Solomon Islands have become so intense in other parts of the Developing World that they have produced changes in the traditional systems of farming. This can be clearly seen in the Gambia in West Africa (Fig. 4.16). Here a complicated system of shifting cultivation has developed, producing both subsistence and commercial crops.

Social organisation and land holding

The Gambia is a land of small villages and larger market towns.

1   Each village has an area of land at its disposal.

2   Each year part of this land is allocated to the families in the village by the headman.

3   The family group is an extended family, i.e. it includes the head of the family, his wives and children and several other relatives. They live in a compound in the village. Each compound will include several huts.

4   This large family group works the land it has been allocated and its activities are controlled by the head of the family.

5   The land is allocated in the form of a number of scattered

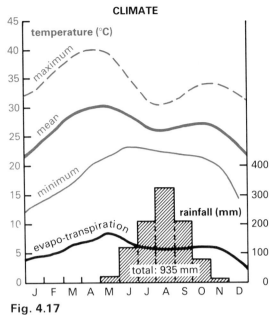

CLIMATE

Fig. 4.17

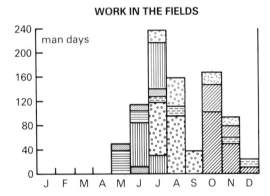

WORK IN THE FIELDS

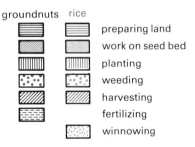

groundnuts	rice	
		preparing land
		work on seed bed
		planting
		weeding
		harvesting
		fertilizing
		winnowing

Fig. 4.18

plots. This ensures that the best land is more equally shared. In addition, however, because most villages in the Gambia are situated near to the river it means that each compound can be given different types of land, e.g. on the floodplain, on the plateau and on the gently sloping land between the two. This is particularly important since these different types of land are used to grow the different crops needed by the family.

a   The main food crop, rice, is grown on the alluvial soils of the floodplain.

b   The major cash crop, groundnuts, is grown on the sloping land above the floodplain and on the lower slopes of the plateau.

c   Around the village the emphasis is on vegetables and cereal crops such as millet and maize.

6   The women of the compound grow the food crops, the men grow the cash crops and look after the cattle which graze on the land which is not in cultivation at the time.

7   Attempts are made to maintain the fertility of the land by applying fertilisers and by rotating the crops on the land not affected by the river floods. In most cases, however, the normal method is still to leave part of the land fallow. If the village has a surplus of land extra plots may be allocated from the unused land.

8   These new clearings tend to be further away from the village and this can involve long walks between the rice fields on the floodplain and the groundnut and cereal fields away from the river. Some attempt is always made, however, to keep some land near the village for growing vegetables and grazing goats, sheep and cattle.

9   The role of animals is important since they are used to indicate wealth as well as to provide food. For this reason families are unwilling to slaughter their stock and herds tend to be large. The animals are kept in the compound at night but during the day they are grazed communally over the unused village land and over fallow land. In return they manure the land. Because of the long dry season, grazing is often in short supply and overgrazing has resulted in the destruction of vegetation and erosion of the soil.

10   Most of the work is done by the members of the compound. If there is a shortage of labour, however, workers are hired in return for the right to work part of the land. If there is a surplus of labour, young men leave the compound to work elsewhere.

The working of the system

This system of farming is obviously very complicated, combining subsistence and cash cropping; arable and pastoral elements; and permanent and shifting cultivation. It can best be understood by looking at a single example – a village near Toniataba in the Lower River Division of the Gambia.

The village has a population of 1130, housed in 54 compounds. Each compound (Fig. 4.20) is a collection of huts bonded by a fence woven out of grass and branches. Within the fence there is room for a small maize and vegetable plot and an enclosure for the animals owned by the family group. Living and sleeping quarters are segregated with separate areas for men and women.

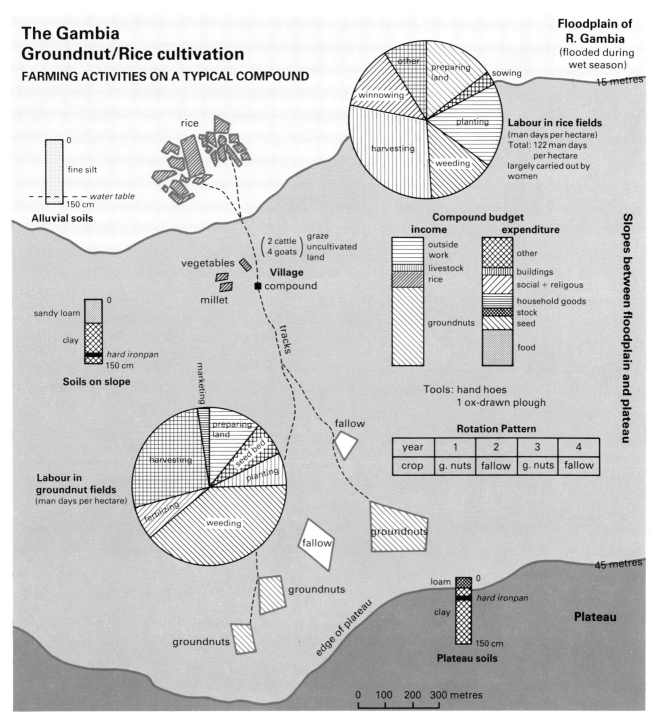

The Gambia
Groundnut/Rice cultivation
FARMING ACTIVITIES ON A TYPICAL COMPOUND

Floodplain of R. Gambia (flooded during wet season)

15 metres

rice

Alluvial soils
- 0
- fine silt
- water table
- 150 cm

Labour in rice fields (man days per hectare) Total: 122 man days per hectare largely carried out by women

preparing land — sowing — planting — weeding — harvesting — winnowing — other

Slopes between floodplain and plateau

vegetables
millet

Village ■ compound

(2 cattle / 4 goats) graze uncultivated land

tracks

Soils on slope
- 0
- sandy loam
- clay
- hard ironpan
- 150 cm

Compound budget

income	expenditure
outside work	other
livestock	buildings
rice	social + religous
	household goods
	stock
groundnuts	seed
	food

Tools: hand hoes
1 ox-drawn plough

Rotation Pattern

year	1	2	3	4
crop	g. nuts	fallow	g. nuts	fallow

Labour in groundnut fields (man days per hectare)

marketing — preparing land — seed bed — planting — weeding — fertilizing — harvesting

fallow
fallow
groundnuts
groundnuts
groundnuts

edge of plateau

Plateau soils
- loam
- 0
- hard ironpan
- clay
- 150 cm

45 metres

Plateau

0 100 200 300 metres

Fig. 4.19

The village has 2275 hectares of land at its disposal. Only one third of this area is allocated to the compounds, the remainder being kept in reserve to meet future population growth and to allow exhausted areas to be rested. The area available to our study compound is 13.3 hectares. About one quarter of this is left fallow and the remainder is equally divided between alluvial land for rice growing and sloping land used for groundnuts (Fig. 4.19). Farming in both areas is limited by the nature of the soils and the length of the dry season (Fig. 4.17).

COMPOUND HOUSING FAMILY GROUP OF 24 PEOPLE

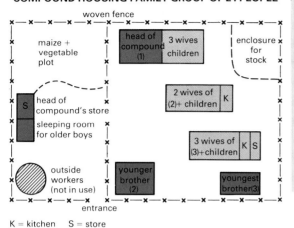

K = kitchen   S = store

	Area (hectares)	
Land use	Village	Compound
Cultivated	482	10.7
Fallow	286	2.6
Uncultivated	1507	—
Total	2275	13.3
Population	1130	24

Fig. 4.20

Using information given on the previous pages complete the following exercise.

a i Describe the farming activities of the compound, paying particular attention to: type of land available, location of the fields, size of fields, crops grown, system of farming the main crops, and the role of animals.

b i Describe the main features of the climate.
  ii During which months is water available for farming?
  iii Explain how the climate influences the pattern of farming during the year.
  iv Describe the year's work in the cultivation of rice and groundnuts.

Fig. 4.21 *A typical village scene in the Gambia*

GROUNDNUT/RICE FARMING: INPUTS AND OUTPUTS

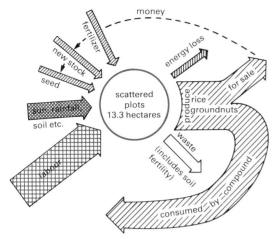

Fig. 4.22

This farming system in the Gambia (Fig. 4.22) is obviously much more complicated than the basic system of shifting cultivation seen in the Solomon Islands and it supports a much greater density of population (approaching 50 per square kilometre compared with less than 5 per square kilometre). At the same time the pressures produced by population growth and the demands of commercial agriculture are even stronger. In some places the reserve of uncultivated land upon which the villages depend has been reduced to danger point and periods of fallow have sometimes disappeared. This has resulted in soil exhaustion and declining yields – a trend which can only be overcome by introducing new methods of farming. Unfortunately this is very difficult given a system in which no individual owns land, holdings are usually small and scattered and there is little capital with which to make improvements. As a result hoe cultivation is still important and the introduction of simple implements such as ox drawn ploughs has been very slow. Such problems, together with the low rainfall of the last decade, have meant that many villages fail to produce enough food to last throughout the year and this has led to even more emphasis being placed on crops which can be sold.

Sedentary farming: Newalpur, Nepal

All systems of shifting agriculture are wasteful of land since, in order to maintain soil fertility and to keep crop yields at a reasonable level, only a small proportion of the land can be used at any given time. This limits the number of people who can be fed. As the population increases, the system can come under severe strain, with periods of fallow being reduced to dangerously low levels. As a result, soils deteriorate and crop yields begin to decline so that the land can support fewer people rather than more.

High population densities are possible only when more efficient use is made of the land and this usually means the development of continuous cultivation of one kind or another. Many systems have developed, ranging from comparatively simple ones in the Developing World to highly complex ones in developed countries. All have to overcome the same basic problem – how to maintain soil fertility without using periods of fallow. Many efficient methods have been developed to achieve this, including heavy manuring, the use of chemical fertilisers and the rotation of crops.

One of the simplest systems can be seen in the Newalpur district of Nepal (Fig. 4.23) where a highly productive system of farming has been developed.

Physical conditions

The main farming areas of the district are located in the valley of the River Gandak (a tributary of the River Ganges) and its tributaries. Since the rivers are deeply cut into the foothills of the Himalayas, slopes are steep and this limits the amount of land which can be cultivated. In fact, most of the farmland is located near the valley floor. Even here, however, there are different types of land which are of different value to the farmers (Fig. 4.24).

Location: Newalpur, Nepal

Climate: Hot summers, warm winters
Heavy summer rainfall

Farming: Sedentary, subsistence

Crops: Rice and wheat

Fig. 4.23

CROSS SECTION OF FARMING AREA

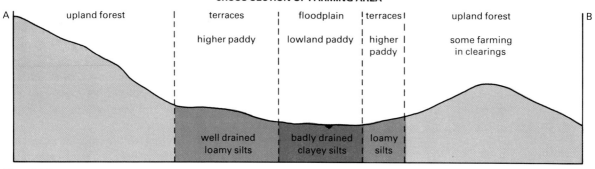

Fig. 4.24

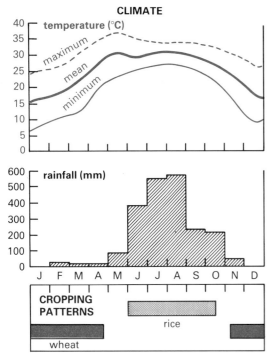

Fig. 4.25 (a)

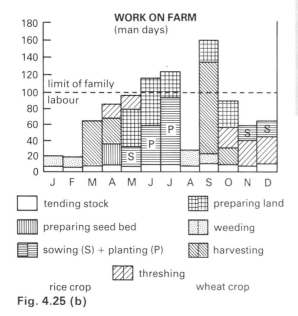

Fig. 4.25 (b)

Land in the upland forest is of least value and clearing has taken place only on a very small scale. By contrast, the land on the floodplain of the river is highly prized since it has a plentiful supply of water and cultivation is restricted only by waterlogging. On the terraces the land is better drained but successful rice cultivation depends upon the development of irrigation schemes. When water is available, however, yields can be very high.

The problems of water supply and drainage are, of course, strongly influenced by the climate (Fig. 4.25). The entire area comes under the influence of the monsoon and there is a marked contrast between the drought of the winter and the heavy rainfall of the summer months. During the wet season the lower paddy near the river is flooded and conditions are ideal for rice cultivation. On the terraces, even during the wet season, water supply is a problem and irrigation is necessary.

The farm

Refer to Figs 4.24–29 and complete the following exercise.

a   i   Where is the farm located? What type of land is it situated on?
   ii   What is the size of the farm? How many people does it support?
b   i   Name the two crops grown.
   ii   Describe the year's work on the farm, relating it to climatic conditions.
   iii   Why does rice cultivation require more labour than the cultivation of wheat?
   iv   During which months is hired labour likely to be necessary? Why?
c   Describe the irrigation system used by the farmer.

The farm shown in Figs 4.24–29 is typical of farms in the area.

1   It is very small and farmed by the family who own the land.

2   In order to feed the family, land use has to be intensive and every effort is made to obtain both wet season and dry season crops.

3   The land is located on the lower terraces of a tributary of the River Gandak and is not subject to flooding during the monsoon rains.

4   Soils are fertile loams and silts and are well drained.

5   As a result, water supply is a major problem, particularly for the growing of rice. For this reason irrigation is important.

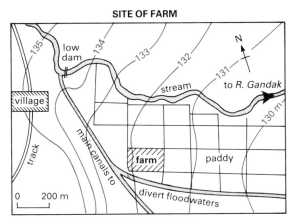

SITE OF FARM

Fig. 4.26 (a)

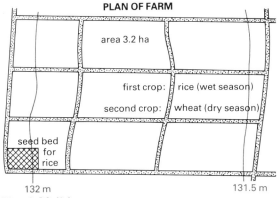

PLAN OF FARM

area 3.2 ha

first crop: rice (wet season)

second crop: wheat (dry season)

seed bed for rice

132 m   131.5 m

Fig. 4.26 (b)

SECTION THROUGH FARMLAND

flow of floodwaters   (average slope 1:500)

embankment to retain water

220 metres

Fig. 4.26 (c)

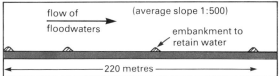

PRODUCTIVITY OF FARM

income

for sale   rice 600 kg / wheat 380 kg

output

2 buffalo husks +   rice 3500 kg
3 cows   straw   wheat 650 kg
2 goats   feed

consumed by family (4 adults, 3 children)
rice 2900 kg
wheat 270 kg

graze stubble (manure land)
graze nearby forest

Fig. 4.26 (d)

tools	plough	spade	axe	sickle	leveller
number	1	3	2	3	1

6 Methods of irrigation are very simple but they require communal effort on the part of the entire village. A small earth dam has been built to raise the water level in the stream and to control flood waters. From the dam water is diverted along canals which carry it to the higher terraces further down the valley. From here the water is allowed to flow from one stepped field to another. Earth banks are built to retain water in the fields long enough for the land to be puddled in preparation for transplanting of the rice.

7 Given an adequate water supply, two crops can be obtained each year. Of these crops, rice – the wet season crop – is by far the most important both in terms of output and in terms of the labour involved.

Rice is a labour intensive crop, requiring growing in nursery beds before it is transplanted into the flooded paddy. A large amount of time is spent ploughing the waterlogged soils of the paddy (Fig. 4.27) and transplanting the individual rice plants by hand. The rice then ripens as the paddy dries out and from then until the harvest little labour is needed. Once the rice crop has been harvested, a second crop of wheat or barley is immediately sown to make use of any remaining moisture. Yields of the dry season crop are generally low but it does provide a surplus which can be sold to raise money. This, in turn, can be used to hire labour during the summer and early autumn when work in the fields is at its peak.

8 Against this, continuing use of the land creates many problems and great care is needed in the preparation and manuring of the fields prior to planting. This problem is particularly severe on the higher paddy which is not flooded by the river and therefore receives no fresh silt – a natural fertiliser.

The farming system

Although productivity is much higher than in any of the systems of shifting agriculture, this system of farming is still comparatively simple.

The land is intensively used and two crops a year are obtained from it. However, a very high input of labour is necessary (Fig. 4.29).

Good use is made of waste products (manure, straw, etc.) which are used to maintain soil fertility and to feed a small number of animals. Despite this, however, yields are generally low, particularly when the second crop is taken into consideration. Any improvement will require a more regular supply of water which involves building a more efficient system of irrigation. This will only be possible when more capital is available – a situation which is unlikely to exist as long as farms are so small and yields so low. Some improvements have been made. Crops other than wheat or barley are now grown and this lessens the risk of exhausting the soil. In addition, higher yielding types of rice have been introduced so that food production has been increased without changing the traditional methods of farming. Beyond this other major improvements are unlikely. For

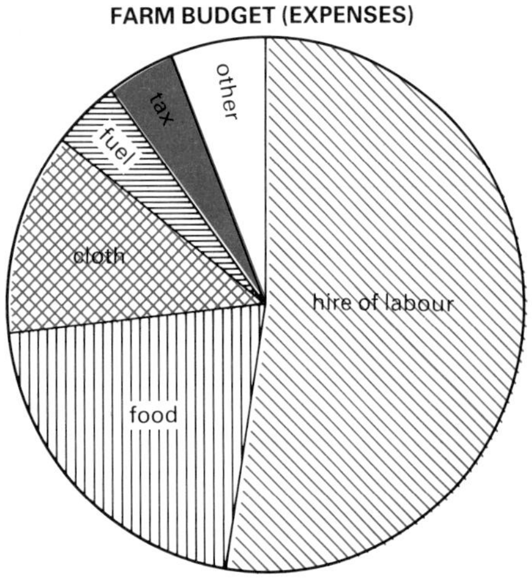

FARM BUDGET (EXPENSES)

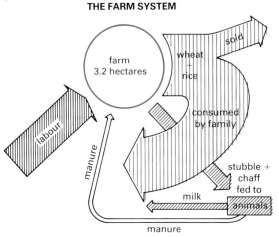

Fig. 4.28

THE FARM SYSTEM

Fig. 4.29

Fig. 4.27 *Oxen ploughing paddy fields*

example, mechanisation would be difficult to introduce because of the small size of farm and in any case it is questionable whether it would be wise to replace labour with machines when no alternative work is available.

Such problems are not found only in Nepal. They are shared by almost all subsistence farming systems in the Developing World and many attempts have been made to overcome them.

The Green Revolution

The rapid increase in population throughout the Developing World has placed many of the traditional farming systems under strain and brought parts of the world to the verge of starvation. The only lasting solution may be to slow down the rate of population growth. Until this happens, however, the countries of the Developing World, in particular, are committed to a race to increase food production simply in order to feed their growing populations. As can be seen from the diagram, Fig. 4.30, the developing countries have so far been successful in this race and food production has generally kept pace with the rising population. The methods used to achieve this success have varied enormously, but together they make up the so-called Green Revolution.

Most of the traditional systems of subsistence farming appear to be inefficient and those based on shifting cultivation or nomadic

FOOD PRODUCTION AND POPULATION

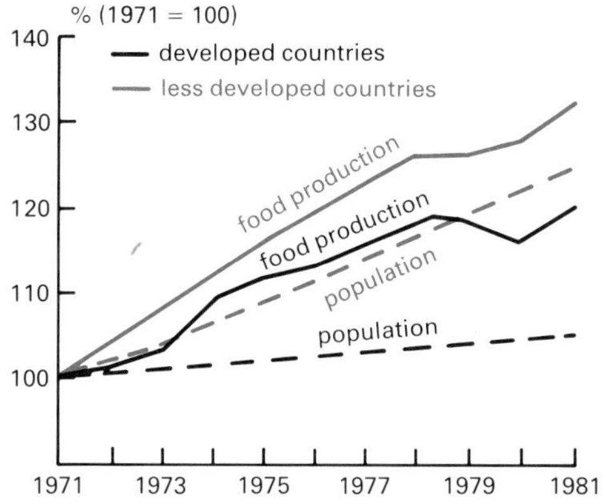

% (1971 = 100)

Fig. 4.30

AGRICULTURAL PRODUCTIVITY AND FERTILISER USE (BY COUNTRY)

	Fertiliser use (kg/ha)	Agricultural production ($/ha)
Canada	41	70
Egypt	212	85
Guatamala	59	49
India	30	24
Japan	478	2144
Kenya	17	60
Sweden	169	295
Tanzania	6	8
United Kingdom	323	275
USA	111	74

herding do require large areas of land. Initially, therefore, an attractive option seemed to be to make use of the land left unused by shifting cultivators to produce food, often using the most up to date techniques available. This resulted in the development of ambitious schemes such as the Groundnut Scheme in East Africa which became an expensive failure. Large areas of land were cleared and ploughed, using modern machines, and a single crop was sown. The result was the rapid exhaustion of the poor tropical soil, leading eventually to soil erosion. Yields began to decline alarmingly and eventually crops could be grown only by using expensive chemical fertilisers. There was a constant battle to keep the farms clear of the encroaching forest. In addition to these problems, many of which might have been predicted, there were unexpected difficulties such as the failure of modern machines and the fact that steel plough blades were worn away by the coarse crystalline soils.

Failures of this kind led to such methods being called 'inappropriate technologies' (see page 191). They also led to a growing interest in adapting existing methods instead of introducing more advanced technologies from the Developed World. Even this has proved difficult for, as we have seen, a change in one part of a farming system is likely to have repercussions – some of them unexpected – in other parts of the system. This applies even to the small scale changes which have tended to make up the Green Revolution.

1   Of all the methods of farming, it is the systems of shifting cultivation which seem to be least efficient and which have been subjected to the greatest change. Population growth generally has put such systems under strain. In addition, in many areas the spread of commercial agriculture has taken some of the best land. As a result, attempts have been made to end the practice of shifting cultivation and to replace it with permanent cultivation. Such a change immediately raises the problem of maintaining soil fertility. This can be achieved by manuring, by rotating crops or by using chemical fertilisers.

2   The use of artificial (chemical) fertilisers (see Table) is one of the more controversial aspects of the Green Revolution. Fertilisers have undoubtedly increased yields enormously but few developing countries have the capacity to produce them and this means that the bulk of the fertilisers have to be imported. Furthermore, since many artificial fertilisers are oil based, the cost has increased enormously in recent years. This has caused great difficulties for developing countries.

3   Less dramatic but of more lasting value have been the increased yields produced by the improvement of traditional farming methods. At its simplest this can mean nothing more than making more effective use of natural fertilisers such as manure or vegetable waste. At the other end of the scale, however, it can involve the introduction of new crops which make more intensive farming possible.

4   The effect of the introduction of new types of crop can be seen in two important areas:

a   Most striking has been the increased yield obtained from new varieties of staple crops. In some parts of the world, for example, yields of rice, wheat and maize have more than doubled,

67

Fig. 4.31 *Large scale food production in the Developing World: new technology aids rice production in the Philippines*

largely because new high yielding varieties have been introduced.

b Equally important, the development of quick ripening varieties has helped the introduction of a second crop in many parts of the tropics. This type of multiple cropping is one of the best ways of increasing food production in less developed countries.

Attempts to introduce completely new crops have been less successful, often because of the unwillingness of people to accept unusual foods.

Overall these developments have been very successful. There are, however, problems to be faced. For example, there are the obvious dangers of exhausting the soil. In addition there is some evidence that the new crops may be less resistant to disease than the old. If this is so it leads to a greater dependence on weed killers and insecticides.

5   The control of pests and weeds was an early and effective means of improving yields. This depended on the use of chemicals, most of which were produced in the developed countries. Not only were these expensive to buy, there is growing evidence that they gradually became less effective and that some, e.g. DDT, were poisoning the environment.

6   In many parts of the world one of the most effective ways of increasing food production has been to improve the supply of water to the fields. At first many expensive large scale irrigation schemes were built. Experience has shown, however, that money is often better spent on small scale projects such as the sinking of wells or the installation of electric pumps, both of which can make the supply of water more regular. Farmers are also taught how to make more efficient use of the water already available (see page 104).

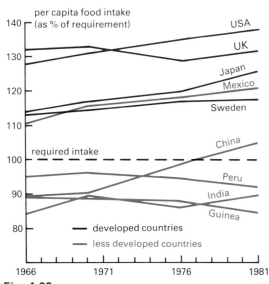

PER CAPITA FOOD INTAKE (by country)

Fig. 4.32

The success of the Green Revolution can be measured by the fact that, during a period of extremely rapid population growth, food production has more than kept pace with the increase in population. At the same time it is important to remember that many problems remain:

1   Food production per capita has increased most rapidly in the countries of the Developed World (Fig. 4.32).

2   In some of the less developed countries food production has barely kept pace with population growth in spite of many attempts to change farming methods.

3   Within individual countries large areas remain which have not benefited from the Green Revolution.

4   Even more important, there is evidence that it has been the wealthiest farmers who have benefited most from the changes. They have used their success to buy more land. This in turn has left other people without land and has increased the gap between rich and poor.

Commercial agriculture in less developed countries

Attempts to introduce modern methods to the traditional subsistence farming systems are comparatively recent. This is not true of commercial agriculture in the less developed countries – the most up to date methods of farming have been used from the earliest days of colonisation by European nations. Nowhere is this more clearly seen than in the spread of plantation agriculture throughout the tropical world.

MODEL: A PLANTATION

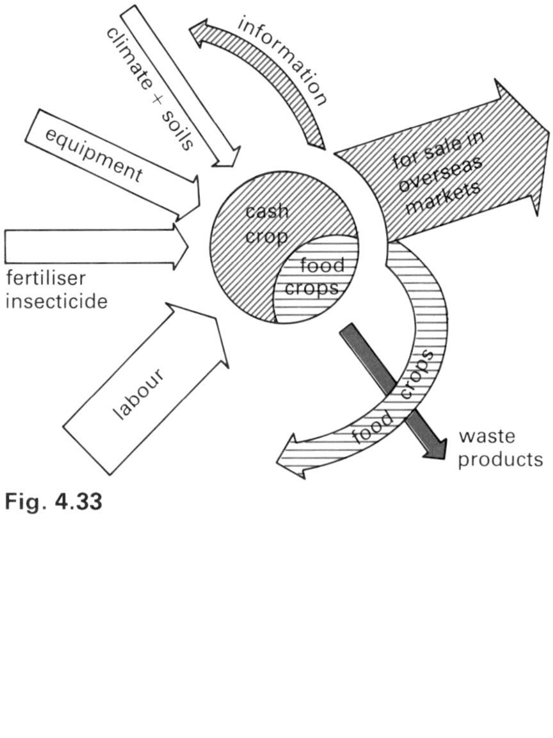

Fig. 4.33

The plantation system

Plantation agriculture is a highly specialised system of farming (Fig. 4.33). The first plantations were established by the Spaniards and the Portuguese in the sixteenth century to grow sugar cane in their new American colonies. Since then the plantation system has been taken to all parts of the tropical world and has been used to grow a variety of commercial crops, including tea, cotton, rubber, palm oil, tobacco and coffee.

The modern plantation is very distinctive.

1   The main crops are cash crops. They are often produced for overseas markets, particularly markets in the industrial world. As a result, plantations are strongly influenced by changes in these markets.

2   Production is on a large scale.

3   Most of the land is used to grow one or two cash crops. In addition a small area is granted to the families who work the estate so that they can grow their own food crops.

4   The labour force is large. Until the nineteenth century many plantations used slave labour. With abolition of slavery, however, labour had to be hired and wages (often low) paid.

5   As the cost of labour increased so it became more important to use it efficiently, so much so that crops were chosen to provide employment throughout the year. This is one reason why tree crops such as rubber, cocoa and coffee have become so important.

6   The plantation is run as a single unit with a strong central management. The management is often European or American; the labour force almost always native. This partly reflects early fears that Europeans could not work in the tropics.

7   Farming methods are generally efficient. This is often the result of large scale investment by the owners (usually large industrial companies).

Plantation agriculture varies from place to place and according to the type of crop grown, but many of these features can be seen in the organisation of any individual farm or estate.

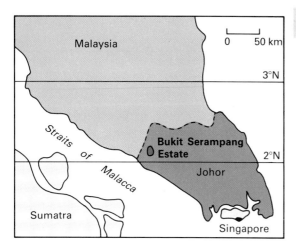

Location: Bukit Serampang
                      Johor State, Malaysia

Climate: Hot throughout the year
                      Heavy rainfall throughout the year

Growing season: 365 days

Farm type: Plantation

Crops: Rubber, palm oil

Fig. 4.34

Rubber estate: Johor, Malaysia

Bukit Serampang estate (Fig. 4.34) was cleared from the dense rain forest in 1926, and the first rubber trees were planted the following year. At that time Malaya (now Malaysia) was part of the British Empire and it was a British company – Dunlop – which made this investment. Initial costs were high, involving the clearing of dense jungle and the maintenance of that clearing in the face of encroaching undergrowth. In addition service roads were built and houses were provided for a large labour force.

The main features of the estate (Fig. 4.36) were laid down at that time.

1 Strong central management was provided by the parent company.

2 Native labour (Malay or Chinese) was employed.

3 Three villages were built to house the workers and their families and, over the years, the amenities of the villages were improved (Fig. 4.37).

4 Planting of the rubber trees was spread over a period of years so as to allow different parts of the estate to reach maturity at different times. This means that production can continue without interruption. It also makes it possible to spread replanting over a long period of time and this allows labour to be used most efficiently.

5 Methods of production are usually the most modern available. Each area of rubber is carefully laid out to give easy access (Fig. 4.38). Service roads are driven into the trees to allow machines to be used. Modern fertilisers, weed killers and insecticides are applied and light machines are used to cut back the surrounding undergrowth which grows rapidly in conditions of high temperature, heavy rainfall and high humidity (Fig. 4.35).

CLIMATE

total: 2350 mm

Fig. 4.35

Tapping a rubber tree

Bukit Serampang Estate, Johor, Malaysia

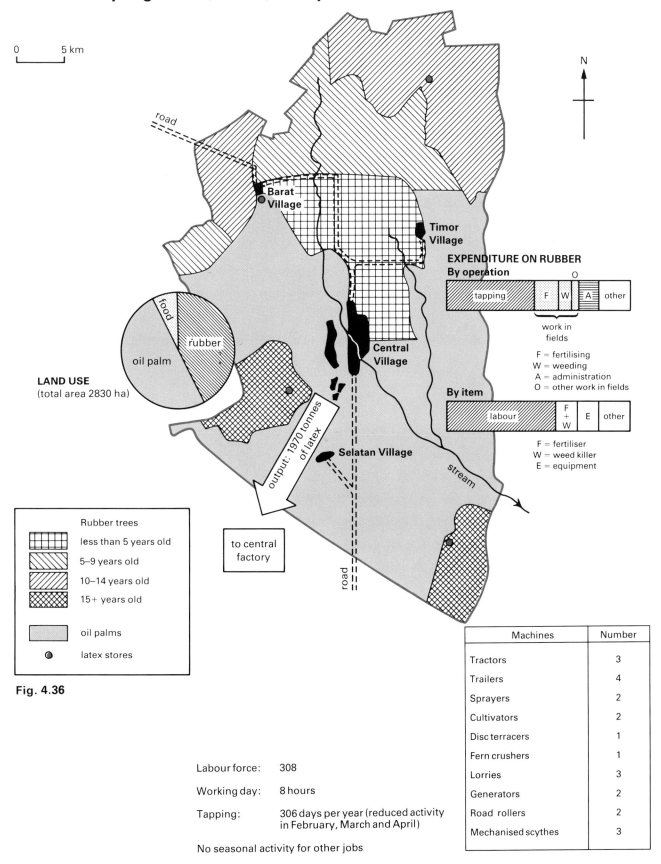

0   5 km

road

N

Barat Village

Timor Village

EXPENDITURE ON RUBBER

By operation

O

| tapping | F | W | A | other |

work in fields

F = fertilising
W = weeding
A = administration
O = other work in fields

Central Village

By item

| labour | F + W | E | other |

F = fertiliser
W = weed killer
E = equipment

LAND USE
(total area 2830 ha)

food
rubber
oil palm

output: 1970 tonnes of latex

Selatan Village

stream

to central factory

road

Rubber trees

less than 5 years old

5–9 years old

10–14 years old

15+ years old

oil palms

latex stores

Fig. 4.36

Machines	Number
Tractors	3
Trailers	4
Sprayers	2
Cultivators	2
Disc terracers	1
Fern crushers	1
Lorries	3
Generators	2
Road rollers	2
Mechanised scythes	3

Labour force: 308

Working day: 8 hours

Tapping: 306 days per year (reduced activity in February, March and April)

No seasonal activity for other jobs

PLAN: CENTRAL VILLAGE

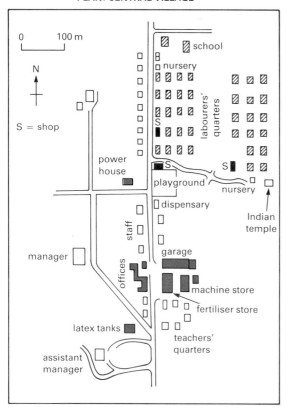

Fig. 4.37

6   The large labour force is occupied mainly in tapping the trees and collecting the latex (sap). It is important, therefore, that this operation should be spread throughout the year so as to provide full employment. The combination of a climate which gives a year long growing season and modern chemicals which can be used to stimulate the flow of latex allows this to be achieved for all but a short period in February, March and April when production slows down.

7   Because the estate is one of several owned by Dunlop in the area the latex is sent in liquid form to a central factory for processing into either concentrated latex which is exported to Britain, Western Europe, Japan and Australia, or block rubber for which the main market is the United Kingdom.

8   Although they are thousands of kilometres away, the influence of these markets is strong. For example, in the years following the Second World War synthetic rubber (derived from oil) challenged natural rubber in the world markets (Fig. 4.39). As a result of this competition, a large part of the estate was planted with oil palms to supply vegetable oils to a rapidly growing world market. This continued until 1972 by which time the area of oil palm had outstripped that of rubber. Recent oil price rises have forced a reconsideration of this policy. It is possible that, with the increasing cost of oil and the growing appreciation of the dangers of a world oil shortage, areas of the plantation will be put back to rubber.

Fig. 4.38 *Rubber trees on an estate*

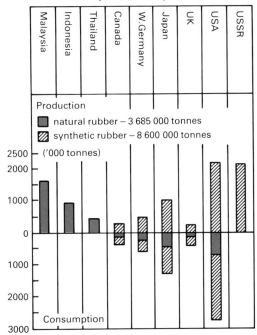

WORLD RUBBER PRODUCTION AND CONSUMPTION (BY COUNTRY)

Production
- ■ natural rubber – 3 685 000 tonnes
- ▨ synthetic rubber – 8 600 000 tonnes

Fig. 4.39

Using information given in this section, complete the following exercise.

a i Describe the main features of the climate at the Bukit Serampang estate.
   ii How does the climate help in the organisation of work on the estate?
b i Refer to the list of features characteristic of plantations given on page 69 and describe the ways in which the Bukit Serampang estate resembles the typical plantation.
   iii Draw an input/output model of the estate and compare it with Fig. 4.33 on page 69.
c Why is rubber an ideal plantation crop?
d Using information given in Fig. 4.39.
   i What proportion of the world rubber market is held by natural rubber?
   ii Name the three largest rubber producers.
   iii Name four major rubber importers.

As we have seen, plantation agriculture had strong associations with colonialism and with slavery. Furthermore, it meant that large international companies could control the lives of thousands of native workers and sometimes even bring in labour from other parts of the world. It is not surprising, therefore, that when countries gained independence many of the large estates, regardless of their efficiency, were broken up and the land was distributed to the native population. As a result, the proportion of cash crops grown on small farms in the tropics has increased enormously in the last 30 years.

Small scale production of cash crops in the tropics: Grenada, West Indies

Grenada (Fig. 4.40) is typical of this pattern of development. The most southerly of the Windward Islands, it was discovered by Columbus in 1498. During the seventeenth century the French colonised the island. In the process the native Carib population was virtually wiped out. This meant that Negro slaves had to be imported from Africa to work the small sugar plantations which had been established. The descendants of these slaves make up the bulk of the population today.

In 1762 the island was occupied by the British and it remained a British colony until independence in 1958. At first there was little change to the existing system of plantation agriculture. However, in 1834 slavery was ended and changes began which were to create the present system of farming.

For a while the plantations continued, often using workers brought in from the East Indies. These workers were sometimes given small areas of land to work for themselves. This was the beginning of the break up of the large estates which was to continue slowly for the next 100 years. It was after the Second World War that the spread of small scale farming became rapid and today the small farms produce a large proportion of Grenada's export crops.

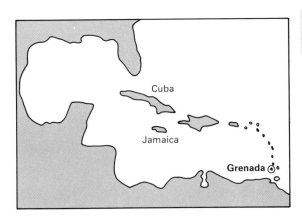

Location:	Grenada, West Indies
Climate:	High temperatures throughout the year Growing season 365 days Rainfall over 1250 mm Spring dry season
Farming system:	Commercial Small scale crop production
Crops:	Cocoa, bananas, coconuts, nutmeg, vegetables

Fig. 4.40

CLIMATE AT FARMHOUSE

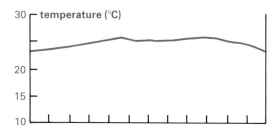

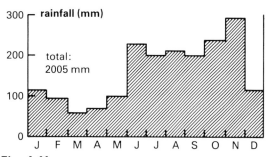

Fig. 4.41

Two factors have influenced the pattern of land holding on the island:

1 When a landowner dies the estate is divided among the heirs. Families are large in Grenada and this has led to a rapid increase in the number of small plots of land.

2 Population densities are generally high and this has caused the price of land to increase rapidly. This means that few people can afford to buy large plots of land.

As a result few farms in Grenada are more than six hectares in extent and most of them consist of three or more widely scattered small plots. The land use on each of these plots varies considerably but the main crops are likely to be bananas, cocoa, nutmeg, sugar or vegetables.

Study the information given in this section and complete the following exercise.

a i How many separate plots make up the farm?
   ii What is the approximate distance of each plot from the farmhouse?
b i For each plot state the two most important crops grown.
   ii Describe how the pattern of cropping changes with distance from the farmhouse.
   iii Why do you think these changes take place?
c i Give two possible reasons for the lack of mechanised equipment on the farm.

Homestead farms in the mountains, Grenada

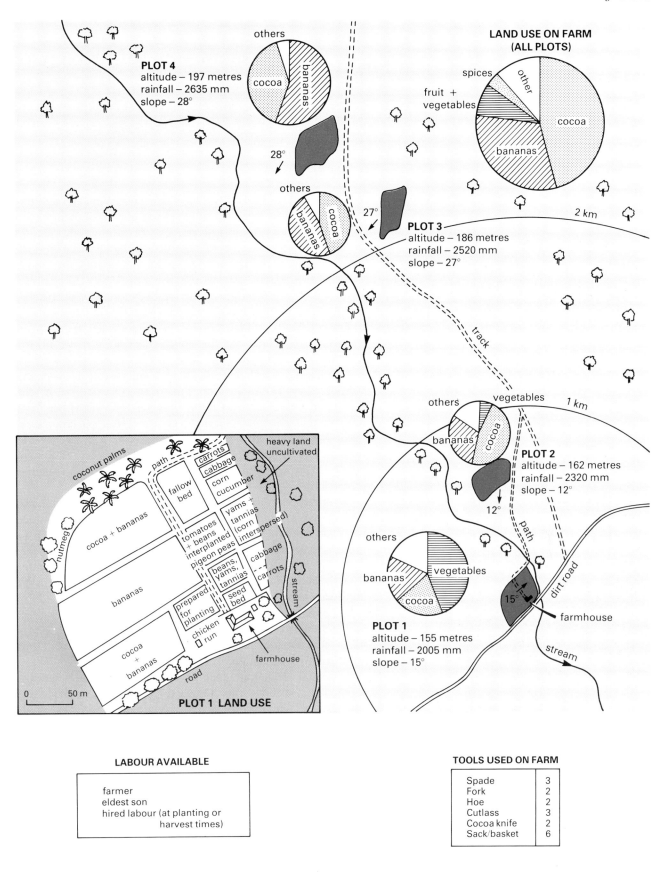

PLOT 4
altitude – 197 metres
rainfall – 2635 mm
slope – 28°

others
cocoa
bananas

LAND USE ON FARM
(ALL PLOTS)

spices
other
fruit +
vegetables
bananas
cocoa

others
bananas
cocoa

27°
28°

PLOT 3
altitude – 186 metres
rainfall – 2520 mm
slope – 27°

2 km

track

others
vegetables
bananas
cocoa

PLOT 2
altitude – 162 metres
rainfall – 2320 mm
slope – 12°

12°

1 km

path

others
bananas
vegetables
cocoa

PLOT 1
altitude – 155 metres
rainfall – 2005 mm
slope – 15°

15°

farmhouse

dirt road

stream

coconut palms
path
nutmeg

heavy land
uncultivated

carrots
cabbage
corn
cucumber

fallow
bed

cocoa + bananas

tomatoes
+ beans
interplanted
pigeon peas

yams +
tannias
(corn
interspersed)

cabbage

bananas

beans,
yams,
tannias

carrots

prepared
for
planting

seed
bed

chicken
run

cocoa
+
bananas

farmhouse

road
stream

0   50 m

PLOT 1 LAND USE

LABOUR AVAILABLE

farmer
eldest son
hired labour (at planting or
            harvest times)

TOOLS USED ON FARM

Spade	3
Fork	2
Hoe	2
Cutlass	3
Cocoa knife	2
Sack/basket	6

Fig. 4.42

    ii   Which aspects of the farm would you describe as simple?
    iii Which are advanced?
d i   For each plot state whether the land is flat, gently sloping or steeply sloping.
    ii   Suggest one serious problem likely to be caused by the steepness of the slopes.
    iii How has the farmer organised the pattern of farming to overcome the problem of the sloping land?
e   Why is the rearing of livestock relatively unimportant?

The farm (Fig. 4.42) is typical of small farms in Grenada. It is made up of four separate plots, the most distant of them nearly 4 kilometres away from the farmhouse. These have been bought at different times over a period of 20 years by a farmer who left Grenada to work in the United Kingdom so as to raise the money to start farming. His greatest problem was to buy the first plot upon which the farmhouse was built. Later plots were more steeply sloping and were therefore cheaper.

The organisation of the farm reflects the steepness of the slopes, the increased rainfall on the higher plots and, above all, the distance of the land from the farm.

Around the farmhouse the land is intensively farmed and vegetables are the main crop. Part of the crop is used by the family. The rest of it is sold in the market at St David. Other crops are grown on the same plot and a system of multiple cropping is used. This means that only small areas of bare earth are ever exposed to erosion. The tree crops such as coconut and mango which are grown along the boundaries of the plot offer further protection.

Beyond the farmhouse plot the pattern of cropping changes, with cash crops such as bananas dominating the middle distance plots and tree crops taking over on the more distant land. There are two major reasons for this:

1   The distant plots are higher and are generally much wetter than the land around the farm. Such conditions favour tree crops like cocoa and nutmeg.

2   More important, the distance of the land from the farm buildings, together with the lack of roads, means that such land is likely to be less intensively worked. This again makes tree crops an attractive proposition.

Because the individual plots of land are so small and because most of the farmers have little capital, farming methods are usually fairly simple. Most of the tools are hand tools, although motor vehicles are often used to carry the crops to market. Against this fertilisers, including chemical fertilisers, are widely used and most of the crops grown are for export. In other words this is genuine commercial farming carried out on a very small scale.

Commercial farming systems in the Developed World

Virtually all farming systems in the Developed World concentrate on the production of crops and animal products for the market, i.e. they are commercial rather than subsistence systems. It is not surprising, therefore, that in most countries outside the Communist bloc, the influence of the market is very strong. At the same time the influence of the market is rarely allowed to work unchecked. In recent years there has been increasing interference as governments have tried to maintain a prosperous agricultural base in the face of strong competition from other countries. This, of course, is most clearly seen in Communist countries where government control of prices and marketing is virtually complete. However, in most developed countries, subsidies, artificially high prices and import duties are now imposed.

The effects of such influences can be seen in most of the farming systems of the Developed World.

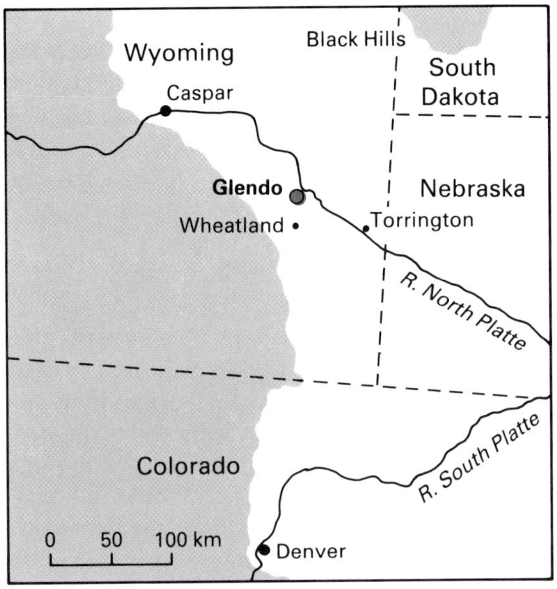

Location: Glendo, Wyoming, USA

Climate: Hot summers, cold winters
Low rainfall, mainly in summer

Farming: Extensive commercial stock rearing

Products: Beef, wheat.

Fig. 4.43

Extensive pastoral farming: Great Plains, USA

The Diamond A cattle ranch is situated on the west bank of the North Platte River as it flows out of the Front Ranges of the Rocky Mountains on to the High Plains (Fig. 4.43). The land rises from 1400 metres near the river to 1650 metres in the west and there is a change of soil from recent alluvium to soils derived from the sedimentary bed rock.

Climatic conditions (Fig. 4.44) are extreme. High summer temperatures (over 20°C) and low winter temperatures (-5°C) reflect the position in the centre of the North American landmass. This continental location also helps produce low rainfall (less than 350 mm) with a marked summer maximum.

These conditions have played an important part in the agricultural development of the area and ever since white settlers displaced the Indians towards the end of the nineteenth century the emphasis has been on stock rearing of various kinds. At first this simply meant the rearing of beef cattle on the open range. Within a few years, however, the first homesteads were established in the area and the pattern of farming began to change. (A homestead was a land grant of 160 acres (65 hectares) made by the government of the United States to new settlers in the West.) The origins of the Diamond A ranch can be traced back to a homestead claim taken out in 1888. The present ranch, comprising 8390 hectares, is the result of the joining together of many homesteads, all of the same size, all rectangular in shape. This regular shape is the product of the original government survey which divided the land into sections of one square mile (2.6 square kilometres) and quarter sections of 160 acres.

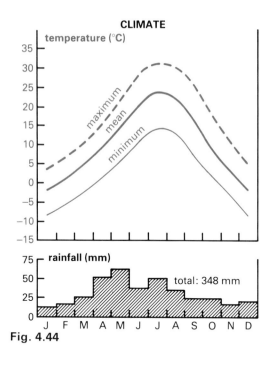

CLIMATE

temperature (°C)

maximum

mean

minimum

rainfall (mm)

total: 348 mm

J F M A M J J A S O N D

Fig. 4.44

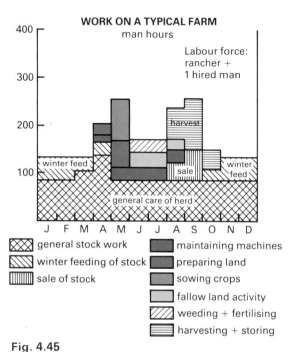

WORK ON A TYPICAL FARM

man hours

Labour force:
rancher +
1 hired man

winter feed

harvest

sale

winter feed

general care of herd

J F M A M J J A S O N D

☒ general stock work

▨ winter feeding of stock

▥ sale of stock

◼ maintaining machines

◼ preparing land

◼ sowing crops

▢ fallow land activity

▨ weeding + fertilising

▤ harvesting + storing

Fig. 4.45

The rearing of beef cattle remains the main activity on the ranch (Fig. 4.45) although the methods used have changed considerably since the days of the open range. Today, for example:

1   The ranch is now completely enclosed by a barbed wire fence and individual areas within it are fenced as necessary.

2   The division of the land into summer and winter ranges (Fig. 4.46) prevents overgrazing.

3   The major factor limiting the development of the farm is undoubtedly the low rainfall and its unreliability. This has to some extent been overcome by the sinking of wells in the drier parts of the range.

4   Another limiting factor is the shortage of winter grazing. Conditions are so severe during the winter that the grass dies back and has very little food value. As a result additional feed is needed. Some of this is bought in but in recent years efforts have been made to irrigate land near the river. This is now used to grow crops for winter feed, particularly corn which is harvested before it is ripe and made into silage. The number of animals kept is small for a farm of this size and any improvement is likely to depend on future success in increasing the amount of winter feed. Unfortunately this will not be easy since the river valley is steep sided and land for irrigation will have to be levelled. This is very expensive. Other alternatives, such as improving the quality of the pasture by sowing new types of grass, are even more difficult because of the extreme conditions and the low rainfall.

5   Attempts have also been made to reduce risks of failure by developing other types of farming. For example, 130 hectares of land, most of it near the river, have been laid down to cereals, with wheat the main crop. Since all of this land is above valley floor, irrigation is impossible and dry farming techniques have to be used. (These methods are described on page 109.) Any extension of grain farming is unlikely because of the risks involved and because of the costs which are higher than in other parts of the United States.

6   It is the shortage of winter feed which encourages the selling of stock at the end of the summer. Most of the animals are transported by road and rail to the mid-West where they are fattened on the farms of the Corn Belt before being sent to market.

The ranch is obviously a fairly simple farming system (Fig. 4.47). At the same time it has strong links with other farming systems in the mid-West. Together they form an extremely complex system. This is reflected in the complexity of links with the markets, both in the local area and in other parts of the United States.

A Ranch, Platte County, Wyoming

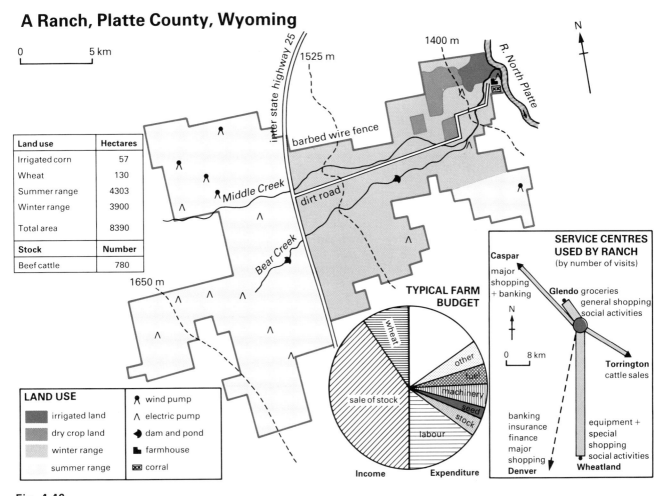

Land use	Hectares
Irrigated corn	57
Wheat	130
Summer range	4303
Winter range	3900
Total area	8390

Stock	Number
Beef cattle	780

LAND USE

- irrigated land
- dry crop land
- winter range
- summer range

- ♀ wind pump
- ∧ electric pump
- ◆ dam and pond
- ▮ farmhouse
- ▨ corral

TYPICAL FARM BUDGET

- wheat
- sale of stock
- other
- fuel
- machinery
- seed
- stock
- labour

Income — Expenditure

SERVICE CENTRES USED BY RANCH (by number of visits)

- Caspar — major shopping + banking
- Glendo — groceries general shopping social activities
- Torrington — cattle sales
- Denver — banking insurance finance major shopping
- Wheatland — equipment + special shopping social activities

Fig. 4.46

INPUT/OUTPUT MODEL OF A CATTLE RANCH

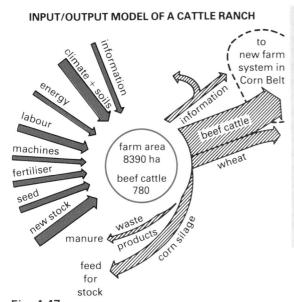

Fig. 4.47

Refer to Figs 4.45–47 and complete the following exercise.

a Five centres are shown as providing services for the ranch.
  i For each centre, list the services provided.
  ii Using the hierarchy given on page 26, list the centres in order of importance, giving reasons for your choice.

b Choose the appropriate missing words to complete the following statements.

The ranch is typical of a fairly *simple/complex* farming system. It covers a *large/small* area and productivity per hectare is *high/low*. Labour requirements are *large/small* for a farm of such a size. Capital investment is *high/low*, largely in the form of *machinery/labour/land improvements*. Effort is concentrated on *one/three* major products, i.e. *beef cattle/wheat/grass*. Attempts have been made to diversify production by growing *wheat and corn/cotton*. The system is an *intensive/extensive* one.

Location: Cereal farm near Saskatoon, Canada

Climate: January temperature −16.9°C
July temperature 19.3°C
Growing season 107 days
Rainfall total 396 mm, of which 305 mm falls during growing season

Vegetation: Prairie grassland

Fig. 4.48

Extensive arable farming: the Prairies, Canada

Although Saskatchewan (Fig. 4.48) lies some 900 kilometres to the north of Wyoming, both the environment and the patterns of farming are remarkably similar. Here, as in the United States, the foothills of the Rocky Mountains merge into high plains (the Prairies) and farming is generally extensive and carried out on a large scale. Furthermore, in the dry rain shadow area of Alberta to the west cattle ranching is important and the farming system resembles that of Wyoming. To the east on the more humid prairie, ranching is gradually replaced by large scale cereal cultivation.

Using information given on page 81, complete the following exercise.

a   i   Write down the mean temperature for January and for July.
     ii   What is the annual temperature range? Why is it so large?
     iii   How long is the growing season? (Plant growth starts when the temperature is above 6°C.)
b   i   What is the total annual precipitation?
     ii   What proportion of this occurs during the growing season?
c   i   What is evapo-transpiration?
     ii   When is evapo-transpiration greatest?
     iii   What effect is this likely to have on plant growth?

The climatic conditions (Fig. 4.49) present serious problems which have been overcome only by the development of a highly specialised system of cultivation known as 'dry farming'. The main problem is the lack of moisture during the growing season when a large proportion of the rainfall is lost through evapo-transpiration from the surface of the land and from the leaves of plants. This, together with the unreliability of the rainfall, caused many crop failures in the early years of settlement. At this time methods developed in areas of regular rainfall were used and the damage was enormous. In fact, the future of the area was threatened by the spread of soil erosion and the present system of land use was developed to combat the problem.

1   As in the United States the land had been surveyed and divided into small farms covering an area of 160 acres (a quarter section). Such farms were much too small and the first step was to join them together to form larger units of production (the shape of the earlier farms can be seen in the regular field pattern of the area).

2   Given a large area of land it was then possible to use a very extensive system of cultivation with half the land under crops and the other half left as fallow. The fallow land is cultivated the following year.

3   The fallow period is of great importance since it is used to build up moisture in the soil. This can then be used to grow future crops. It is essential, therefore, that the loss of water from these fields is kept to a minimum and to achieve this a new approach to farming was necessary. The most obvious cause of water loss was the vegetation which, in the form of weeds, quickly covered the

Cereal Farm, Saskatchewan

CLIMATE

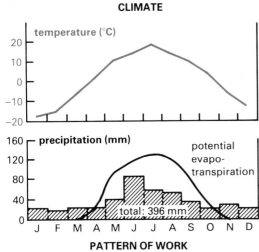

PATTERN OF WORK

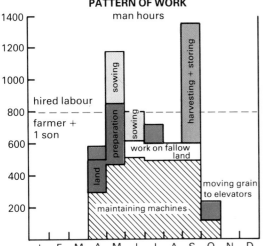

Fig. 4.49

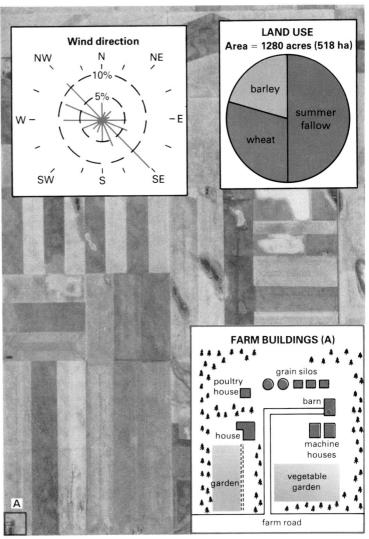

MACHINES

2 large tractors with:
  1 rod weeder   15 m wide
  1 disc harrow   8 m wide
  1 mulch treader   8 m wide
  1 seed drill   11 m wide
  1 sprayer   18 m wide
2 combines   5 m wide
2 grain trucks

ROTATION

Year 1 – grain
Year 2 – fallow
Year 3 – grain
Year 4 – fallow

fallow fields. The control of these weeds occupies a considerable part of the farmer's time during the growing season. Traditional methods of weed control such as ploughing or surface harrowing cannot be used since they would simply expose bare earth to the sun and wind and so increase both evaporation and erosion. To limit this problem machines have been developed which cut through the roots of the weeds at a depth of ten centimetres, leaving the surface undisturbed.

4 If all vegetation is killed, however, there is an obvious danger that the bare earth will be exposed to wind and rain and that soil erosion will become widespread. Such a danger is reduced by the simple policy of not ploughing the land after the harvest in the autumn. This means that the stubble of the previous crop is left standing to protect the soil.

In this way moisture loss by evapo-transpiration is considerably reduced. During the fallow period there is a gradual build up of moisture in the soil and this allows the next crop to be grown. It is, however, a system of farming which can only operate on a very large scale and with the use of a large amount of machinery. Indeed every operation on the farm is mechanised and the need for labour is kept to a minimum.

Refer to Fig. 4.49 and complete the following exercise.

a i Describe the year's work on the farm.
 ii Which of the major operations have been mechanised?
b i How many men are permanently employed on the farm?
 ii When, if ever, is it necessary to hire labour?
c Study the field pattern of the farm.
 i How many fields (not strips) are there?
 ii How big is each field and each strip?
 iii How does this size relate to the original government survey which laid out the land in homesteads of 160 acres?
 iv The division of the fields into strips helps to reduce erosion. Referring to the colour patterns and to the direction of the strips explain how this could be so.
d Why is the layout of the farm suited to the use of large machinery?

The high degree of mechanisation has strongly influenced the layout of the farm, with large regular fields (Fig. 4.50) and a very simple pattern of cropping, centred entirely on the production of cereals. Such a system of cultivation is called 'monoculture'. There are, however, limits to the size of individual areas of cultivation and the threat of soil erosion has led to the subdivision of fields into a number of strips. This allows the farmer to alternate cropland and fallow in any given year so that the standing crop acts as a windbreak, protecting the fallow land from erosion.

Fig. 4.50 *Large scale commercial cereal farms, Saskatchewan*

GRAIN EXPORTS FROM THE CANADIAN PRAIRIES, 1982
(total 18 million tonnes)

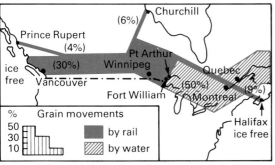

figures in brackets indicate grain movements in 1965,
(as % of total)

Fig. 4.51

The combination of a short growing season and a concentration on one type of crop means that the harvest at all farms in the area takes place within a very short period in September. As a result the transport and marketing of the crop becomes a major problem, both for the individual farmer and for the industry as a whole.

Until recently the bulk of the output was moved out of the region along the Great Lakes and the St Lawrence waterway. Since this is closed by ice for five months during the winter, a complicated system of storage was developed, with silos on the farms, at the railway and in the major ports. Changes in the world markets for grain have seen a decline in the importance of the waterways to the east and the development of rail traffic to the Pacific coast of British Columbia (Fig. 4.51).

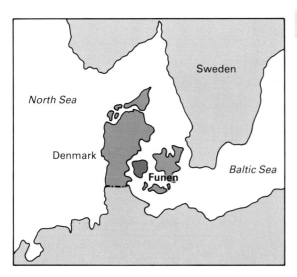

Location:	Funen, Denmark
Climate:	Temperate Growing season 195 days Rainfall 602 mm, throughout the year with a slight summer maximum
Farming system:	Commerical Complex mixed farming
Products:	Bacon + dairy produce

Fig. 4.52

Mixed crop and cereal farming: Denmark

Although heavily mechanised and often making use of sophisticated modern techniques, the farm systems developed for the large scale production of crops and animals are generally fairly simple. The same cannot be said of the other great farming system of the Developed World – the mixed farm which produces both crops and animals. This type of farming is widespread in the developed countries where it appears in many different forms.

In Denmark (Fig. 4.52), for example, interest centres on dairy farming. However, it is a different type of dairy farming from that found in countries like the UK.

In the first place, throughout the twentieth century milk production has greatly outstripped the demand for liquid milk in Denmark and this has led to an ever increasing dependence upon export markets, particularly in Britain and North West Europe. As a result it has been the production of high cream milk – suitable for processing into butter and cheese – which has grown most rapidly. Linked with this is the rearing of bacon pigs fed on the main by-product of the dairies – skimmed milk.

A second major difference is that physical conditions in Denmark do not favour the laying down of large areas of land to permanent pasture. This has led to the development of a pattern of farming very different from that found in other long established dairy farming regions in Europe and North America.

Using information given in Figs 4.53–57 complete the following exercise.

a   i   What is the size of the farm?
    ii   How many fields make up the farm? What is their average size?
b   i   What proportion of the farm is laid down to grass (not cereals)?
    ii   What type of grassland is it?
    iii   How does this type of pasture differ from permanent pasture?
    iv   How is the grassland used to feed the dairy cattle?

CLIMATE

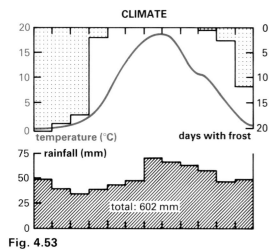

Fig. 4.53

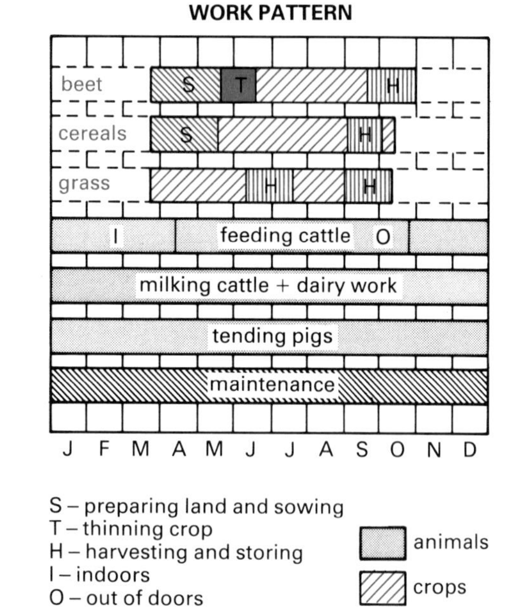

WORK PATTERN

	J	F	M	A	M	J	J	A	S	O	N	D
beet			S	T					H			
cereals		S						H				
grass				H			H					
feeding cattle												
milking cattle + dairy work												
tending pigs												
maintenance												

S – preparing land and sowing
T – thinning crop
H – harvesting and storing
I – indoors
O – out of doors

animals

crops

Fig. 4.54

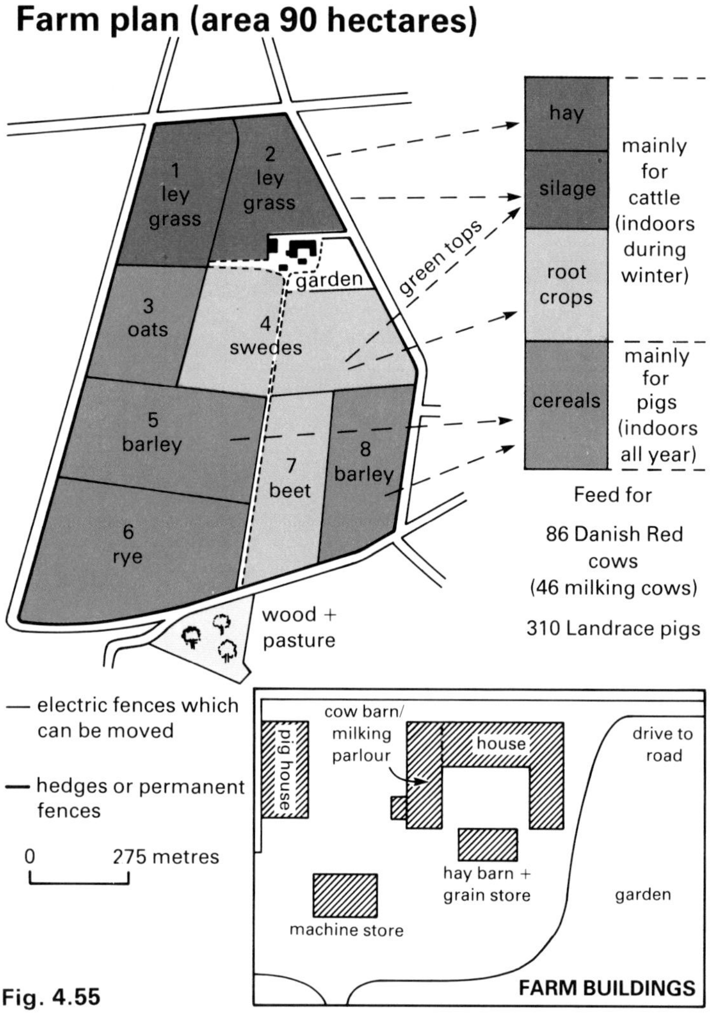

Farm plan (area 90 hectares)

hay
silage — mainly for cattle (indoors during winter)
root crops
cereals — mainly for pigs (indoors all year)

green tops

Feed for

86 Danish Red cows
(46 milking cows)

310 Landrace pigs

1 ley grass
2 ley grass
garden
3 oats
4 swedes
5 barley
6 rye
7 beet
8 barley

wood + pasture

— electric fences which can be moved

— hedges or permanent fences

0   275 metres

FARM BUILDINGS

pig house
cow barn/ milking parlour
house
drive to road
hay barn + grain store
machine store
garden

Fig. 4.55

c i For how long are the cattle kept out of doors?
  ii When are they taken indoors? What is the reason for this?
d i List the other crops grown on the farm.
  ii Describe the main uses of the crops.
e i How many milk producing cows are kept?
  ii Why is the production of beef cattle a worthwhile activity for the farmer?
f i How many pigs are kept?
  ii How are they fed?
g Describe the pattern of work on the farm and explain how it is related to climatic conditions.
h Describe the way in which the farm system works, paying particular attention to the inputs and outputs and to the ways in which different parts of the system are related.

In its complexity the farm (Fig. 4.55) is typical of the farming systems of Denmark as a whole and of large areas of many other developed countries.

1 The farm itself is comparatively small and it is very intensively worked, i.e. the inputs of labour and capital are large and output of milk and bacon is very high.

2 The labour force of the farmer, his two sons and one hired labourer, is very large for a farm of less than 100 hectares in a developed country.

CROP ROTATION PATTERN

Field \ Year	1	2	3	4	5	6	7	8
1	grass	grass	oats	swedes	barley	rye	beet	barley
2	barley	grass	grass	oats	swedes	barley	rye	beet
3	beet	barley	grass	grass	oats	swedes	barley	rye
4	rye	beet	barley	grass	grass	oats	swedes	barley
5	barley	rye	beet	barley	grass	grass	oats	swedes
6	swedes	barley	rye	beet	barley	grass	grass	oats
7	oats	swedes	barley	rye	beet	barley	grass	grass
8	grass	oats	swedes	barley	rye	beet	barley	grass

3   In addition almost every activity on the farm is highly mechanised.

4   This is necessary because the main activity on the farm is stock rearing and animals, particularly dairy cattle and pigs, need attention throughout the year. As a result there are few periods when little labour is needed.

5   To support the production of livestock, all the farmland is given over to the production of crops which are used to feed the animals. These range from ley grass (sown pasture), through root crops, to cereals. The crops are planned to provide feed throughout the year. All parts of the crops are used: the green tops of the root crops are made into silage, the straw from the cereal crop is used as bedding in the cowbarns and pig houses. Even so the farmer has to buy in some feed.

Fig. 4.56 *Mixed farming land in Denmark*

6   In order to keep production at a high level virtually the entire land area of the farm is cultivated each year. To maintain soil fertility under these conditions a complicated system of crop rotation, spread over eight years, is used. In addition, the fields are heavily manured and large amounts of chemical fertiliser are applied.

7   The prosperity of the farm depends upon milk production from a herd of 46 Danish Red cattle. The size of the herd is limited by the need to feed the cattle during the six months of winter when they are kept indoors and by the amount of labour required.

8   The success of this system depends upon an efficient system of marketing. Farmers in Denmark were among the first to set up a co-operative system of collecting and processing the products of the farms. Many of the factories are large – the dairy which handles the milk produced at the farm in the case study serves 263 other farms in the area. This means that the farmers can gain the benefits of bulk production in spite of the small size of individual farms. Such dairies are large enough to ensure that products are of the highest quality and also to organise the distribution of by-products such as skimmed milk which are used to feed other animals on the farms.

9   Stock rearing is often associated with dairy farming. Cows produce milk after they have calved. Some of these calves are sold off immediately. Others are kept on the farm and fattened for meat. Even more important, more than 300 pigs (in our case study) are kept for bacon production. These are kept indoors throughout the year and are fed on skimmed milk, cereals and imported feedstuffs.

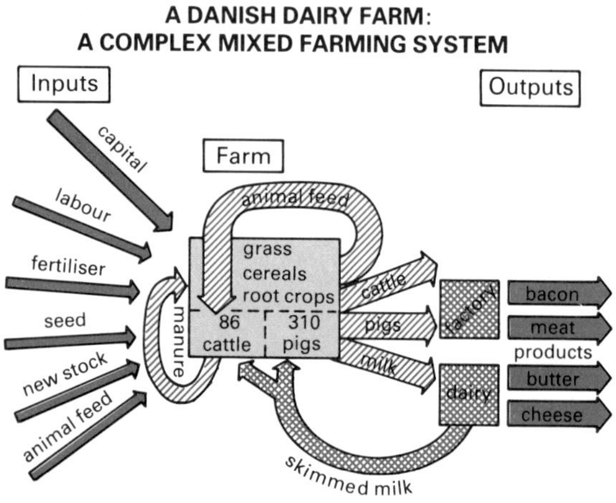

A DANISH DAIRY FARM:
A COMPLEX MIXED FARMING SYSTEM

Fig. 4.57

This is one of the most efficient farming systems in the world. Output per hectare is very high and unit costs are relatively low. However, at the same time it is producing food (butter, cheese, milk and bacon) which is in surplus throughout Western Europe. In fact, production can be maintained at present levels only because of the agricultural policy of the EEC (see page 87) which pays fixed prices for all food produce and buys up all surplus production. In this way Denmark makes its contribution to the 'milk lakes' and 'butter mountains' of the EEC. Without support of this kind there would probably be more pressure for change in Danish farming.

Agriculture and politics :

THE EEC SYSTEM OF PROTECTING AGRICULTURE

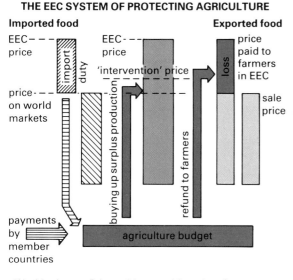

World price — Price paid on world markets for any commodity, e.g. wheat or butter

EEC price — The price paid to farmers within the EEC

Intervention price — If too much food is produced and prices fall to this point the EEC buys up the food produced by the farmers. This is stored and sold later when the market has recovered.

Fig. 4.58

As we have seen, few countries have allowed agriculture to develop freely and in most developed countries there is now strong government control. Examples of this are numerous.

Britain, for example, became so dependent upon cheap imported food that by the beginning of the twentieth century farming was in decline. As a result, the country experienced serious food shortages during the First World War when imports were threatened by German U-boats. This led successive governments to support farming in Britain by giving subsidies to farmers so that home produced food could be sold at prices which could compete with the price of imported foods. During the Second World War farm production reached record levels and, when the war ended, the system of subsidies was extended so that the dependence upon imported food was kept within limits.

When Britain entered the European Economic Community in 1972 other methods of protecting agriculture from cheaper imports were introduced (Fig. 4.58). These methods, known as the Common Agriculture Policy (CAP) had been developed in Europe when the EEC was established and they were based on paying farmers a fixed price for their produce. At the same time food imports were controlled by imposing dues which raised the cost of imported foods above those which existed within the Community. The change for Britain was dramatic: before 1972 subsidies had given low prices to consumers, with additional money coming from the tax payer; since 1972 the EEC system has produced high prices for the consumer.

Most governments today try to control the development of agriculture, usually by controlling the prices paid to farmers. In some cases, however, the control is much more direct. This is most clearly seen in the Communist world where two distinct systems of farm organisation have developed – the collective farm in the USSR and the commune in China.

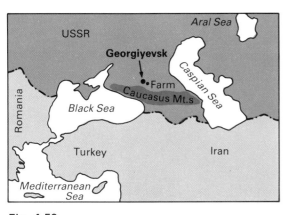

Fig. 4.59

A collective farm: near Georgiyevsk, USSR

Collective farms are not special types of farm designed to produce specific crops or animal products. In fact collectivisation is a system of organising agriculture almost regardless of farm type or product. It was introduced into Russia during the 1920s after the Communist revolution. Land was acquired by the state and any opposition by landowners was ruthlessly put down. The entire system of farming was then reformed and state owned collective farms were established throughout the country. Production targets were then established for the collectives by the government in a series of five year plans.

The development of the collectives near Georgiyevsk, SE Ukraine, USSR (Fig. 4.59), is typical.

Collective farm: USSR

CLIMATE

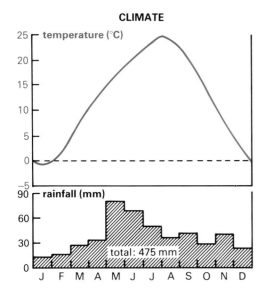

PATTERN OF WORK

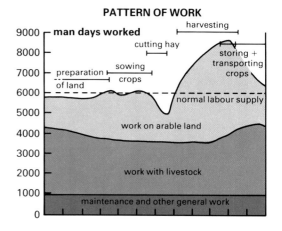

LIVESTOCK

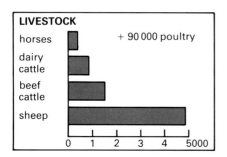

LAND USE

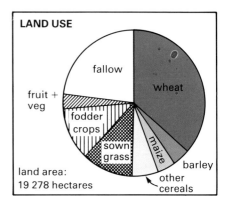

Fig. 4.60

Fig. 4.60 (a)

TYPICAL ORGANISATION OF A COLLECTVE

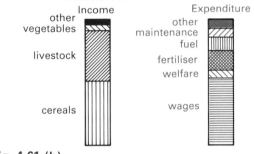

total labour force
670 men
490 women

machines
70 tractors
9 combines
3 harrows

Fig. 4.61 (a)

COLLECTIVE: BUDGET

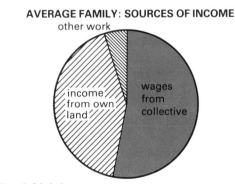

Fig. 4.61 (b)

AVERAGE FAMILY: SOURCES OF INCOME

Fig. 4.61 (c)

Using information given in this section, complete the following exercise.

a Describe the climate of the area in which the collective is located.
b Describe the natural vegetation of the area.
c Write a brief summary of the development of the collective farm.
d i   What is the area of the farm today?
    ii Compare this with other large scale farming operations, e.g. a plantation, a cattle ranch, a cereal farm.
e i   What is the population of the collective?
    ii What is the labour force employed?

The scale of operation is obviously enormous. The area of the first collective was 12 000 hectares but this was almost doubled when a second farm was added to it in 1962. This new area, which lies more than 100 kilometres to the east, is more arid and the land has been developed mainly for pastoral farming, particularly sheep rearing. Villages have been built on both sections and the collective operates as a self contained community with its own schools, nurseries, hospital, library, cinema and sports centre.

The farm has a complicated system of management (Fig. 4.61). Orders are sent from the national and regional governments and from the Communist party. These set the targets which should be reached.

The management of the farm itself is in the hands of a committee and a chairman. This committee takes advice from a group of trained specialists – on this farm there are 40 such people, ranging from veterinary officers to skilled mechanics. The workforce, which numbers more than 1200 men and women, is divided into 15 brigades each with responsibility for a different type of work.

Some of the produce is processed on the farm which operates its own flour mill, abattoir, cold store, oil press, bakery and winery. The produce is sold to the state at prices fixed by the state. This has not encouraged efficiency and an increasing proportion of the output of the farm is grown on the small plots of land which are rented by the families working on the collective. These garden plots are used to grow fruit and vegetables and to rear livestock. This produce can be sold privately. Such sales now make up more than 50% of the total sales of the collective.

On the farm itself the variety of produce is great and the pattern of farming is complicated.

Using information given in this section, complete the following work.

a i   List the crops in order of importance.
    ii What proportion of the farm is under cereals?
b What evidence is there that cereal farming is on a large scale and probably uses methods similar to those used on the Canadian Prairies? (See page 80.)
c What proportion of the land is used to produce feed for animals?

On many occasions the farm has failed to reach its planned output. To some extent this is due to the variability of the rainfall which has resulted in serious crop failures. Attempts have been made to reduce this risk by building irrigation reservoirs in the hills. Unfortunately the area of land suitable for irrigation is small and future success will probably depend upon the introduction of more efficient methods of dry farming similar to those used in North America. As it is, yields still remain far below those obtained in other countries in spite of a high degree of mechanisation and widespread use of chemical fertilisers. This is true of collective farms throughout the USSR.

As a result, it has been necessary to import large amounts of grain, in spite of the vast area of land laid down to cereals. It has also led to the questioning of the efficiency of such vast farms and to the encouragement of commercial farming on the small family plots. This has been so successful that on some collectives food production from private land has outstripped that from the rest of the farm.

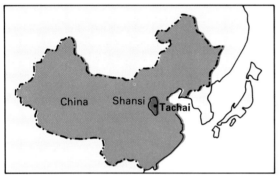

Tachai Village, Tachai Commune, Hsi-Yang County, Shansi Province, People's Republic of China

MAIN EVENTS
1949 – Communist Government established in China
– Mutual Aid Team set up in Tachai
1953 – Reorganisation as a co-operative
1958 – Commune established, with Tachai a brigade
1963 – Severe flooding destroyed terraced land, large scale rebuilding necessary
– All private landowning abolished
1964 – Commune headquarters established at Tachai

Fig. 4.62

Tachai commune, Shansi Province, China

The large scale reorganisation of Chinese agriculture began after the Communist take-over in 1949. At first the farmers were allowed to retain ownership of the land but tools and draught animals were shared by groups of families. These groups were often too small and eventually large areas of land were merged to form co-operatives which sometimes included as many as 2000 families. Even with these larger units problems remained, particularly if major developments such as drainage or irrigation schemes were planned. In the late 1950s, therefore, a decision was taken to merge co-operatives and to form larger units known as people's communes.

The Tachai commune in northern China (Fig. 4.62) has a population of more than 10 000. There are 2700 households and the workforce is organised into 26 brigades, each of which works a district or area of the commune.

The commune is situated on the loess belt of China. Loess is a fine wind blown deposit which covers large areas of the country. In places it can be very deep, completely covering the earlier landscape. This is not the case in Shansi, however, and here the older rocks penetrate the loess cover, forming rocky and infertile uplands. In the valleys the loess is thick, but here there has been widespread erosion. Stormwater, running off the uplands, has carved steepsided ravines, so narrow that there is very little land flat enough to cultivate.

In spite of this the valley floor areas were the first to be farmed – largely because there was water available for the crops. Elsewhere the loess was so porous that rainwater passed through it, leaving the surface layers too dry to produce good crops. Even so some of the hillsides were terraced and grain crops were grown when there was sufficient rainfall. All too often, however, the

TACHAI VILLAGE 1949–78

	1949	1978	% change
Population	248	440	+77
Households	49	88	+79
Work force	96	157	+63.5
Cultivated area (ha)	50	56.7	+13.4
Irrigated area	—	39.7	—
Number of fields	4700	1800	−162
Grain output (tonnes)	101	482	+377
Grain yield (tonnes per ha)	1.8	9.8	+444

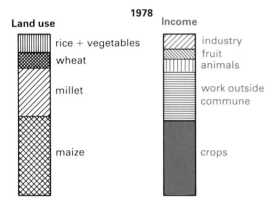

1978

Land use — rice + vegetables, wheat, millet, maize

Income — industry, fruit, animals, work outside commune, crops

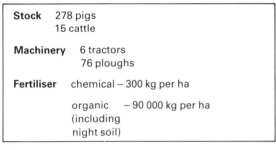

Stock	278 pigs
	15 cattle
Machinery	6 tractors
	76 ploughs
Fertiliser	chemical – 300 kg per ha
	organic – 90 000 kg per ha (including night soil)

Fig. 4.63

RECLAMATION OF A LARGE GULLY IN TACHAI

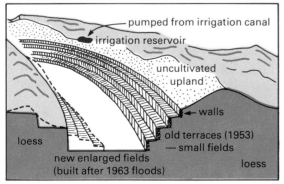

pumped from irrigation canal — irrigation reservoir — uncultivated upland — walls — old terraces (1953) — small fields — loess — new enlarged fields (built after 1963 floods) — loess

Fig. 4.64

rains failed or in wet years the terraces were washed away by run-off from the surrounding hills.

In 1963 there was a particularly severe flood which destroyed large areas of terraced land. As a result, it was decided to begin a massive land improvement project. This involved building a system of permanent terraces (Fig. 4.65) along with a series of dams to control flood waters and to provide water for irrigation. Within 20 years the life of the commune was transformed. The cultivated area was increased, the irrigated area doubled and, by using improved farming methods and chemical fertilisers, grain yields more than trebled.

The scale of this development is best understood by looking at the activities of one brigade in the commune – the Tachai brigade (Fig. 4.63).

Using information given in Fig. 4.63, complete the following exercise.

a i What is the area of cultivated land available to the Tachai brigade?
  ii What proportion of the cultivated land is irrigated?
b i List the crops grown by the brigade.
  ii List the animals reared. Why is stock rearing of no great importance?

In spite of the comparatively recent introduction of several tractors and some basic mechanical equipment, the success of the Tachai brigade (its district is now one of the show places of Communist China) has largely depended on the use of manual labour. The entire population which worked the fields during the summer turned to improvement work during the winter months. This work included:

1 The blasting of rock outcrops so as to enlarge the fields.
2 The building of large permanent terraces on the valley sides.
3 In places small valleys were filled in to provide flat land for farming.
4 Where this has happened tunnels were built to carry away the flood waters which used to occupy the valleys. In this way the risk of erosion was reduced.
5 The building of small reservoirs to store this water draining from the fields and terraces. This was used to increase the area of irrigated land.
6 The sinking of six wells to add to the water available for irrigation.

All of this was achieved by moving tens of thousands of tonnes of rock and soil, usually with no tools other than shovels and baskets. Entire fields were built by carrying back up the hillsides the soil which had been washed down valleys during storms (Fig. 4.64). Most of these fields were large (more than 1.5 hectares) and this meant that for the first time farming could be partly mechanised.

The efforts of the Tachai brigade have changed one of the poorest districts in China into a fairly prosperous farming area. There has, however, been a price to pay. Unlike the collective farms, communes were established not only to control agricultural production but also to encourage industrial development within their boundaries. Some communes have been very successful in this and a number of industries have been set up, many of them related to improvements in agriculture and most of them making use of surplus labour within the commune. In the Tachai district the entire workforce was involved in land improvement schemes and this delayed industrial development (see page 191).

It is also true that communal efforts such as those seen in Tachai were favoured during the years of the Great Leap Forward (1959) and of the Cultural Revolution (1968). Today, however, private land owning is encouraged as a means of increasing food production – a trend already seen on the collective farms in the USSR. Such a development has been difficult in areas like Tachai where so much of the land has been created by communal effort.

Fig. 4.65 *Terracing in the loess belt, Shansi Province, China*

The economics of agriculture

Almost all agricultural systems are today strongly influenced by economic factors. Only in the most remote and isolated areas are these influences relatively unimportant and even here change is taking place at a rapid rate.

There are two major types of economic influence:

Farm inputs:
the price paid for land
the cost of:
seed
fertiliser
stock
feedstuffs
labour
machinery
fuel and power

Outputs:
the cost of transport to
markets
the price fetched by produce
in the market

Three of these influences are more important than the others – the value of the land, the accessibility of markets and the prices paid in those markets. Such factors are so important that they appear to influence not only the working of individual farms but also the general pattern of farming in a region.

Many attempts have been made to explain the relationship between the pattern of farming and economic influences. Most are based on a number of relatively simple ideas:

1 That most farmers will be trying to obtain the highest possible profit.

2 That land values will be highest near the city centre and will decrease as distance from the city increases.

3 That as a result agricultural systems which produce high returns per hectare will be found on land near the city, i.e. the intensity of agriculture will tend to decrease with distance from the city centre (Fig. 4.66).

4 That ease of access to the market and costs of transport emphasise this pattern. For example, the production of vegetables, soft fruit and milk (all highly intensive forms of farming) was traditionally located near to the city. This was because the city was the main market for produce which deteriorates quickly and which had to be consumed within a short time of harvesting.

The combined effect of such influences was to produce a series of concentric zones around the city. Obviously such a simple pattern rarely existed in reality and factors such as variations in relief and accessibility caused considerable distortion. In spite of this, however, traces of such zones can be found. This is particularly true in less developed countries where the transport of goods is still a major problem and the effects of distance can be striking.

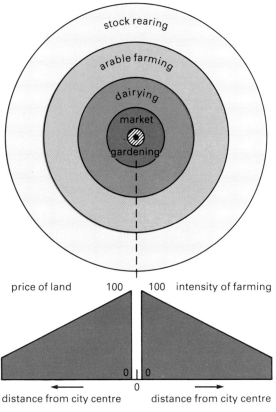

PATTERN OF FARMING AROUND A CITY

stock rearing
arable farming
dairying
market gardening

price of land   100   100   intensity of farming

0   0

0

distance from city centre   distance from city centre

Fig. 4.66

A VILLAGE NEAR JODPHUR, RAJASTHAN, INDIA

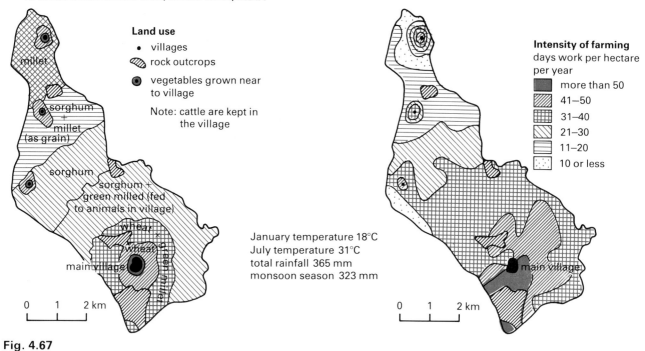

Land use
- villages
- rock outcrops
- vegetables grown near to village

Note: cattle are kept in the village

millet

sorghum + millet (as grain)

sorghum

sorghum + green milled (fed to animals in village)

wheat

wheat

main village

green millet

0   1   2 km

January temperature 18°C
July temperature 31°C
total rainfall 365 mm
monsoon season 323 mm

Intensity of farming
days work per hectare per year
- more than 50
- 41–50
- 31–40
- 21–30
- 11–20
- 10 or less

main village

0   1   2 km

Fig. 4.67

Study Figs 4.66–68.

a   Fig. 4.67 shows the land use around a village near Jodphur in Rajasthan, India.
   i   Measure the average distance from the centre of the main village to each crop division.
   ii Relate these changes in crop to the intensity of farming.
   iii The crop zones are not concentric circles. Which factors may have caused distortion?
b   Fig. 4.68 shows a generalised pattern of land use in South Australia, around the city of Adelaide.
   i   Measure the distance of each land use division from the centre of the city.
   ii How does this pattern differ from that seen near Jodphur?
   iii Why do you think these differences occur?

The Indian example given in Fig. 4.67 also raises a further point. The village is not only the main market for much of the produce, it is also the chief source of labour. Families living in the village have to walk to the land which is under cultivation. Therefore greatest effort is put into the land near the village and farming becomes less intensive in the outlying fields.

In developed countries the pattern is very different. Improvements in transport have meant that distance from markets is no longer critical. As a result the zones, where they exist, tend to be much wider. The area around the city of Adelaide in South Australia (Fig. 4.68) illustrates this point. Distinct zones do occur and these zones follow the pattern suggested in the diagram on page 93. However, they occur over a distance of more than 150 kilometres and the pattern is far from simple. It is of course strongly influenced by relief, with the Mount Lofty Range restricting agricultural development inland. Even more im-

LAND USE: ADELAIDE, SOUTH AUSTRALIA

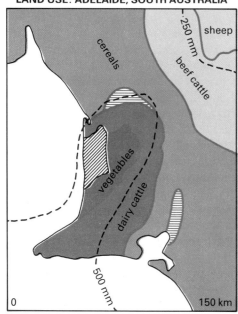

sheep

cereals

250 mm

beef cattle

vegetables

dairy cattle

500 mm

0   150 km

Fig. 4.68

94

% INPUTS ACCORDING TO FARM TYPE: SOUTH AUSTRALIA

		Land	Machinery	Labour
Vegetables		37	23	40
Dairying		45	19	36
Intensive cultivation		23	28	49
Cereals		28	52	20
Pastoral		63	16	21

Fig. 4.68 (a)

portant, there is a strong relationship between rainfall and agriculture. The coastal lowlands are generally wetter than the interior and this has undoubtedly encouraged the development of horticulture, dairying and intensive forms of agriculture such as fruit growing. These physical influences have tended to emphasise a pattern of farming which developed around the city at a time when transport was poor.

It is, however, a pattern which has tended to break down as the dependence on nearby markets has become less marked. Two important influences have led to this breakdown:

1   The spread of the city itself has led to industry and housing taking over large areas of land which were once used to grow vegetables. This has happened on the fringes of most large cities and, although in some cases vegetable production continues in new locations near the city, in many cases it ceases.

2   Modern methods of transport are much more efficient and they allow fresh vegetables and fresh milk to reach the markets from great distances. New methods of preserving food, particularly freezing and quick drying, have encouraged this trend.

This is particularly true in the Developed World where patterns of farming have become very complicated and where there has been a strong move towards specialisation in all branches of farming. Nowhere is this more clearly seen than in the Netherlands which has become one of the leading producers of vegetables, with markets throughout the world.

Market gardening in the Netherlands

The Netherlands is one of the most densely populated countries in the world. In addition, more than 50% of the land area has been reclaimed either from inland lakes and marshes or from the sea itself (see page 106). The cost of draining such land was very high and this combination of farmland which is both expensive to maintain and in great demand has helped to give rise to systems of farming which are among the most intensive in the world. The Naaldwijk area of Zuid (South) Holland (Fig. 4.69) is typical in this respect.

The land is below sea level and is protected from the North Sea only by the zone of coastal dunes. It was drained by building dykes to reduce the danger of flooding from the River Lek, the northern distributary of the River Rhine. Once drained the land was improved by careful cultivation (see page 108) and a pattern of farming developed which was strongly influenced by the nearness of large urban markets such as Rotterdam. The market influence has remained strong but it has changed significantly in recent years.

Using information given in Figs 4.70–71, complete the following exercise.

a   i   What is the area of the farm?
   ii   How is the soil fertility maintained on the farm?
b   i   What is the length of the growing season (i.e. the period when the temperature is above 6°C)?
   ii   Are there likely to be any other problems caused by the climate?

MARKET GARDENING IN THE NETHERLANDS: LOCATION OF STUDY FARM

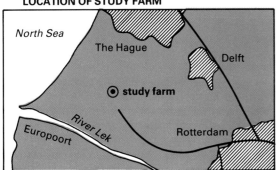

Fig. 4.69

FARM PLAN

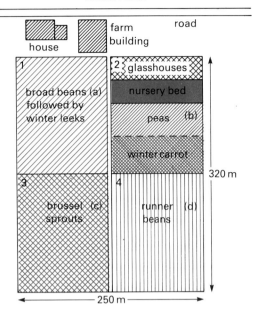

CROP ROTATION

Field	Year			
	1	2	3	4
1	a	b	c	d
2	b	c	d	a
3	c	d	a	b
4	d	a	b	c

FARM BUDGET

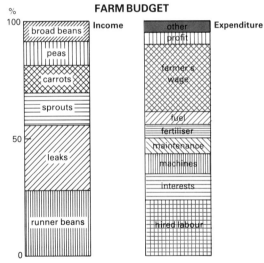

Fig. 4.70

RANK ORDER OF IMPORTANCE

Crop	Costs per are*	Labour input per are
Broad beans	6	5
Winter leeks	3	2
Brussel sprouts	5	6
Runner beans	1	4
Carrots	2	3
Peas	4	1

* 1 are = 100 sq metres, i.e. $\frac{1}{100}$ hectare

Fig. 4.71 *Spraying the fields on a market garden. Note the flatness of the land*

c
  i   How many people work on the farm?
  ii   Calculate the average number of man hours worked per hectare (1 hectare=10 000 square metres).
  iii   Calculate the comparable figure for the Canadian cereal farm (see page 81). What does this tell you about the intensity of farming in each case?
  iv   During which part of the year will the demand for labour be greatest?
  v   What causes this increased demand?

d   Using the details given in the farm budget:
  i   List the sources of income in order of importance.
  ii   Calculate the average percentage return for each crop per are (1 are=100 square metres). List these returns in rank order.
  iii   Compare these figures with the details given of labour input.
  iv   Do these comparisons indicate an intensive system of farming?

e   Describe the working of the farm using the following headings – farm size and layout; crops grown; the pattern of work during the year.

The Farming Year

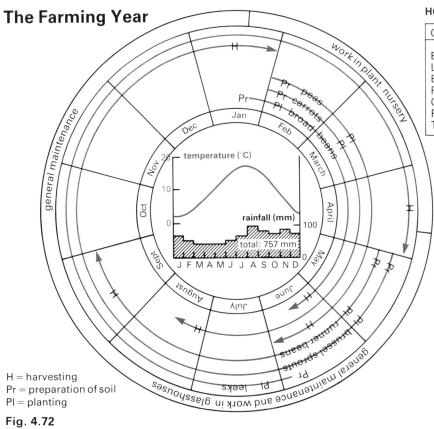

H = harvesting
Pr = preparation of soil
Pl = planting

Fig. 4.72

HOURS OF LABOUR

Crop	Cultivation	Harvest
Broad beans	280	1200
Leeks	440	2000
Brussel sprouts	200	500
Runner beans	450	1340
Carrots	70	500
Peas	350	850
Total	1790	6390

LABOUR FORCE

Farmer	2500 hrs
2 hired helpers	4000 hrs
Part time help	1680 hrs

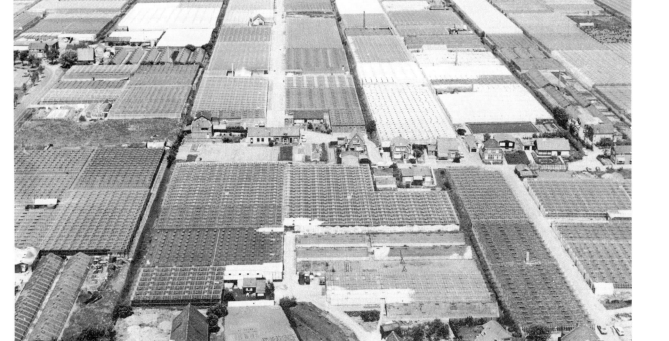

Fig. 4.72 (a) *Market gardens in the Netherlands*

MARKETS FOR HORTICULTURAL PRODUCE

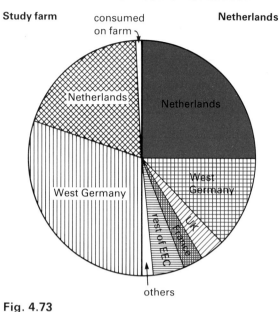

Study farm   consumed on farm   **Netherlands**

others

Fig. 4.73

This system of farming is obviously very intensive.

1 The land is used continuously, soil fertility being maintained by rotating crops and by using large amounts of chemical fertiliser.

2 The number of man hours worked on each field is very high.

3 In addition to this large labour input, many of the operations are mechanised.

4 Crops which give high returns are grown and output is very high.

5 The entire operation is highly specialised and most of the produce is sold.

Because farming has become so specialised, the market gardens of the Netherlands supply markets throughout Western Europe (Fig. 4.73). For example, more than half of the output of the study farm is sent by road to the industrial regions of West Germany. This development has been made possible only because road links are good and because methods of storing and packaging have been developed which slow down the rate at which the produce deteriorates after harvesting. To serve such a system large co-operative packing plants have been established and farming has been organised on the lines of a factory industry. Many of the farms in the Naaldwijk area even look like factories since a large area of farmland is under glass. The availability of a cheap source of energy (natural gas from the Gröningen field) has allowed the growing season to be lengthened so that crops are grown under artificial conditions. The costs are very high, however, and the industry depends not only on the high prices guaranteed by the EEC but also on aid from the government in the form of cheap energy.

WORLD POPULATION AND GRAIN PRODUCTION

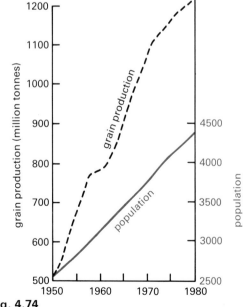

Fig. 4.74

Food production and population growth

As we have seen, it is population increase more than anything which has placed the existing systems of food production under strain. So far, in spite of this increase, food production has kept pace with population growth (Fig. 4.74). This has been achieved in two ways – by increasing the area of farmland and by increasing the output of the land which is being used.

FACTORS CONTRIBUTING TO INCREASED CROP PRODUCTION IN INDIA

	1961	1981
Developing new land	59	48
Irrigation	22	20
Application of fertiliser	5	15
Other e.g. new crop types	14	17
All	100%	100%

The area of agricultural land

Throughout the nineteenth century a growing world population was fed by opening up new areas of farmland, particularly in the Americas, Australia and Southern Africa. The area of land under cultivation increased rapidly. During the twentieth century this rate of increase has slowed down as the best and most accessible land has been used. Today the problems of increasing the area of farmland are much greater.

In some areas, such as the tropical rainforests, land is still being cleared for agriculture. Almost always it is land which was once thought to be too difficult to cultivate. In most areas, however simple clearance of new land is not possible and alternative methods of increasing the farmed area have been used. These are usually expensive and make use of modern technology. The most obvious method is to bring water to land which was previously too dry to produce crops. This is irrigation and it makes an important contribution to increased food production. At the other end of the scale, some countries like the Netherlands have increased the area of agricultural land by draining large areas of marshland and even by reclaiming land from the sea. This is an expensive alternative and is found mainly in the wealthy developed countries.

Of more immediate interest, therefore, is the attempt to introduce new crops and new techniques of farming which will allow farming to spread into areas which could not previously be cultivated. This 'marginal' land is usually too cold or too dry to produce crops using normal methods of farming. By introducing new methods of farming or by using new varieties of crops, it is sometimes possible to open up new lands for agriculture. This has been seen on the Great Plains of North America.

All of these methods are expensive and difficult to introduce. It is not surprising, therefore, that in recent years more interest has been shown in increasing yields from existing land. This has often meant simply increasing the amount of chemical fertiliser used.

Developing new land

The largest area of lowland which is climatically suitable for cultivation but which has not yet been developed is the tropical rainforest. This covers much of the equatorial regions of Africa, South America and the East Indies. Elsewhere new farmland is available only along the present margins of cultivation.

In tropical rainforest areas the growing season extends throughout the year and rainfall is abundant. Furthermore, farming – usually a form of shifting cultivation – was already practised in many areas. These developments were, however, on a very small scale, largely because of the problems presented by the environment. In fact the difficulties were so great that it was only the recent rapid increase in population in the Developing World which has encouraged attempts to develop these areas for agriculture. In some countries, notably Brazil, these attempts have been on a large scale with a view to establishing both plantations and farms for individual families.

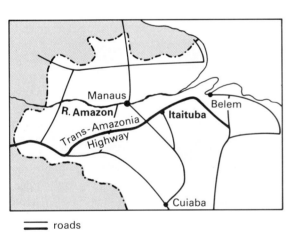

roads

Location: Itaituba, Brazil

Climate: Equatorial
                 High temperatures throughout year
                 — over 15°C
                 Rainfall more than 2000 mm, no dry
                 season

Growing season: 365 days

Farming system: Subsistence/commercial
                 Mixed farming

Produce: Cattle + pigs for sale
                 Cassava, corn, beans

Fig. 4.75

99

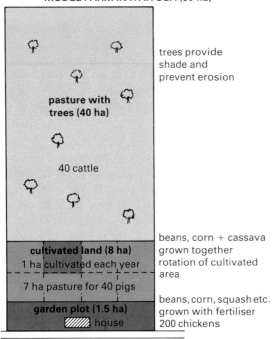

MODEL FARM IN ITAITUBA (50 ha)

pasture with trees (40 ha)

40 cattle

trees provide shade and prevent erosion

cultivated land (8 ha)
1 ha cultivated each year

7 ha pasture for 40 pigs

garden plot (1.5 ha)
▨ house

beans, corn + cassava grown together rotation of cultivated area

beans, corn, squash etc. grown with fertiliser
200 chickens

Fig. 4.76

One of the first and most adventurous of these developments took place at Itaituba (Fig. 4.75), deep in the Amazonian forests, and its history has been typical of such attempts.

From the outset the problems were enormous:

1 In common with many areas of rainforest, access was difficult. For a long time rivers provided the only routeways but for a modern system of farming roads had to be provided. These were often unsurfaced and were easily washed out by the heavy storms which are frequent in such areas. Add to this the fact that the main markets for any commercial crops are hundreds, if not thousands of kilometres away, and the problems are obvious.

2 This leads to a second point. The rainforests themselves are sparsely populated and the pressure which has led to their development stems from population growth in cities in other parts of Brazil. As a result any agricultural development depends on families being encouraged to move into the area. This has not always been successful.

3 One reason for this is the problem of disease which is widespread in the Amazon Valley. It was this which helped slow down early development and, although modern medicine can control diseases such as malaria, the threat remains and the health and strength of the population can still be affected.

4 Using modern equipment, the clearance of the forest presents few problems – the trees are large, the root systems shallow and easy to remove, and there is little undergrowth. Once cleared, however, the spread of undergrowth is rapid and maintaining the clearings becomes a serious problem.

It was not until development began, however, that the most serious problem emerged. The soils which supported the luxuriant rainforest proved to be unsuitable for cultivation. The layer of leaf litter and humus was thin and, after two years, it had virtually disappeared. Beneath these surface layers the soil was laterite – a tropical soil which contained large amounts of iron. Once exposed to the sun and rain this soil baked and became so hard that even modern ploughs could not break it up for cultivation. Where this happened farming ceased and the land was abandoned. Elsewhere, as the soils became exhausted, erosion increased and large areas of farmland were lost.

The entire experiment was a disastrous failure but, in spite of this, new attempts have been made to develop the rainforests. Much of this development has been for timber or to exploit minerals, but large areas of rainforest are still being cleared for farming (Figs 4.76 and 4.77). In fact, with many thousand of hectares being cleared each year, it is feared that the balance of the atmosphere could be changed by the release of the carbon dioxide which is stored in the forest. This in turn could change the pattern of climate by causing an overall rise in temperature on the earth's surface.

There are few parts of the world where new land is available for cultivation and, as we have seen, the development of this land is rarely easy. If this were not so it is probable that such lands would have been developed long ago. In most areas there is a shortage of land suitable for agriculture and great efforts have been made to increase the area of farmland, usually by reclaiming land or by building irrigation schemes.

Fig. 4.77 *A typical farmstead, Amazonia*

Fig. 4.78 *Traditional method of irrigation, Egypt*

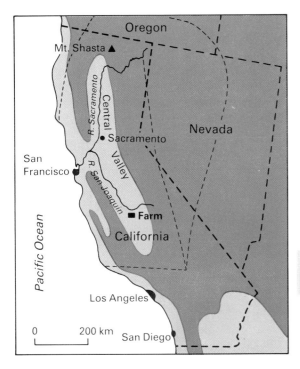

Location:	Fresno County, San Joaquin Valley, California
Climate:	Mediterranean January temperature 12°C, July temperature 23°C Rainfall 295 mm, dry season May–October
Growing season:	365 days
Farm system:	Intensive commercial crop production using irrigation
Products:	Cotton, tomatoes, fruit, cereals

Fig. 4.79

Irrigation

This is the most obvious and most widely used method of bringing new land into cultivation. It involves introducing a controlled supply of water into areas which are too dry for cultivation or in which the rainfall is so seasonal that the growing of crops is very difficult.

Irrigation was first practised in the ancient world. In Egypt, for example, the Nile overflows its banks every year with remarkable regularity and it was not difficult to hold back some of the flood water by simply building low mud walls around some of the fields. This water could then be used to grow crops at a time when the land would normally be too dry for cultivation. The next step was to take water from the river – usually by means of nothing more than a type of bucket – and to channel it into nearby fields.

Irrigation on a larger scale became possible when canals could be built to divert water from rivers and streams. By using the fall of the valley, water could be supplied to fields downstream which were at a distance from the river itself and considerably above its level. This method was developed at an early date, as can be seen from the irrigated terraces of South East Asia and the Andes in South America.

All of these early systems of irrigation depended upon the natural flow of the river and this could vary enormously. It was obvious, therefore, that it would help if the river itself could be controlled. This was achieved by building weirs or low dams and by the end of the nineteenth century rivers as large as the Nile and the Indus were controlled by means of a series of low dams or barrages. These were not designed to store water. They simply raised the level of the water in the river and regulated its flow into the irrigation systems which, as a result, could be greatly enlarged.

Large scale irrigation: Central Valley, California, USA

The twentieth century has seen the construction of massive irrigation projects. One of the best examples is in California (Fig. 4.79) – an area of the United States which has experienced its own population explosion, largely as the result of immigration from other parts of the country. Many of these immigrants have settled in Southern California, an area of low and unreliable rainfall. To supply water to this growing population and to expand crop production in the area, water management has taken place on a scale seen nowhere else on the earth's surface.

By 1981 no less than 25% of the farmland of Southern California was irrigated (an example of one farm is given in Fig. 4.82). In places the irrigation schemes are small, depending upon reservoirs in the surrounding hills or upon wells which tap local supplies of groundwater. For the most part, however, the schemes are large and, of these schemes, the largest and most impressive is the Central Valley Project (Fig. 4.80).

Central valley scheme

Total area – 45 000 sq km

Water transferred from the Sacramento to the San Joaquin Valley – 8250 million cubic metres per year

Water taken from the San Joaquin River – 1950 million cubic metres per year

Irrigated area – 8500 sq km

Major dams – 35

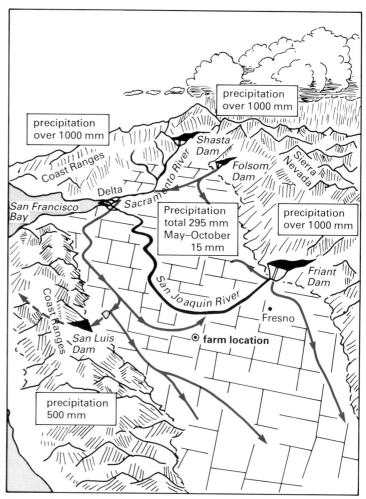

Fig. 4.80

Fig. 4.81 *Large scale irrigation project in Southern California, USA*

Study Farm

PLAN OF IRRIGATED FARM, FRESNO COUNTY, CALIFORNIA (total area 130 ha)

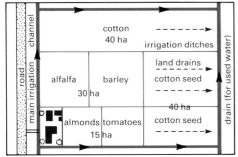

Fig. 4.82 (a)

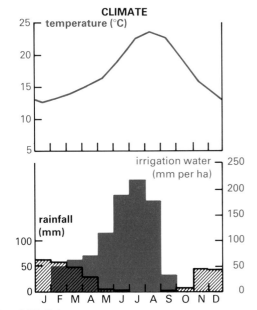

Fig. 4.82 (b)

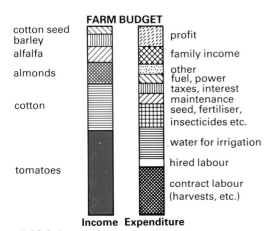

Fig. 4.82 (c)

The cost of these schemes can be enormous. To supply parts of Southern California, for example, the Colorado River has been dammed at many points. Canals have been built to carry the water more than 500 kilometres to lowlands suitable for irrigation. In the Central Valley scheme the upper reaches of the Sacramento River, which flows in an area of high rainfall, have been dammed and the water has been diverted more than 500 kilometres to the south, into the dry San Joaquin Valley. Here the water is allowed to enter the San Joaquin River where it is used to irrigate large areas on the valley floor.

Given engineering projects on this scale, it is hardly surprising that the irrigated land has been used to grow fruit and vegetables and other crops which give a high return per hectare.

Similar large scale schemes have been attempted in other parts of the world, including many developing countries. The problems associated with large scale irrigation have become very obvious:

1 Good sites for dams on large rivers are very difficult to find. If the site is not good, the cost of building can be very high.

2 Once built, silting can become a serious problem. The lakes behind some of the smaller dams in the Colorado system have been completely filled and even some of the large lakes have been greatly reduced in size. Furthermore, in many countries the silt is one of the main sources of fertiliser for farms on the floodplain of the river. The dam deprives these areas of silt because it controls flooding.

3 The most serious and perhaps the most surprising problems concern the nature of the land which is to be irrigated. If the fall of the valley floor is not sufficient, fields tend to become water-logged. The result is that evaporation increases enormously and, since river water usually contains minerals in solution, this causes salts to be deposited in the surface layers of the soil. In time this can prevent crops growing.

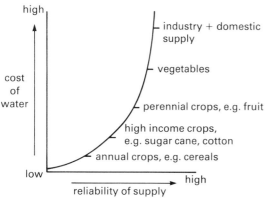

THE EFFECT OF THE COST AND RELIABILITY OF WATER SUPPLY ON ITS USE

Fig. 4.83

4   The building of large scale irrigation schemes can even change the environment, sometimes with serious consequences. For example, so much water is now taken from the Colorado River that it no longer reaches the sea. As a result, beaches in the Gulf of California are beginning to disappear as the supply of sediment from the river ceases. In addition, the river enters the sea in Mexico and there is little or no water left to extend irrigation schemes in that country.

5   The costs of irrigation are usually high. It is necessary, therefore, to use the irrigated land to grow crops which give high returns (Fig. 4.83). These are often cash crops; not always the best crops for a developing country trying to increase its production of basic foods. In fact it is now felt that in such countries the emphasis ought to be on building small scale projects.

Small scale irrigation: Varanasi, Uttar Pradesh, India

The irrigated area of India is about 30 million hectares. Of this, about 40% is irrigated by damming streams and rivers and by building complex systems of canals. Some of these schemes are very large.

The remaining 60% of the irrigated area is in small scale schemes – usually based on tanks or wells. For tank irrigation small storage reservoirs are built, either by damming very small streams or by digging pools to collect rainfall or flood water. This water can then be used to irrigate a small area of land around the tank. There is, of course, considerable water loss by evaporation from the tanks. Furthermore, in some areas the tanks also provide breeding grounds for malarial mosquitoes and this can have a serious effect on the health of the local population. It is not surprising, therefore, that where supplies of groundwater are available – and this is true of vast areas of India to the south of the Himalayas – well irrigation has become more popular. Varanasi (Fig. 4.84) is one area which has plentiful supplies of groundwater and in some villages minor improvements, which cost very little, have transformed the pattern of agriculture.

The villages around Banwaripur, near Varanasi, are typical. The land area of these villages is 323 hectares and the population is 1253 – this represents an increase of more than 25% in less than 20 years. During this period food production has more than kept pace with population growth, largely as a result of improvements in irrigation.

IRRIGATED LAND IN INDIA (BY TYPE OF IRRIGATION)

Type of irrigation	% of irrigated land in		
	1901	1950	1980
Canal	53.0	40.2	40.4
Tank	11.9	17.2	10.4
Well	24.0	28.2	42.7
Other	11.1	14.4	6.5

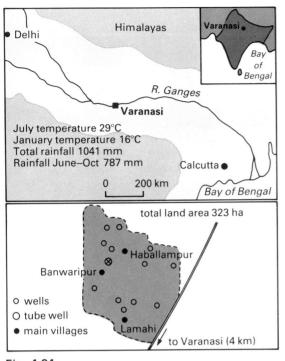

Fig. 4.84

Irrigation has long been practised in the area and a number of simple wells had been sunk to tap supplies of groundwater. The water was raised either manually or by using draught oxen to lift large buckets. It was carried to the fields along a simple system of canals. As part of a government scheme to improve agriculture, a modern tube well was drilled and an electric pump was installed. This increased the flow of water and made it more regular. As a result the pattern of farming was transformed.

Using information given in this section, complete the following exercise.

a The area has a monsoon climate.
  i   When does the wet season occur?
  ii What proportion of the total rainfall occurs during this season?
  iii During which part of the year is the rainfall least reliable?
b Before the sinking of the new tube well:
  i   What was the total cultivated area?
  ii What proportion of this land was irrigated?
  iii What were the main food crops? List them in order of importance.
c After the sinking of the new well:
  i   What was the increase in the cultivated area?
  ii What was the increase in the irrigated area? Had the proportion of irrigated land increased or decreased?
  iii What were the main food crops in order of importance?
  iv Describe the changes which took place in agricultural output.
d The crops can be divided into wet and dry season crops. (The major wet season crop is rice.)
  i   Which group has shown the greatest improvement as a result of the improvement in irrigation?
  ii Why do you think this is so?

RAINFALL AT VARANASI

	June-Oct	Oct-Feb	March-June
Rainfall (mm)	787	108	146
% variability	26.3	76.3	71.5
Total rainfall	1041 mm		

LAND USE AND FARM PRODUCTION IN VARANASI

Before new well		After new well
140	Cultivated area (ha)	180
65	Irrigated area (ha)	94
	Major crops (tonnes)	
4.2	Rice	6.8
8.2	Maize	22.8
9.4	Wheat	55.0
19.6	Barley	23.4
4.7	Peas	14.5
63.7	All food crops	136.0
366.6	Sugar	766.9

The effects of a relatively inexpensive development were as follows:

1 The area of cropland has been increased.

2 Improved water control has led to increased yields. This, together with the introduction of higher yielding varieties of crops, has led to a doubling of output.

3 Improvement has been greatest among dry season crops which were at greatest risk from variations in rainfall.

4 The area of land which can be double cropped, i.e. produce both wet and dry season crops, has increased threefold.

Government action led to the installation of the existing well. It is hoped that landowners will soon be able to afford to sink more wells and install electric pumps.

In some parts of the world – particularly the oil rich countries of the Middle East – this has been done on a large scale. Large areas are irrigated by slowly moving sprinkler booms and circular patches of cropland form a distinctive feature of the landscape in deserts (Fig. 4.85). In India, however, it is likely that modern tube wells will be used largely to increase the availability of water in areas which are already irrigated.

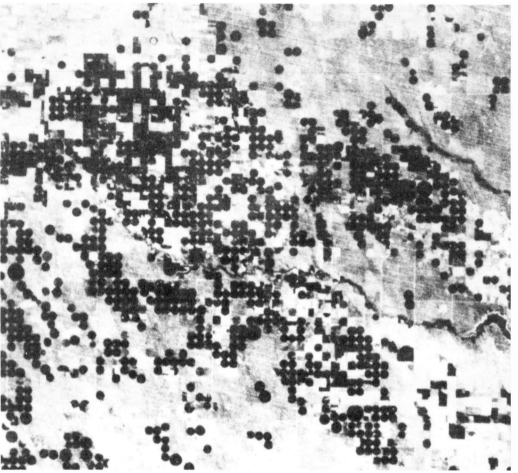

Fig. 4.85 *Circular irrigation plots, Chase County, Nebraska, USA*

Reclaiming land

In some parts of the world the only remaining uncultivated land appears to be unsuitable for agriculture. Occasionally, however, land subject to flooding – either by rivers or the sea – can be reclaimed. In this case the costs are almost always greater than the value of the land brought into cultivation. As a result land reclamation is important only in areas which are densely populated and which have a serious land shortage.

The reclamation schemes in the Netherlands are among the most impressive in the world. Here, within the space of 100 years, the population has increased from 3.5 million to more than 13 million and densities now exceed 400 per square kilometre. Furthermore, more than 50% of the land area has been reclaimed. Most of this land is 'polderland' (Fig. 4.86).

There are three types of polderland:

1   Areas which are above sea level but which are subject to flooding during storms. Such areas could be reclaimed simply by building protective embankments or dykes. This type of reclamation began more than 400 years ago.

2   Areas which are below the high tide level. Such areas can be reclaimed only by building a complicated system of drains. The main drains, which are often canalised rivers, are built to carry

the water to the sea. These drains often flow above the level of the surrounding land, and water in the smaller field drains has to be pumped into them. Reclamation began only in the seventeenth century when windmills became available to drive the pumps. The development of more efficient pumps powered by steam, electric and diesel motors led to a rapid increase in the area which could be drained.

3   The areas below the level of low tide presented the greatest difficulties. Reclamation required the building of massive dykes and the installation of huge pumps. As a result the drainage of these areas has only taken place during the present century. The largest of the schemes is the Zuider Zee/Ijsselmeer project which was started after the First World War.

The Zuider Zee was a large freshwater lake. At the end of the fourteenth century it was invaded by the sea and the water became salty. Plans to reclaim this shallow sea were first drawn up during the nineteenth century but work did not begin until 1919. By this time the technology was available to build a main dyke large enough to cut off the Zuider Zee from the North Sea. This was completed in May 1932. Sluices in the dyke allowed floodwaters from the land to escape and there were massive gates to keep out the tides. Within five years the sea water had been replaced by freshwater and the drainage of large areas of land could begin.

In fact drainage of the first polder began before the main dyke was closed. In the north west 20 000 hectares of land were enclosed by a secondary dyke and water up to a depth of five and a half metres was pumped out to expose the sea bed. To drain this land 40 500 kilometres of ditches were dug and these were fed by a dense network of field drains. This allowed rainwater to pass through the soil and helped wash out the salt which made farming impossible. As a result farming began at a very early date. Within two years the first crop of grass had been sown. This was followed by crops of beans and peas which helped fix nitrogen in the soil. Then, as fertility increased, the first cereal crops could be sown.

The pattern of drains has also influenced the shape and layout of the farms (Fig. 4.87).

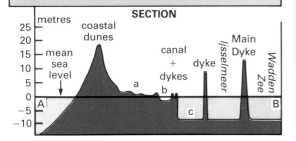

POLDERS IN THE NETHERLANDS, WITH DATES OF RECLAMATION

Using information given in this section, complete the following exercise.

a   Using the photograph, Fig. 4.87, describe the landscape of the polderland.

b   i   Why is the shape of a typical polder farm so regular?
    ii   Why are farms generally small in this area?

c   On the section three drained areas are labelled a, b and c.
    i   Give the approximate date of draining of each polder.
    ii   Give the height of each polder in relation to sea level.
    iii   Explain the methods used to drain each type of polder.

d   Write a brief history of the draining of the Zuider Zee and describe the situation today.

Fig. 4.86

Today 2336 square kilometres of the Zuider Zee have been reclaimed for farming. The reclaimed land represents little more than 70% of the original area. The remainder has been left undrained and it forms a shallow freshwater lake known as the Ijsselmeer. This has been retained to provide a storage basin for water from the surrounding land at times of high tide or storm when the sluice gates in the main dyke are closed. It also provides water for irrigation since during the summer the polderlands can become too dry. Irrigation is important not only because it improves yields but because it prevents salt from rising as the soil dries out.

Even more ambitious plans have been drawn up to reclaim more land from the sea in the Netherlands, particularly in the area of the Rhine Delta. This is an option open to few other countries, however, simply on account of cost.

Fig. 4.87 *Recently reclaimed land on the Ijsselmeer Polders, the Netherlands*

Bringing 'marginal' land into cultivation

Crops can be grown only if warmth, moisture and sunlight are available. The conditions under which any crop grows best are known as the optimum conditions and these will be found in few places. Most parts of the earth's surface present some problems which combine to reduce yields; and in some areas the problems are so serious that the risk of crop failure is very high. Such land is said to be marginal and it is this land which is now being brought under cultivation in many parts of the world.

As we have seen, one approach is to irrigate land in arid areas. This has been very successful, but the amount of land which can be irrigated is limited and the costs are almost always high. Other approaches practised in recent years have been to develop new methods of cultivation, such as dry farming, or to introduce new varieties of crops which can be grown under difficult conditions.

a   Dry farming techniques

These were developed to grow cereals in parts of the Great Plains and Prairies of North America (Fig. 4.88).

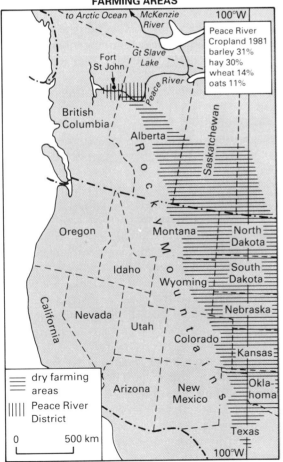

WESTERN NORTH AMERICA, SHOWING THE PEACE RIVER DISTRICT AND THE MAIN DRY FARMING AREAS

Peace River
Cropland 1981
barley 31%
hay 30%
wheat 14%
oats 11%

dry farming areas

Peace River District

0   500 km

Fig. 4.88

Using information given on pages 80–83, relating to a cereal farm in Saskatchewan, complete the following exercise.

a   i   Which type of land use takes up the largest area of the farm?
  ii   Crops are grown on the same land *every year/every other year/ once in three years.*
b   Why is so much land left fallow?
c   i   Why is the stubble left standing in the fields during the period of fallow?
  ii   Why are the crops grown in alternating strips, separated by fallow land?
  iii   Why is an underground harrow used in the fields?
d   The purpose of these techniques is *to expose bare earth to the sun/to reduce water loss by evapo-transpiration/to reduce the dangers of soil erosion/to reduce the labour force on the farm/to store water in the soil.*
e   Using the information given, write a brief account of dry farming methods.

Dry farming methods have been successful in developed countries like the United States and Australia where they have been used to increase grain production and to reduce soil erosion. They have to be undertaken on such a large scale, however, that they are difficult to introduce into developing countries where land holdings are generally small.

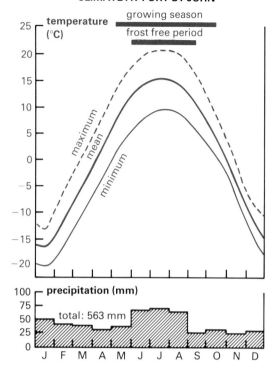

CLIMATE AT FORT ST JOHN

growing season

frost free period

temperature (°C)

maximum
mean
minimum

precipitation (mm)

total: 563 mm

J F M A M J J A S O N D

EFFECT OF CLIMATE ON FARM OUTPUT
(output expressed as % of maximum
yearly output during period)

Year	Wheat	Barley	Climatic problems
1965	55%	77%	
1966	—	—	cool and wet
1967	48%	97%	drought
1968	100%	92%	killing frost in August
1969	54%	100%	severe frosts in June & August

Note: 1 The greater resistance of barley to climatic problems
2 The area under wheat more than doubled in 1969

Fig. 4.89

Methods of preventing soil erosion
1 Use of small areas of cleared land
2 Abandoning clearings after a short time
3 Use of regular fallow
4 Use of crop rotation
5 Movement of animals to prevent overgrazing
6 Use of wind breaks e.g. strip cultivation on the Canadian Prairies
7 Covering exposed soil
8 Use of manure to maintain soil fertility

b Improved crops

One of the main improvements in farming in recent years has been the development of new varieties of crops. Some of these are simply more resistant to disease or give higher yields, but others ripen more quickly. This last development has meant that cultivation can be extended into areas which have very short growing seasons (Fig. 4.89). For example, new varieties of quick ripening wheat have allowed cultivation to spread from the Canadian Prairies to the lowlands of the Peace River Valley, 300 kilometres to the north.

Even more important, the development of quick ripening strains of rice made it possible to grow two or even three crops a year in many developing countries. This has increased yields enormously and has helped food production to keep pace with population in these countries. More details of this development are given on pages 66 to 68.

The loss of agricultural land

Agricultural production has increased enormously in recent years. At the same time serious problems have become apparent. In particular, attempts to bring new land into cultivation have to be set against a steady loss of agricultural land. The causes of this loss are varied.

1 The increase in population has meant that more land is needed for houses.

2 Land is also needed for industry, roads and railways, airports etc. This type of loss is greatest in developed countries but it is becoming more important in the Developing World.

3 Much more serious, however, is the loss of agricultural land as a result of soil exhaustion and soil erosion. Soil erosion is the removal of parts of the surface layers of the soil. Individual particles are freed from the soil mass and are then transported by agents of erosion such as wind and running water. Soil erosion takes place everywhere but, with a natural vegetation cover, it takes place only slowly and presents few problems. This is because the vegetation canopy protects the soil from the worst effects of wind and rain, while the plant roots bind the soil together. Protection of this kind is particularly important on hillsides since the rate of soil erosion is strongly influenced by slope.

Problems occur when the natural vegetation cover is destroyed. This can take place naturally – following a volcanic eruption, for example. In most cases, however, it is a result of land being cleared, usually for agriculture. Even then soil erosion need not become a serious problem. As we have seen, most methods of farming – including the most simple – are designed to safeguard the soil. The extent of soil erosion in the world today (Fig. 4.90) is a measure of the failure of these methods.

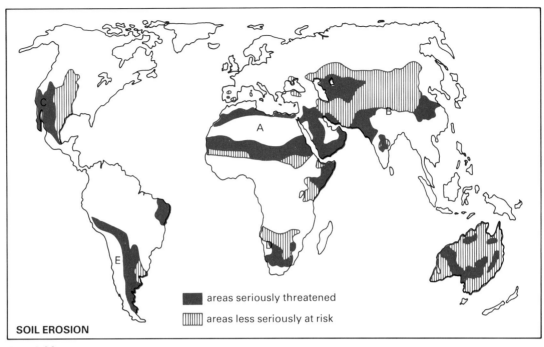

areas seriously threatened

areas less seriously at risk

SOIL EROSION

Fig. 4.90

Compare the map of rainfall distribution on page 7 with the map of soil erosion, Fig. 4.90.

a   Look at the map showing the distribution of rainfall.
   i   The areas lettered A–E on the map above have one thing in common. What is it?
   ii   Name the areas A–E.
   iii   Describe the distribution of soil erosion in the world and relate it to the pattern of rainfall.
b   i   Which continent is suffering most from soil erosion?
   ii   Which continent is suffering least?

Soil erosion became a major problem when new land was developed for farming in the Americas, Australia, Africa and Asia. This was because the methods of farming used were often inappropriate for the environment. It remains a major problem today, particularly in the areas bordering the great deserts of the world.

Using the information on page 114, answer the following.

a   i   What is the average annual rainfall of the Sahel area of Africa?
   ii   Describe the pattern of rainfall between 1950 and 1980 (see graph in Fig. 4.93).
   iii   Would you describe this pattern as regular or irregular?
   iv   The area is experiencing drought conditions today. How long has the drought lasted?
   v   Which type of erosion is likely to be experienced here? (Examine the two case studies on page 112.)
b   i   What effect is population growth likely to have on the main types of farming, i.e. nomadic pastoralism and sedentary cultivation? (See case studies on pages 55 and 63.)
   ii   Why is pressure on the farm systems likely to cause soil erosion here?

The causes of erosion are complicated and can best be understood by comparing two areas.

	Tennessee Valley: USA (1850 onwards)	The Dust Bowl of Kansas and Oklahoma: USA (1930s)
Natural vegetation	Deciduous and coniferous forest	Prairie grassland
Rainfall	1125 mm	750 mm
Slopes	Steep	Gentle
Size of farms	Small	Small farmers failed and land was taken over to form large farms
Crops	Corn, tobacco and cotton	Cereals and cotton
Factors encouraging soil erosion	1 Clearance of the natural vegetation. 2 Continuous cultivation without adequate rotation or manuring. 3 Steep hillsides ploughed, often up and down the slope.	1 Destruction of the natural vegetation. 2 Monoculture of cereals or cotton. 3 Successive years of drought. 4 Crop failures left bare earth exposed to strong winds.
Type of erosion	1 Sheet erosion (soil particles washed down steep slopes). 2 Large gullies.	1 Wind erosion. 2 Large gullies, formed during storms. 3 Formation of shifting dunes.
Methods of reclamation	1 Planting ground cover on steep slopes. 2 Replanting forests. 3 Contour ploughing on farmland, i.e. furrows which follow the contours rather than running up and down slopes. This reduces run-off. 4 Improved methods of farming.	Reclamation difficult and slow because of the low rainfall. 1 Planting grasses to stabilise dunes. 2 Planting or building wind breaks. 3 Strip farming to reduce wind erosion. 4 Pastoral farming rather than cultivation.

Fig. **4.91** *Soil erosion in the Tennessee Valley. Note the size of the gulleys and the lack of vegetation*

Fig. **4.92** *Soil erosion in the Dust Bowl of Oklahoma (the combined effects of wind and rainstorm erosion)*

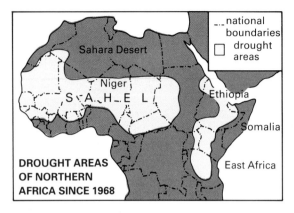

DROUGHT AREAS OF NORTHERN AFRICA SINCE 1968

RELIABILITY OF RAINFALL: SAHEL REGION,
annual rainfall (expressed as a % of the average)

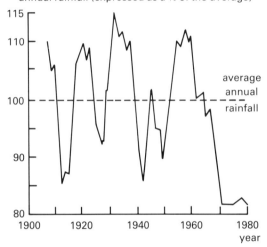

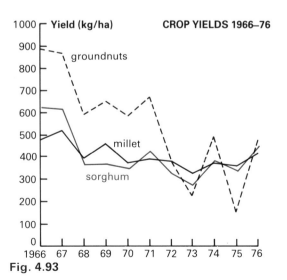

NIGER		
Area 1 266 700 sq km		
1969		1981
3.9 m ha	Population	6.0 m ha
2.9	Cropland	3.4
15.6	Pasture	9.6
96.0	Other	113.5

In the Sahel (Fig. 4.93) the destruction of the natural vegetation during droughts led to soil erosion. This happened during all the previous droughts but the area recovered. The damage produced by the drought which started in the early 1970s has been much more severe. This is because the drought coincided with a period of rapid population growth in the area. The land, already heavily used for both stock rearing and cultivation, was put under further pressure. The result has been the overgrazing of pasture and the exhaustion of farm land. Soil erosion has been on a scale so great that large areas of once productive land have been reduced to shifting sand, no different from the desert itself. This process is called 'desertification'. Reclamation will be far from easy and probably beyond the resources of a developing country.

Approximately 80 000 square kilometres of land are lost in the Sahel each year. Similar, if less serious losses, are taking place in other parts of the world and the problem is a major one.

Fig. 4.93

Fig. 4.94 *The effects of overgrazing in the Sahel*

5 Energy

WORLD CONSUMPTION OF ENERGY (per capita)

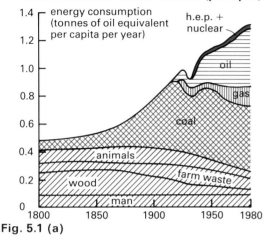

Fig. 5.1 (a)

ENERGY CONSUMPTION IN INDIA AND THE USA
(million tonnes of coal equivalent)

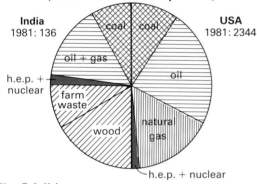

Fig. 5.1 (b)

ENERGY CONSUMPTION AND DEVELOPMENT
IN 1982 (development measured by GNP)

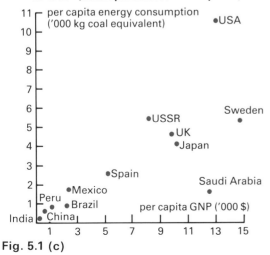

Fig. 5.1 (c)

All human activity depends upon the availability of an effective supply of energy. At its simplest this can involve no more than a man hunting for food or cultivating his own fields – the energy supply will be the food he produces. At its most complex, in a modern industrialised country, it can involve the use of energy on a vast scale, and the sources of that energy can be very varied. It follows, therefore, that the pattern of energy consumption will vary greatly from country to country and that the amount of energy used will probably reflect the extent of economic development in a country (Fig. 5.1).

Using information given in Fig. 5.1 complete the following exercise.

a i When did world consumption of energy begin to rise rapidly?
  ii Why did this sudden rise take place?
  iii There has been one period of decline since that date. When and why did it take place?
  iv The rate of increase has slowed down in recent years. Why has this happened?
b i List the main sources of energy in the world in 1800. Arrange them in order of importance.
  ii Make a similar list for 1980.
  iii Describe the main changes which have taken place in the pattern of energy use during this period.
c i List the sources of energy in India and the USA and, in each case, arrange them in order of importance.
  ii Describe the main differences between the two patterns.
d Write down each of the following sentences, completing it with one of the alternatives given.
  i Per capita (i.e. per person) energy consumption in the United States is *twice/half/ten times/more than twenty times* as great as in India.
  ii Overall energy consumption in the United States is *ten/twenty/forty/more than one hundred* percent more than in India.
  iii There is *a very strong/a strong/a weak/no* relationship between development (as measured by Gross National Product) and energy consumption.
  iv The relationship (if it exists) can be described in the following terms: *energy consumption generally decreases with development/energy consumption generally increases with development/energy consumption always increases with development*.

The pattern of development is very clear. Energy consumption has increased rapidly throughout the world since the last quarter of the nineteenth century. This increase has been most rapid in the developed countries which today, with 125% of the world's population, consume 175% of the world's energy.

During the same period there has been a dramatic change in the forms of energy used. Throughout the nineteenth century most countries depended upon wood and farm waste for fuel. Only in the developed countries of Europe and North America was coal an important fuel. Today almost all countries are heavily dependent upon oil and coal and even in the poorest developing countries dependence upon traditional fuels has declined.

Consumption of energy is greatest in the USA and if other countries were to approach such levels of consumption there would be an immediate shortage of energy in the world. The threat of such a shortage became apparent in the early 1970s and since that time attempts have been made to reduce energy consumption. Even more important, attempts have been made to reduce dependence upon fuels, such as oil, which in the near future will be in short supply. It is against this background that any study of energy – both fuels and secondary sources such as electricity – must take place.

Firewood and other traditional fuels

The effects of any energy crisis are most severe in the developing countries – the very countries which use least energy (see Fig. 5.1). One reason for this has been the failure of traditional sources of energy to keep pace with population growth. This is particularly true of the most important of the traditional fuels – firewood.

Nine tenths of the people in the world use firewood as fuel. In spite of the vast growth of commercial forestry (see page 143), at least half of the timber in the world today is used to heat houses or to cook food (Fig. 5.2).

Timber is, of course, a renewable source of energy. If cutting is not more rapid than tree growth, the needs of people in developing countries can be met indefinitely. Traditional farming systems took this into account and sources of timber were made available to the farmers. In recent years, however, the rapid increase in population has led not only to an increased demand for firewood but also to the clearing of areas of forest which once provided the fuel. The results have been disastrous in countries like India and the semi-arid areas of Africa and Latin America. Here:

1   Every available source of fuel is used (Fig. 5.3). Leaves and litter are scraped from beneath the trees and even the tree roots are removed for firewood. This kills the trees, reduces the amount of plant food returning to the soil and eventually causes severe soil erosion.

2   The collection of firewood – usually done by women – now takes many hours. This reduces the amount of time spent running the home or working in the fields.

USE OF TIMBER

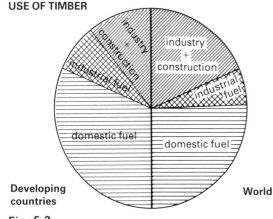

Developing countries

World

Fig. 5.2

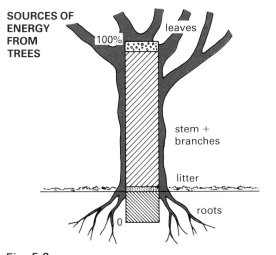

SOURCES OF ENERGY FROM TREES

leaves
100%
stem + branches
litter
roots
0

Fig. 5.3

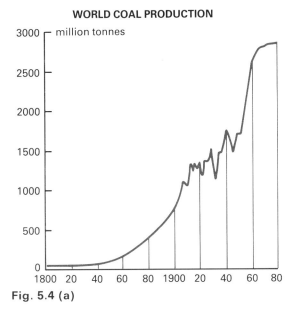

WORLD COAL PRODUCTION

million tonnes

Fig. 5.4 (a)

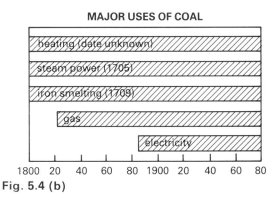

MAJOR USES OF COAL

heating (date unknown)
steam power (1705)
iron smelting (1709)
gas
electricity

Fig. 5.4 (b)

3   It is often necessary to buy firewood. This is expensive and takes up money which could otherwise be used to buy food or to improve the farm.

4   The use of other fuels such as dried animal dung has increased and this, in turn, has led to a reduction in the amount of manure available in the fields. As a result food production is again affected and there is an increased danger of soil exhaustion.

For a time it was hoped that kerosene (obtained from oil) could be used instead of firewood. The oil price rises of the 1970s have made this virtually impossible and in many developing countries governments have been forced to turn to the growing of timber as a crop. In some forested areas this has been successful. However, in most places, the destruction of the few remaining trees continues and, with it, the destruction of the soil and (in arid areas) the spread of deserts.

Coal

The first alternative to timber as a fuel was coal (Fig. 5.4). Coal is a rock which is formed when the remains of ancient vegetation are metamorphosed, i.e. changed by heat and pressure. This occurs when the thick layers of partly decomposed vegetation are buried under later sedimentary deposits. Eventually layers (seams) of coal will be formed. In some parts of the world many coal seams have been laid down, separated by bands of other rocks such as sandstone and shale. The entire complex of rock, including the coal seams and the rocks between, is called the coal measures.

Because vegetation varies enormously and because the pressure and heat which form the coal have differed from place to place, no two coal deposits are alike. For convenience, however, certain major types of coal are identified. These range from peat and lignite, which are soft and contain partly decomposed plant remains, through to anthracite which has been exposed to such enormous heat and pressure that it is hard and rock-like and is almost pure carbon. In terms of quantity mined, however, the most important type is bituminous coal.

The use of coal dates back more than 2000 years. For most of this period production was small and limited to places where coal was found on the surface. Trade in coal began in the fourteenth century when, for example, London was supplied by sea from the coastal coalfields of North East England. Even then, it was used almost entirely for domestic heating and cooking and demand was small. Large scale production began only with the use of coal as a source of energy for industry. There were several important developments:

1   The use of coke in iron making: 1709.
2   The development of the steam engine: 1712.
3   The commercial extraction of gas from coal: 1812.
4   The generation of electricity: 1882.

As a result of these developments demand for coal increased enormously and during the eighteenth century new methods of mining were developed to increase production. These methods are still in use today.

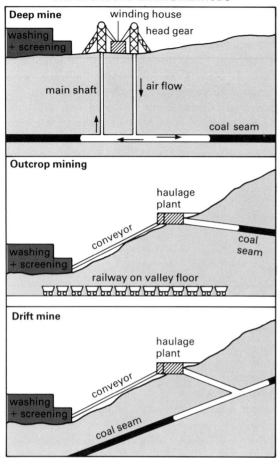

UNDERGROUND MINING METHODS

Deep mine — washing + screening, winding house, head gear, main shaft, air flow, coal seam

Outcrop mining — haulage plant, conveyor, coal seam, washing + screening, railway on valley floor

Drift mine — haulage plant, conveyor, washing + screening, coal seam

Fig. 5.5 (a)

Underground mining

For centuries mining was restricted to the surface working of outcrops or, at most, to the sinking of small, shallow pits to reach seams which were near the surface. This obviously limited output severely and it was not until methods of underground mining (Fig. 5.5) were developed that the large scale production of coal could begin. For this to happen a number of technological advances had to take place.

1 Large shafts had to be dug and lined so that the best coal seams could be reached. By 1800 some of these shafts were more than 100 metres deep.

2 Engines had to be developed to lift the coal and the waste products to the surface.

3 To make a profit, mines had to be large and seams were worked at great distances from the bottom of the shafts. This required a haulage system (usually primitive railways) to bring the coal to the face from the pit bottom.

4 As the workings spread out from the shafts the need for ventilation became greater. Air circulation was created using two shafts (a downcast and an upcast) and large pumps.

5 Pumps were needed to remove surplus water from the mine.

Such an operation was obviously very expensive but, because demand for coal was high and because no alternative method was available, most coal was deep mined until the beginning of the twentieth century. Methods of mining were gradually improved. Coal cutting machines were introduced at the face and conveyor belt systems replaced the old haulage systems. However, the basic methods remained unchanged. It is not surprising, therefore, that, when machines were developed which were large enough to remove the overlying rock (the overburden), the working of coal in open pits (Fig. 5.8) became an attractive proposition.

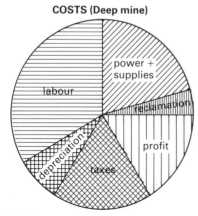

COSTS (Deep mine)

labour, power + supplies, reclamation, profit, taxes, depreciation

Fig. 5.5 (b)

Fig. 5.6 *A modern drift mine. Note the housings for the belts that carry coal from the pit head*

Modern open cast or strip mining

Advantages (compared with underground mining)

1 Cheapness – mining is highly mechanised and labour costs are therefore comparatively low.

2 Greater efficiency – less coal is left in the ground (more than 80% can be extracted, compared with 50% in deep mines).

3 Safety – the risk of explosion or rock falls is low.

4 Fewer problems during mining, e.g. no need for ventilation, and haulage by conveyor and truck is much easier.

5 Land can be restored within ten years. In modern surface or strip mines the pit is filled continuously and top soil (which is stored away from the overburden) can be replaced quickly.

Disadvantages (compared with underground mining)

1 The number of seams which can be reached is limited. Costs increase rapidly with the thickness of overburden which has to be removed.

2 The seams near the surface do not always contain the best coal.

3 Open pit mining is not possible on all types of terrain.

4 Reclamation is sometimes difficult and expensive. This is particularly true in areas of low or irregular rainfall where plant growth can be slow.

5 It looks a mess and destroys the environment for several years.

Fig. 5.7 *A modern open pit mine. Note the size of the earth moving equipment*

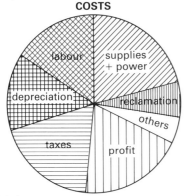

Fig. 5.8 (a)

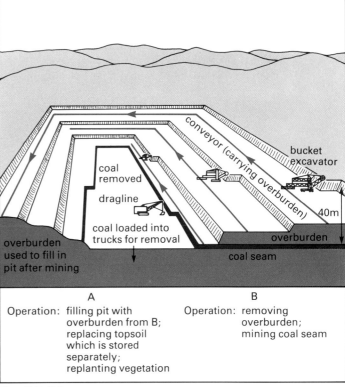

Fig. 5.8 (b)

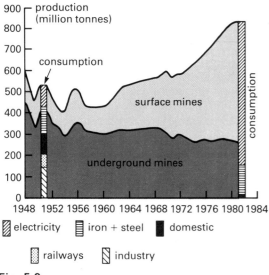

USA: COAL PRODUCTION, CONSUMPTION AND METHOD OF MINING

Key: electricity, iron + steel, domestic, railways, industry

Fig. 5.9

Coalmining in the United States

The United States consumes more energy than any other country in the world and coal supplies 16% of that energy. Demand for coal is now increasing and the coal mining industry has developed rapidly in recent years so as to meet this growing demand (Fig. 5.9). The changes which have taken place reflect those seen in many countries in the Developed World.

Using information given in Figs. 5.9 and 5.10, complete the following exercise.

a i   In 1950 coal supplied 38% of the energy used in the United States. What was the comparable figure in 1981? (See Fig. 5.1.)

   ii How much coal was produced in the United States in 1950 and in 1980?

   iii Compare the figures given in your answers to i and ii. What does this tell you about the amount of energy used in the United States during the period 1950 to 1980?

b   Complete the following statements:

   i   In 1950 *one half/one quarter/three quarters/four fifths* of USA coal production was from underground mines.

   ii In 1980 *one third/one half/two thirds/four fifths* of USA coal production was from underground mines.

   iii What proportion of USA coal production was from the eastern fields in 1950?

   iv What proportion of USA coal production was from the eastern fields in 1980?

   v   During this period the rate of growth in mining has been greatest in the *eastern/western* fields.

THE COALFIELDS OF THE USA

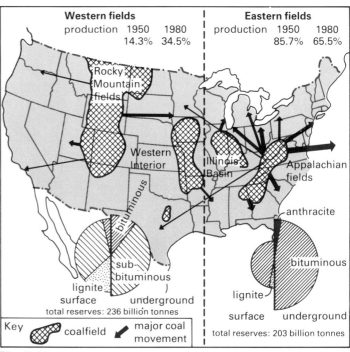

Fig. 5.10

Note:
1 The size of the reserves
2 The size of the coalfields in the western states
3 The proportion of surface reserves in the west

120

c i What are the advantages and disadvantages of surface as opposed to underground mining?

　　ii Surface mining is usually cheaper than underground mining. Which of the following have helped to reduce costs: *mining is more heavily mechanised; labour costs are lower; the coal is of better quality; little coal is left in the ground; the surface fields are near the main markets*?

d i Demand for coal is likely to increase in the future. Why?

　　ii Which fields are likely to be developed to meet this demand? Give reasons for your choice.

　　iii What are the main problems facing the development of coalmining in the western states?

The oil price rises of the early 1970s, which took place at a time when the United States was becoming increasingly dependent upon imported oil, led to a renewed interest in coal as a source of energy. Production was increased and new mines – most of them open pits in the coalfields of the mid and far west – were opened. Here the coal was generally of poorer quality than that obtained from the deep mines of the Appalachian region but, using modern highly mechanised methods, it was cheap to mine. In fact it was so cheap it could compete in the main markets several hundred kilometres away in the north east of the country. Because costs are so low it is likely that any further increase in demand will be met from strip mines in the western states. This means that the problems of restoring land in areas of low rainfall will have to be overcome.

Coal in the Developing World

Coal is the most abundant source of energy available in the world today. If present levels of mining continue the known reserves (Fig. 5.11) will last for the foreseeable future. Furthermore, even if production is increased to replace declining supplies of oil, it is unlikely that there will be a shortage of coal.

Like oil, however, coal reserves are not evenly distributed throughout the world and in certain areas, particularly South America, Africa and South East Asia, they are almost completely lacking. Unfortunately it is in these areas that most of the developing countries of the world are located. This means that for them coal is unlikely to provide a cheaper alternative to oil which is already expensive and which in the future is likely to be in short supply.

It is the availability of oil which will play an important part in the development of coal mining throughout the world. As long as oil was cheap and plentiful coal could not compete. Price rises and dwindling oil reserves have made coal more attractive. Also, if new methods are found of using coal more efficiently, both as a source of energy and as a raw material for the chemical industry, production is likely to increase rapidly.

WORLD COAL RESERVES (billion tonnes)

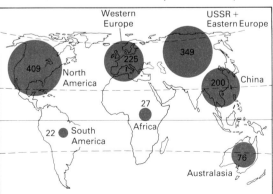

Fig. 5.11

121

WORLD OIL AND NATURAL GAS PRODUCTION

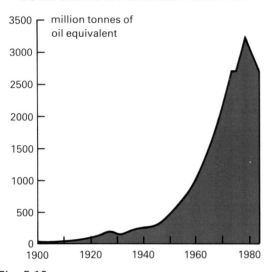

Fig. 5.12

Oil and natural gas

We have seen that, although the amount of coal mined in the world has continued to increase, its importance as a source of energy has tended to decline when compared with other fuels. This pattern is largely the result of the massive increase in the consumption of oil and natural gas which has taken place since the end of the First World War in 1918. Prior to this date oil was comparatively unimportant and used mainly in the form of kerosene for lamps and heaters. Since that time, however, oil and gas have become increasingly important both as a source of energy and as the raw material for the petro-chemical industry (see page 171). In fact, by 1970 they had replaced coal as the main source of energy in the world.

There are many reasons for this rapid growth (Fig. 5.12), most of them stemming from the advantages of oil and gas when compared with other sources of energy.

1   They occur naturally as liquids or gases. This means that they can be extracted from the ground more easily than solid fuels such as coal.

2   Extraction is highly automated and therefore cheap.

3   Because they are liquid or gaseous they can be transported cheaply and easily by bulk tanker or along pipelines.

4   Both are more 'efficient' fuels than coal, i.e. when they burn they give more heat and produce little or no waste.

5   Any waste produced – usually in the form of gases – does less harm to the environment than the waste associated with other fuels.

6   Both are extremely 'versatile', i.e. they have a large number of possible uses. These include the provision of direct power to the internal combustion engine and the generation of secondary sources of power such as electricity.

WORLD OIL RESERVES (1982): BY REGION

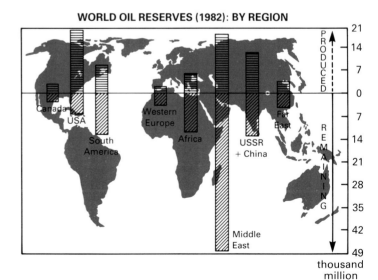

Fig. 5.13

A TYPICAL OIL PRODUCTION SYSTEM

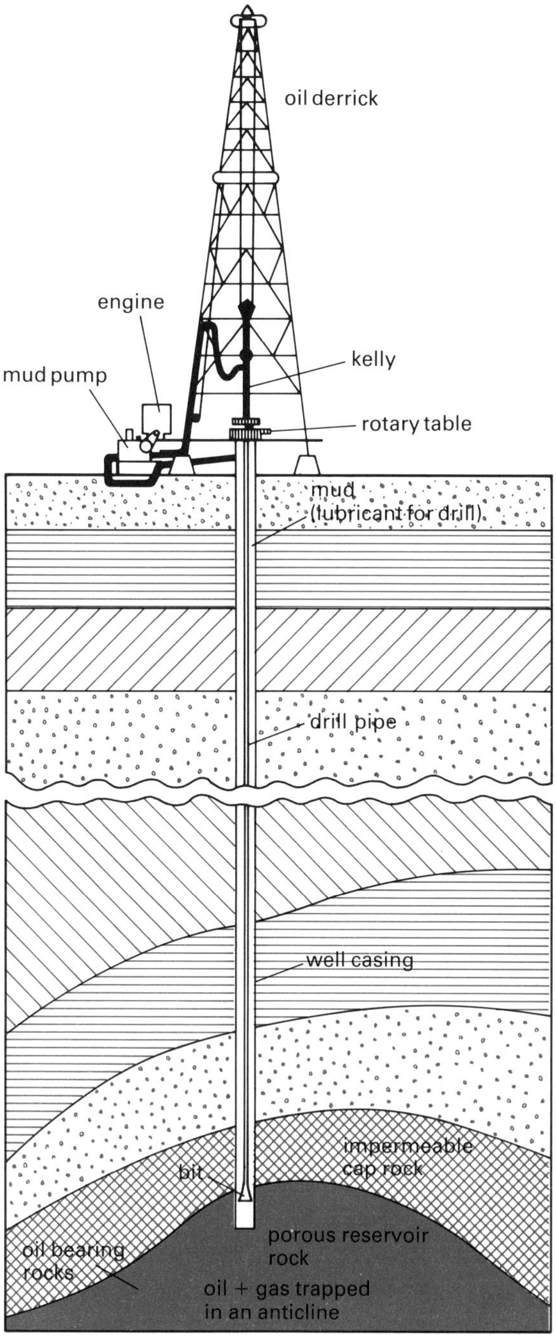

oil derrick

engine

kelly

mud pump

rotary table

mud
(lubricant for drill)

drill pipe

well casing

impermeable
cap rock

bit

porous reservoir
rock

oil bearing
rocks

oil + gas trapped
in an anticline

Fig. 5.14

However, there are many problems to be overcome in maintaining adequate oil supplies for the world. Most of these problems stem from the way in which the oil was formed. It is thought that the oil originated as organisms which lived in shallow tropical seas thousands of years ago. Sediments deposited on the sea bed contained the remains of these organisms and when these sediments were covered by later deposits pressure and temperature increased. Under these conditions oil was formed. Seas of this kind covered large areas of the earth's surface and large amounts of oil were formed. Unfortunately little of the oil laid down can be extracted. Some of it remained locked in tar sands and oil shales and even where these are found on the surface, extraction is difficult and expensive (see page 126). A proportion did, however, escape into surrounding porous rocks and it is this oil which is today extracted from wells. Once again, only a small proportion of the oil available in such rocks can be extracted. In most cases the oil is spread thinly through the rock and it cannot be separated from the rock particles. Only where geological conditions are such that the oil is trapped in a comparatively small area, e.g. on the crest of an anticline or dome (see Fig. 5.14), or between faults is the oil found in sufficient quantity for it to flow out of the rock.

Given such limitations, it is not surprising that the area of workable oil fields is comparatively small or that reserves are limited (Fig. 5.13). What is more surprising is the fact that these reserves are widely scattered over the earth's surface. They may even be found in polar regions, far from the tropical areas in which the oil was formed. (This, of course, is the result of the movement of the 'plates' which make up the earth's surface.)

Using information given in this section, complete the following exercise.

a i Name two early uses of oil.
   ii Name the new uses which gave rise to the rapid expansion of oil production after 1930.
b i List the areas with the largest reserves of oil, arranging them in order of importance.
   ii List the areas which produce most oil, arranging them in order of importance (see table on page 125).
c Name one country or region which has:
   i Large reserves but still imports a large amount of oil.
   ii The largest reserves, highest output and exports a large amount of oil.
   iii A large demand for oil but is almost totally dependent upon imports.
   iv Has large reserves and comparatively low output.
d Describe the method of extracting oil from the ground.

The major problem is obvious. With the exception of the USA, USSR and the United Kingdom the world's major consumers of oil produce little or no oil themselves and have virtually no known reserves. In fact, most of the world's oil reserves are found in a small number of countries, mainly in the Middle East. As a result, a massive trade in oil has grown up between the producing

DISTILLATION PROCESS AT AN OIL REFINERY

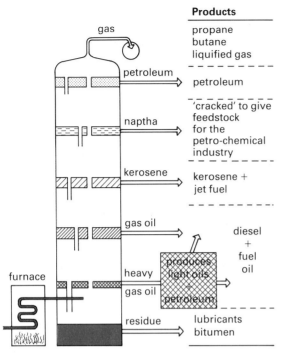

Fig. 5.15

countries in the Middle East and the industrialised areas such as Europe, Japan and, more recently, the United States.

Most of this trade is in crude oil, i.e. the oil as it emerges from the well. In this form it can be transported easily and cheaply – usually by bulk tanker – to the markets. Before it can be used, however, the oil is processed in a refinery (Fig. 5.16). Here the crude oil is broken down into its constituent parts.

The basic process in the refinery is distillation (Fig. 5.15). Crude oil is heated in a furnace before it is passed into a distillation or fractioning tower as a vapour. Inside the tower, the vapour rises and cools rapidly. During cooling the various constituents of the oil become liquid.

Since this takes place at different levels in the tower, each constituent can be isolated and drawn off separately. Distillation is a comparatively simple operation and it rarely produces the most satisfactory range of products. Most crude oil, for example, gives a surplus of heavy oil products while the greatest demand is for the lighter fractions such as petrol and naphtha. As a result it has become necessary to develop techniques which will increase the output of these lighter products. This process, known as 'cracking', is highly complex. However, it means that in the United States, for example, no less than 45% of the refinery product is petroleum – a figure which matches the pattern of demand in that country.

Fig. 5.16 *The BAPCO oil refinery at Sitra, Bahrein*

124

OIL PRODUCTION, OIL CONSUMPTION AND REFINERY CAPACITY

(each expressed as a percentage of the world total)

	Oil production	Oil consumption	Refinery capacity
USA	17.7	25.0	22.5
Mexico	5.4	>0.1	1.7
Saudi Arabia	12.0	>0.1	0.6
Nigeria	2.3	>0.1	>0.1
USSR	22.3	15.9	17.2
United Kingdom	3.8	2.7	3.0
France	0.1	3.3	4.1
Italy	0.1	3.2	5.0
West Germany	0.2	4.0	3.8
Japan	>0.1	7.3	6.9

Before refining, oil can be transported cheaply in a single container, whether it is a pipeline or an ocean going supertanker. After refining, it is broken down into a large number of products each of which needs its own container for transport. For this reason it is more economic to locate the refineries as near to the markets as possible so as to reduce the distances over which the refined products have to be transported. It is not surprising that the oil refining industry is concentrated in the highly developed countries.

Using the statistics given in the table, left, complete the following exercise.

a   **Either**: On two separate scattergraphs, plot the relationships between (i) refinery capacity and oil production (ii) refinery capacity and oil consumption.

Or:i   Make three lists, arranging the countries in rank order according to refinery capacity/oil production/oil consumption.

ii   Calculate the Spearman Rank Correlation Coefficient to show the relationship between (a) refinery capacity and oil production (b) refinery capacity and oil consumption.

b   In each case state whether the relationship appears to be *strong/fairly strong/moderate/weak/*or whether there is *no relationship* apparent.

c   Which of the following statements are supported by the statistics: (i) oil refining capacity increases with oil production (ii) oil refining capacity decreases with oil consumption (iii) oil refining capacity increases with oil consumption (iv) oil refining capacity decreases with oil production (v) there is no relationship between oil refining capacity and oil production (vi) there is no relationship between oil refining capacity and oil consumption?

d   Explain any relationships which you have noted.

The effect of the rising price of oil

Until 1973 oil was cheap and the world economy had come to depend upon ever increasing supplies of cheap oil. In that year, however, a number of the major oil producing countries which had joined together to form the Organisation of Petroleum Exporting Countries (OPEC) decided to increase the price of oil. Within a few weeks prices on the world markets more than trebled (Fig. 5.17) with serious consequences for almost every country in the world. The effects were felt in different ways in developed and less developed countries.

1   The Developed World

As we have seen, oil consumption is greatest in the developed industrialised countries of the world. Because of this, it might be expected that these countries would suffer most from any price increase. In fact, as can be seen from the situation in the United States (the largest consumer of oil in the world), this was not the case (Fig. 5.18).

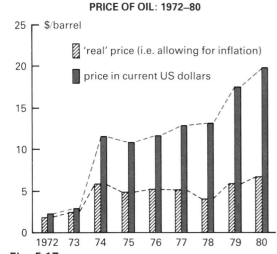

Fig. 5.17

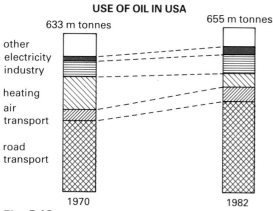

USE OF OIL IN USA

633 m tonnes

655 m tonnes

other
electricity
industry

heating
air
transport

road
transport

1970

1982

Fig. 5.18

In 1972 the USA consumed 775 million tonnes of oil, no less than 30% of world production. Until the mid 1960s virtually all of this vast demand had been met from American oil fields. For this reason it had been possible to establish prices which were far below those charged in other countries. Eventually, however, demand had outstripped the production of these oilfields and the United States became increasingly dependent upon imported oil. When prices were raised adjustments had to be made to limit the effects. Because the United States was a large consumer of energy and had developed many different sources of supply (see page 115), this proved to be easier than was at first expected.

1 Because energy consumption was so high savings could be made quite easily. For example, smaller and more efficient motor car engines were developed – a massive saving in a country where many families owned two or more cars and where the number of vehicles on the road already exceeded 117 million. Better insulation reduced the amount of energy, including oil, required to heat or cool down buildings in a country where air conditioning was widespread.

2 Alternative sources of energy were already in use and wherever possible these were developed so that dependence on oil could be reduced. As we have seen (page 120), the production of coal was increased mainly by opening new strip mines in the Mid West and in the Rocky Mountains. This coal could then be used in power stations to generate electricity which, in many cases, could be used as an alternative to oil. Even more significant, the rate at which nuclear power stations were being built was increased enormously.

3 Alternative sources of oil were sought within the United States:

a Oil fields which were too small or too difficult to exploit when oil was cheap could now be developed.

b Attempts were made to extract a greater proportion of the oil from the ground. The bulk of the oil in a reservoir adheres to the rock particles and will not flow into the wells. Several methods have been developed to improve this rate of flow (Fig. 5.19). By pumping hot water or a combination of heated gases into the rock the proportion of oil extracted can be increased by up to 75%. Improvements of this kind could help resolve any immediate oil shortage but unfortunately such methods are difficult and expensive and have only been tried on a small scale.

c Work was begun on the even more difficult problem of extracting oil from the oil shales and tar sands which occur in vast quantities in the United States and Canada. This oil will not flow out of the rock, so other methods have to be developed if use is to be made of the energy contained in the rocks. Two alternatives have been suggested. The first involves setting fire to the oil while it is still in the rock. In this case it is necessary to harness the heat generated underground to supply usable energy and this is technologically very difficult. The second alternative is to mine the rock and to extract the oil in a specially built plant. This approach has the advantage of making use of existing technology. It is, however, very expensive and the list of adverse effects on the environment is long, e.g. atmospheric pollution

**METHODS OF INCREASING THE PRODUCTIVITY
OF KNOWN OIL FIELDS**

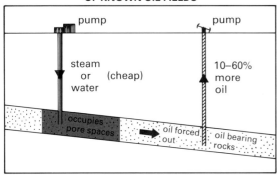

pump

pump

steam
or   (cheap)
water

10–60%
more
oil

occupies
pore spaces

oil forced
out

oil bearing
rocks

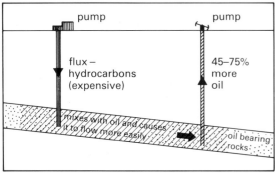

pump

pump

flux –
hydrocarbons
(expensive)

45–75%
more
oil

mixes with oil and causes
it to flow more easily

oil bearing
rocks

Fig. 5.19

ENVIRONMENTAL PROBLEMS CAUSED BY THE EXPLOITATION OF OIL SHALES

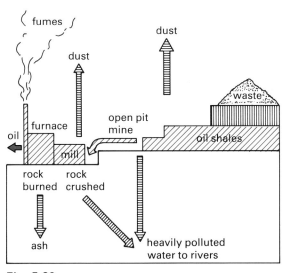

Fig. 5.20

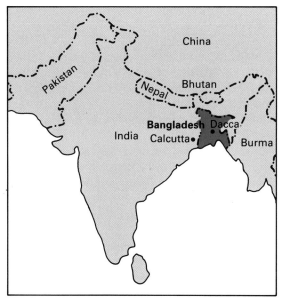

Fig. 5.21

during the crushing and burning of the rock, river pollution caused by the return of mud-laden water to the streams, landscape pollution caused by the dumping of waste and noise pollution caused by mining operations on a very large scale (Fig. 5.20). Many of these problems are made worse by the fact that most of the oil shale and tar sand deposits are found in the far west of North America. Here rainfall is generally low and little water is available either for mining and extraction operations or for the reclamation of the land after mining. It is hardly surprising, therefore, that the exploitation of these vast reserves of oil has taken place only on a very small scale.

In spite of the price rises the decline in the amount of oil used in the United States has been slight. Furthermore, overall consumption of energy has continued to rise, although the *rate* of increase has slowed down considerably. This has been the situation in many of the developed industrialised countries. Most of the decline in oil consumption has been the result of the recession which began in the 1970s. In spite of this recession the countries of the Developed World have remained rich enough to continue buying oil and the effects of the oil price rises, although serious, have not been devastating.

2 The Developing World

In the developing countries the situation is very different. Here oil consumption was often small and it might be expected that any reduction in supply caused by higher prices would have little effect. In fact, the effects were often very serious.

The situation in Bangladesh (Fig. 5.21) is typical. Bangladesh is a newly independent country (until 1971 it formed part of Pakistan) situated at the head of the Bay of Bengal. It covers an area of 140 000 square kilometres and, with a population which now exceeds 100 million, it is one of the most densely populated countries in the world. It is also one of the poorest and is almost totally dependent upon agriculture, particularly rice production on the vast deltas of the Ganges and Brahmaputra rivers. Industry and commerce are generally poorly developed.

In 1971, immediately before the oil price rises, per capita energy consumption in Bangladesh was among the lowest in the world. Little oil was imported and the overall pattern of energy use (Fig. 5.22) suggested that Bangladesh might escape the worst effects of the price increases.

Using the information given in Fig. 5.22, complete the following exercise.

a i List the main sources of energy used in Bangladesh.
  ii For each source of energy state whether it is likely to be imported or produced within the country.
b What is likely to be the main form of energy used by people at home?
c What are the main types of energy likely to be used by each of the following: agriculture, industry, transport?

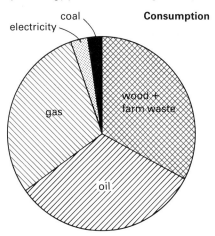

BANGLADESH: ENERGY PRODUCTION AND CONSUMPTION

(per capita energy production – 20 kg coal equivalent)

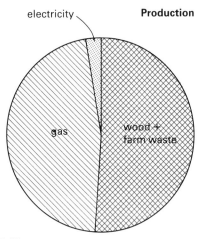

Fig. 5.22

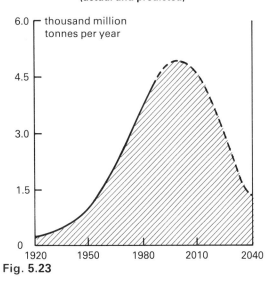

WORLD OIL PRODUCTION 1920–2040
(actual and predicted)

Fig. 5.23

In fact the effects of the oil price rises were very serious. Most of the energy consumed in Bangladesh is used in the home and most of this energy is obtained from firewood or from the waste products of farms. When oil was cheap it was increasingly used to replace these fuels for domestic heating and cooking. This meant that the waste products of the farms, including the stubble left after harvesting and the dung of animals, could be used to maintain the fertility of the soil; and the rate at which the forests were being cleared could be slowed down. This helped to prevent soil erosion and serious long term damage to the environment. The price rises of the early 1970s put an end to such developments. Pressure on the traditional renewable sources of energy increased once again and with it the destruction of farmland and forest.

Equally important has been the effect on agriculture and industry. The latter depends heavily upon electricity, much of which is generated at oil fired power stations. Therefore one of the results of the oil price rises has been to slow down the rate of industrial development. Agriculture, on the other hand, still depends upon manual labour and animals but, as we have seen (page 105), the introduction of simple electric pumps can improve the efficiency of irrigation systems and increase crop yields enormously. This development was just beginning in Bangladesh when the rising costs of oil forced the government to limit imports. For a country with a population increasing by more than one million each year the consequences are serious.

The future of oil

Since the 1970s there have been growing fears about the future of oil supplies. Price rises have helped to push the world economy into recession and this has, in turn, reduced the demand for oil. Nevertheless, it is still generally felt that:

1   Oil production has for the first time begun to exceed the discovery of new reserves.

2   Unless methods are found of obtaining more oil from existing fields, and extracting oil from tar sand and oil shale deposits, there may be a shortage of oil before the end of the century.

3   World oil production is likely to reach its peak within the next 20 years (Fig. 5.23).

4   World oil reserves are likely to be completely exhausted before the end of the next century (Fig. 5.24).

This is the basis of the energy crisis, the first effects of which are already being felt throughout the world. For the oil producing countries price rises have been used as an insurance against the time when the oil runs out. Among consumers the effects have been dramatic. In the developed countries, which were forced to spend more on buying oil, economic growth slowed down. In many parts of the Developing World development came to a virtual halt as countries struggled to find the money to buy oil. Here the answer has been to reduce the amount of oil used.

The result has been that for the first time during the present century the use of oil in the world declined. Since production was

KNOWN OIL RESERVES (changes 1964–82)

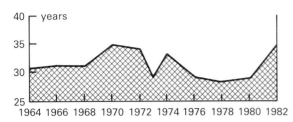

Fig. 5.24

maintained at a high level a surplus developed and prices began to fall. This in turn has affected the oil producing countries. Many of them had started major development projects using money earned from the sale of oil. In addition some countries borrowed heavily, expecting to repay the loans from future oil revenues. When this income proved to be much lower than expected, countries like Mexico, Venezuela and Nigeria were left heavily in debt. (See page 9.)

In the short term, there are serious doubts about supplies of oil. For example, most of the reserves are to be found in politically unstable areas and any conflict in the Middle East is likely to threaten oil supplies and to cause immediate price rises. In the long term, oil will be in short supply. It will also become expensive and this prospect is already causing countries throughout the world to look for alternative sources of energy. In particular they are trying to develop secondary sources of power such as electricity.

Electricity

Coal, oil, gas and timber are primary sources of energy, i.e. they can be used directly to provide power for the home and for industry, commerce and transport. Electricity, on the other hand, is a secondary source of energy and is derived from these primary sources (Fig. 5.25). The conversion, by means of turbines and generators, is expensive and inefficient but the end product – electricity – is the most acceptable form of energy available in the world today. It is cleaner, easier to use and more flexible than any of the primary sources of energy. For this reason, the generation of electricity has increased rapidly not only in the industrialised countries but also in the Developing World (where its introduction can transform both agriculture and industry).

In spite of this, most of the world's supply of electricity (Fig. 5.26) is produced and consumed by the highly developed industrialised countries. In fact consumption of electricity appears to be a more accurate measure of economic development than consumption of energy as a whole. The reasons for this can be traced back to the nature of electricity and the methods by which it is produced. The Table (page 130) gives some of the advantages and disadvantages of electricity as an energy supply. From this it is possible to gain some impression of the problems likely to be faced by less developed countries.

There is obviously a balance between the advantages and disadvantages given in the table. This varies according to the method used to generate the power.

STAGES IN THE GENERATION OF ELECTRICITY

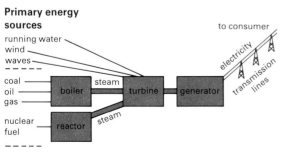

Fig. 5.25

WORLD ELECTRICITY SUPPLY (by type)

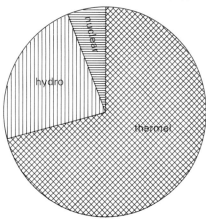

Fig. 5.26

Electricity	
Advantages	Disadvantages
1 The easiest form of energy to use.	a Difficult to produce, requiring complex equipment in large power stations. b Expensive to produce – the costs of modern power stations place a great strain on the resources of most developing countries. c The building of a power station requires advanced technology which has to be imported by developing countries.
2 Efficient to use once a supply has been established.	a Inefficient to produce – energy loss is high, particularly if steam is produced to drive the turbines
3 Versatile – electricity can be used to provide heating and lighting and to drive machines both in the home and in industry.	
4 Flexible – electricity can be transported easily to different locations along power lines.	a A widespread grid of power lines is difficult and expensive to build. b The system is expensive to run since energy loss from the cable system is high. This has important effects on the location of the power supply industry.
5 Clean – there is virtually no pollution during use.	a Pollution can be serious during production, e.g. waste gases and ash from thermal power stations; radio-active waste from nuclear stations. b The effect on the environment can be severe, e.g. large power stations are difficult to disguise; the lakes associated with hydro-electric schemes can change the landscape completely.

Thermal power stations

Nearly 80% of the world's electricity is generated in thermal power stations, i.e. power stations in which a heat source is used to convert water into steam which can then be harnessed to drive the turbines. Furthermore, of this thermal electricity no less than 90% is generated in conventional power stations, i.e. power stations in which the heat source is coal, oil or natural gas.

Fig. 5.27 *West Burton Power Station, UK. (Source: CEGB)*

Energy

131

Of the conventional fuels coal is by far the most important. During the 1950s and 1960s, however, there was a general move towards oil and gas which were more efficient and easier to transport. This trend has continued in countries without supplies of coal of their own although, as we have seen, rising oil prices have slowed down such developments and forced all countries to look for alternative sources of energy. The effects of this have been most marked in the less developed countries where small oil powered generators are widely used to meet local needs.

In most parts of the world, however, the generation of electricity takes place on a massive scale and it is important to locate power stations where the costs of supplying the markets can be kept as low as possible, i.e. the location should be a least cost location.

A TYPICAL THERMAL POWER STATION IN THE USA
(showing average energy losses)

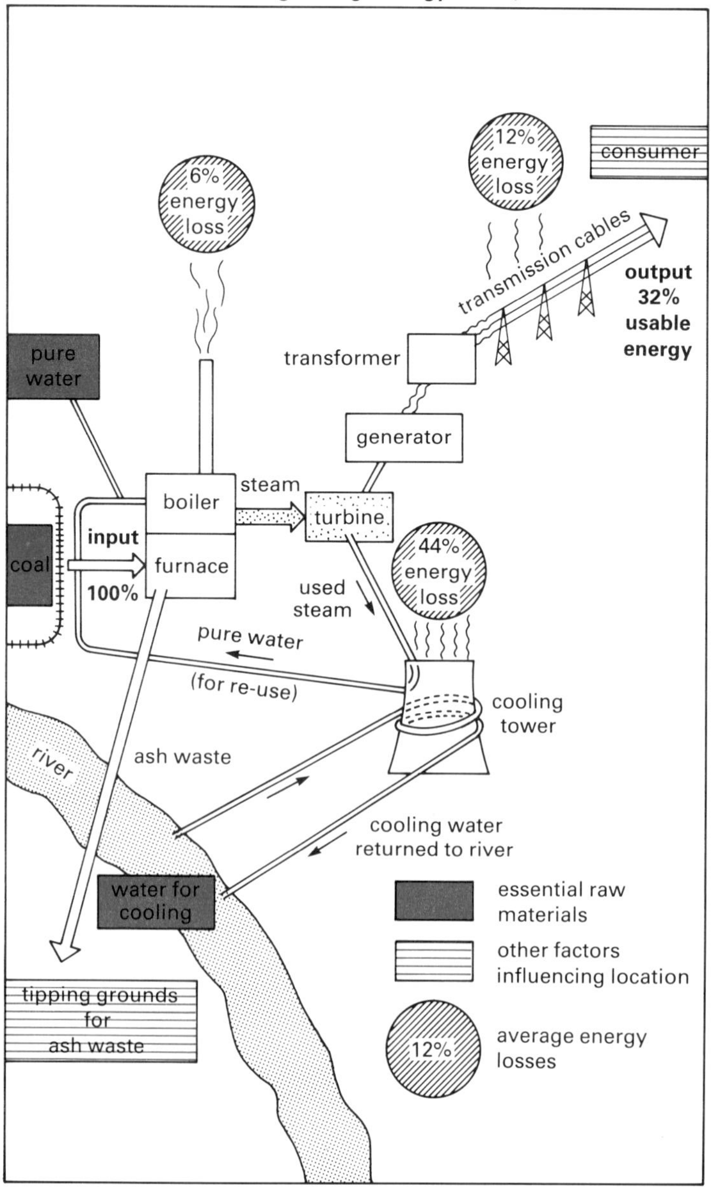

Fig. 5.28

LOCATING A THERMAL POWER STATION

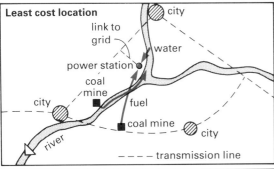

Least cost location

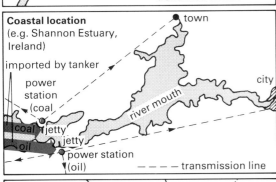

Coastal location
(e.g. Shannon Estuary, Ireland)

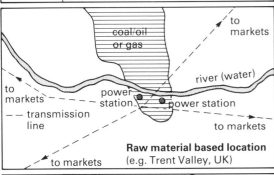

Raw material based location
(e.g. Trent Valley, UK)

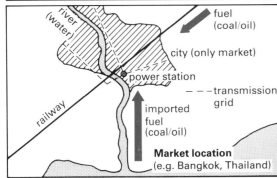

Market location
(e.g. Bangkok, Thailand)

Fig. 5.29

Using information given in this section, complete the following exercise.

a i Is electricity an 'efficient' form of energy?
  ii Is a thermal power station an efficient or an inefficient generator of electricity?
  iii Describe where the main energy losses are likely to occur in supplying electricity from a thermal power station.
b i List the main 'raw materials' used in a thermal power station.
  ii List any other factors which may influence the location of thermal power stations.
  iii Which of the raw materials are expensive to transport?
  iv How is this likely to influence the location of power stations?
c Study the maps in Fig. 5.29 which show typical power station locations in the world. Describe each location.
d Why are oil and gas fired power stations more flexible in their location?

It is obvious that the choice of site for a thermal power station is extremely difficult.

1   The power station is large. Large areas of flat land are required for buildings and, in the case of coal fired stations, for vast stock piles of fuel (Fig. 5.28).

2   Power stations use a large amount of fuel and this is bulky and often expensive to transport. As a result it is sensible to locate power stations near to supplies of fuel, i.e. near coal, oil or gas fields, or on the coast near to the ports which import these fuels.

3   At the same time energy loss from transmission cables is high. It is better, therefore, to locate power stations near to markets so that power lines are as short as possible. Unfortunately not all major markets are near to sources of fuel.

4   An added complication is the fact that most thermal power stations use vast quantities of cooling water to convert the steam back to usable water. This means that the ideal location will be on a river or lake or near the sea (see Fig. 5.29). Once again this may be in conflict with the locations favoured for other reasons. In arid areas where water is not available air cooling is used, but this is less efficient and the cooling towers have to be very large.

Nuclear power stations

Nuclear power stations also produce steam to drive the turbines and they are therefore thermal power stations. At the same time they have features which place them apart from other thermal power stations. For example, the generation of nuclear power is very complicated and the power station is only a small part of the process (see Fig. 5.30). Even more important, there is a great concern about the environmental consequences of building

STAGES IN THE PRODUCTION OF NUCLEAR ENERGY

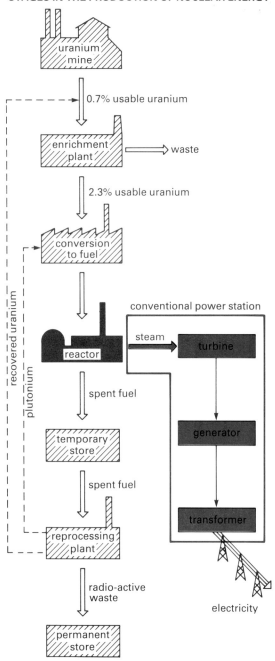

Fig. 5.30

nuclear power stations. The debate about possible dangers in both the production of energy and in the disposal of radio-active waste has strongly influenced the growth of the industry and the location of power stations.

When the first commercial nuclear power station was built at Calder Hall in North West England in the 1950s, it seemed to offer the prospect of unlimited cheap electricity. It was also realised, however, that such power stations would be difficult and expensive to build. While other forms of energy were cheap, nuclear power remained unattractive. Fears about future oil supplies changed the situation and the large scale development of nuclear energy was planned throughout the industrialised world. Following the oil price rises of the 1970s the number of power stations increased rapidly and by 1982 7% of the world's energy came from nuclear sources. This rapid growth led to increasing concern about the dangers of nuclear energy. These include:

1   The difficulties of disposing of the radio-active waste produced in the reactors. At first storage areas were built near to the processing plants but, as the amount of waste increased, more material was stored underground in old mines or dumped into the sea. Objections to these methods of disposal have increased and the problem of radio-active waste – some of which will remain dangerous for several thousand years – has yet to be solved.

2   The fact that the plutonium produced in the reactors can be used to make nuclear weapons.

3   The fear that accidents in a nuclear power station could occur, possibly releasing radio-active gases over the surrounding area. This fear increased greatly following an incident in 1981 at Three Mile Island in the state of Ohio, USA (which resulted not only in that power station being shut down but in demands for the atomic energy programme in the United States to be halted), and more recently, the disaster at Chernobyl near Kiev in the USSR.

Such fears have influenced the location of nuclear power stations in almost every country in the world. Because such power stations use very little fuel it was hoped that they could be located in areas where demand for electricity was greatest – provided, of course, that there was a plentiful supply of water for cooling. This would have enabled transmission lines to be short and energy losses to be kept to a minimum. In fact there were many objections to the siting of nuclear power stations near to centres of population and this often led to the choice of locations far from the nearest markets. Such a policy has increased the cost of nuclear energy and has made it difficult for the industry to compete in countries which have supplies of coal or oil. Further technological advances, particularly in the development of fast breeder reactors which can produce fuel in the process of generating power, will probably reduce the running costs of nuclear power stations. As long as the problems associated with nuclear energy remain unsolved, however, it is likely that conventional power stations will continue to dominate the electricity supply industry. It is also likely that the search for alternative sources of energy will continue.

Fig. 5.31 *Wylfa Nuclear Power Station, Anglesey, United Kingdom*

Hydro-electric power stations

At present the only widely developed alternative to thermal electricity is hydro-electricity or water power. Direct water power is the use of running water to turn a water wheel. This can be used to drive machines. In the late nineteenth century, however, it became possible to harness the power of running water to generate electricity. This was a major breakthrough and within the next 50 years hydro-electricity became a major source of energy in many countries (Fig. 5.32). Hydro-electricity was, and still is, the most attractive energy source available in the world today.

Hydro-electricity is generated when moving water is allowed to strike the blades of a turbine. This causes the turbine to spin so that it can be used to drive a generator (Fig. 5.33). The attractions of such a simple system are obvious.

1   It depends upon a widely available energy source – running water.

2   Unlike thermal electricity, it is not dependent upon fossil or mineral fuels which will one day be exhausted. In fact hydro-electricity appears to be a renewable energy source since it can be generated as long as running water is available.

3   It is efficient because the turbines are driven directly. As a result energy losses are very low (less than 20%) compared with thermal power stations which depend upon steam driven turbines (the energy losses from which often exceed 60%).

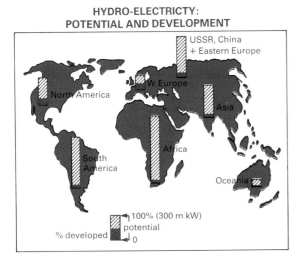

HYDRO-ELECTRICTY: POTENTIAL AND DEVELOPMENT

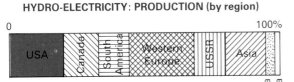

HYDRO-ELECTRICITY: PRODUCTION (by region)

Fig. 5.32

4   It is clean. There is no atmospheric pollution or waste products and the water is returned to the river in an unchanged state.

These are enormous advantages and yet hydro-electricity supplies only a small proportion of the energy used in the world today. There are many reasons for this.

Although all running water contains usable energy, the amount of energy available depends upon the velocity of the water when it hits the blades of the turbine, i.e. the faster the water is flowing the greater the output of energy. The first hydro-electric stations were built at large waterfalls such as Niagara. Unfortunately few sites offer the natural advantages of Niagara and in most cases it has been necessary to improve the sites to allow power to be produced more efficiently. This usually involves the building of dams to increase the head of water and to control flow through the turbines. Two main types of dam are built, depending upon their location on the river.

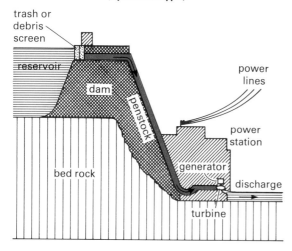

A SIMPLIFIED HYDRO-ELECTRIC SCHEME
(upstream type)

trash or debris screen

reservoir

dam

penstock

power lines

power station

generator

discharge

bed rock

turbine

Hydro-electric power stations: the ideal natural site

1   Great difference in height, giving a large 'head' of water.

2   Regular flow with little seasonal variation. This is produced by a combination of the following:

a   heavy rainfall

b   snowfield 'reservoirs'

c   a large catchment, i.e. water gathered from a large area

d   a large lake above the falls.

3   A site for the turbines below the falls so as to give the largest 'head' of water.

4   Markets nearby so as to reduce transmission costs.

Fig. 5.33

	Location A: upstream	Location B: downstream
Size of catchment	Usually small	Usually large
Volume of water in river	Usually low	Usually high
Regularity of flow	Often irregular and seasonal	Usually more regular
'Head' of water available	Often large	Usually small
Type of dam	Usually high storage dam	Usually low dam or 'barrage'
Purpose of dam	a To create a large reservoir which will allow flow to be controlled b To give maximum head of water	To raise the level of the river so that: a flow can be regulated b the velocity of the water hitting the turbines is increased
Purpose of the power station	Water release to meet peak demands	Continuous running so as to provide 'base load' electricity
Consumers	Often distant and costs of transmission can be high	Often near – transmission costs can be low

Dam and reservoir in the Rhône Valley, France

Whichever type of scheme is planned, however, there are usually serious problems to be overcome. It is these problems which have limited the development of hydro-electricity in the world.

1　There are few sites suitable for the building of large dams. This is because several different characteristics are needed:

a　The bed rock must be strong enough to support the weight of the dam and to allow it to be firmly anchored.

b　Ideally the valley ought to narrow so that the size of the dam can be reduced. This will make it cheaper and easier to build.

c　Above the dam the valley should widen so as to increase the size of the reservoir.

d　Beneath the reservoir the bed rock must be stable enough to support the weight of the water.

e　The rock also has to be impermeable so as to reduce water loss.

2　The costs of building any hydro-electric scheme are high and this to some extent offsets the very low running costs. This is a particularly serious problem for developing countries which would benefit most from the development of hydro-electricity.

3　The effect on the environment can be dramatic:

a　Valleys have to be flooded and this often involves the loss of fertile farmland. This is important, particularly in densely populated developing countries where it has limited the development of downstream sites.

b　The building of large dams has an effect on the wildlife, e.g. it may stop the migration of fish such as salmon.

c　Less obviously, the development of remote sites involves the building of access roads to be used by the contractors during construction. When work has finished these roads allow the development of the surrounding areas, often with disastrous consequences. In some developing countries it has resulted in the wholesale clearance of forest which in turn has led to a dramatic increase in soil erosion.

d　This can have an important effect on the hydro-electric scheme itself. All rivers carry sediment. A large proportion of this sediment will be deposited behind the dam, eventually causing the lake to fill with silt. This means that any hydro-electric scheme has a limited life. In a 'clean' river, i.e. a river carrying little sediment, this life may be more than 500 years; in a 'dirty' river it can be as little as 50 years. Any increase in soil erosion will increase the amount of sediment in the rivers and this will reduce the life of an expensive hydro-electric scheme.

One of the major problems faced by the electricity supply industry is that demand for power varies enormously not only between seasons, but also within the space of a single day. Demand is highest during the day and lowest during the night. In the developed countries where more electricity is used by domestic consumers the pattern is more complicated. There are peaks at breakfast time and in the early evening when the family has returned from work or school. To meet these peaks it is necessary to have spare capacity, i.e. power stations which are used only during periods of high demand and which stand idle for the rest of the time. Hydro-electric plants are ideal in this situation since water can be released when power is needed. Not only this, it is now possible to control the amount of water in the reservoir so that maximum output is available whenever it is needed. This is done by building pumped storage schemes:

1   A small reservoir is built below the dam.

2   Turbines are used which can be reversed to pump water back into the main lake from this lower reservoir.

3   Power from other sources is used to pump the water. This usually takes place during the night when demand for electricity is low and when there is surplus power available.

4   The water is then released during the day to produce maximum power when demand is greatest.

The use of pumped storage increases the efficiency of the hydro-electric plants but it also increases the cost. It is the balance between the obvious advantages of hydro-electricity and the great cost of building the plant which determines the rate of development. This is particularly true in developing countries where most of the remaining undeveloped sites are to be found. One such site is at Itaipu on the Parana River between Brazil and Paraguay.

Fig. 5.34 (a)

The Itaipu hydro-electric scheme

Planning for the Itaipu scheme began in 1966 when an agreement was drawn up between the governments of Brazil and Paraguay. The idea was to exploit the hydro-electric potential of the Parana River which forms part of the border between the two states (Fig. 5.34). The costs of the project and the power produced were to be shared between the two countries. The site at Itaipu (Fig. 5.35) was chosen and work started in 1974. It continued for the next nine years.

A channel was dug so that the Parana River – 400 metres wide and up to 40 metres deep at this point – could be diverted away from the site of the main dam. Two coffer dams, each of them 70 metres high, were built to protect the site from flooding and to allow the dam to be built with a vast power station in its base. The main dam itself was built of concrete and was to be one and a half kilometres in length and up to 180 metres in height. Other large earth and rock dams were built along the shores of the future reservoir to prevent water loss. The entire project cost six billion dollars.

Using information given in this section, complete the following exercise.

a   The site at Itaipu possesses many advantages. Several of them are included in the following list. Copy out the most important.

i   The Parana River drains a *large/small* area and this helps by giving *an irregular/a regular* pattern of flow.

ii   The underlying rock is _____ and this is a *hard/soft* rock which provides a *good/poor* base for the dams.

iii   The underlying rock is *impermeable/permeable* and this *increases/reduces* water loss.

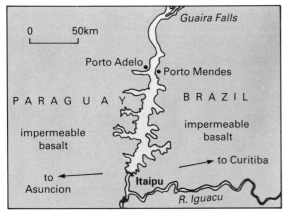

Location: Itaipu, on the Brazil/Paraguay border
Reservoir area: 1460 km²
Flow to each turbine: 625 m³ per second
Number of turbines: 18
Power output: 12600 MW

Fig. 5.34 (b)

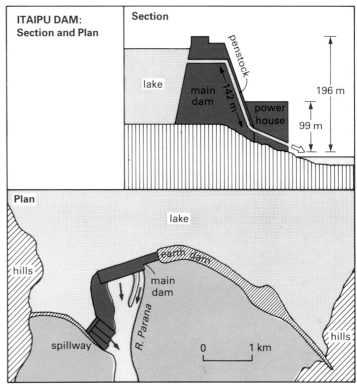

Fig. 5.35

CLIMATIC DATA FOR GOIANIA
(in the Parana catchment above Itaipu)

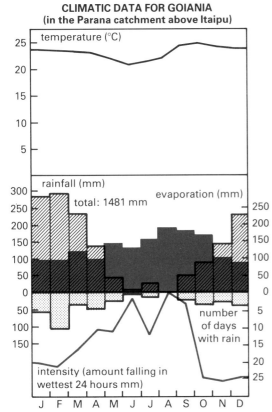

Fig. 5.34 (c)

Fig. 5.36 *Itaipu dam*

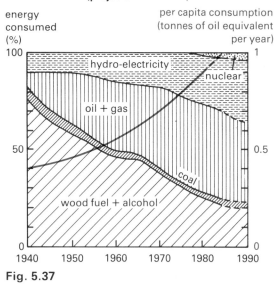

BRAZIL: PATTERN OF ENERGY USE
(projected until 1990)

Fig. 5.37

iv Temperatures are *high/low* and water losses from evaporation are *low/high*.

v Rainfall is *seasonal/regular* and this gives *an irregular/a regular* pattern of flow.

vi The river is *wide/narrow* and this reduces building costs.

b i What is the 'head' of water now that the dam has been built?

ii Why is it better to have a large head of water?

iii How have the engineers positioned the turbines (in the power house) so as to give the largest head of water?

c What is the major problem relating to the site at Itaipu? (Looking at the location of the major cities in Brazil and Paraguay will help.)

d Write an account of the advantages and disadvantages of Itaipu as a site for the development of a hydro-electric power station.

When work began on the Itaipu power station its planned output represented one fifth of the electricity consumed in Brazil at that time. But Itaipu was only one of many projects which were designed to double the production of electricity within the space of ten years – a decision taken to meet a rapidly growing demand for power and to reduce Brazil's dependence upon imported oil and gas.

In many ways the pattern of energy use in Brazil (Fig. 5.37) is typical of that seen throughout the Developing World. For 300 years after its colonisation by the Portuguese, timber was the most important source of energy. Since large areas of the country were forested, this presented few problems. During the twentieth century, however, alternative energy sources were developed, particularly water power, coal and oil. Consumption of oil increased rapidly – in 1940 it represented no more than 10% of the total energy used; by 1970 this figure was approaching 50%. Four fifths of the oil used was imported. As a result, Brazil was seriously affected by the price rises of the 1970s. It was at this time that plans were made to develop alternative sources of energy. In this respect Brazil was more fortunate than most other developing countries.

Although Brazil possesses reserves of coal and oil it seemed unlikely that production could be increased dramatically. The coal, found in the far south near Rio Grande, was of very poor quality and was difficult to use. The known oilfields, situated on the Atlantic seaboard near Santos and Rio de Janeiro, are small and have a limited output. This meant that other alternatives had to be explored. These included:

BRAZIL: LOCATION OF POWER PLANTS

Hydro
△ planned
▲ built

Nuclear
□ planned
■ built

0   500 km

Fig. 5.38

ALTERNATIVE ENERGY SOURCES

1 Geothermal electricity

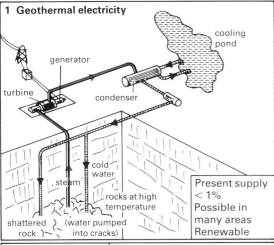

Present supply
< 1%
Possible in
many areas
Renewable

2 Solar energy

Present supply
< 1%

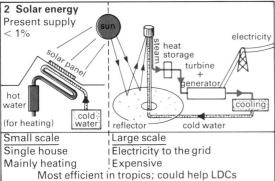

Small scale	Large scale
Single house	Electricity to the grid
Mainly heating	Expensive
Most efficient in tropics; could help LDCs	

3 Biomass

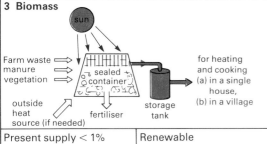

Present supply < 1%	Renewable
Valuable in LDCs when used on a small scale	Large scale development in DCs using rubbish

4 Wind power	5 Wave power
Present supply < 1%	Present supply 0%
Possible in many places	Possible in many areas
Most widely used to power small industries, e.g. a farm	Technology not yet available
Renewable	Renewable

Fig. 5.39

1 The planned use of forests for domestic fuel. Since large areas of the eastern forests have already been cleared for agriculture, this means the exploitation of the Amazon rain forests. As we have already seen (page 100), this is far from easy.

2 The use of vegetation to produce alcohol which can then be mixed with petroleum. Sugar cane is the most efficient source of alcohol and large areas have already been planted for this purpose.

3 Most important of all, a massive expansion of hydro-electricity was planned. Brazil contains two of the largest river systems in the world – the Amazon and the Parana – and there are many sites where hydro-electricity can be generated on a large scale. Few of these sites have been developed and at present production is running at less than 20% of the maximum possible. There are plans for a doubling of output. As we have seen at Itaipu, however, there are many problems to be faced. The most serious of these is that remaining sites are far from the main markets for electricity. The rivers near the Atlantic coasts are already used to supply power to the great cities such as Sao Paulo and Rio de Janeiro. As a result, interest has now shifted to sites on the Parana River (Fig. 5.38). These sites are several hundred kilometres away from the main cities and transmission is both difficult and expensive. When these sites have been developed – and this is planned to take place before the end of the century – only the Amazon will remain. Here the potential is enormous, but few sites are less than 2000 kilometres away from the nearest urban areas. New methods of transmission will have to be developed if power lines of this length are to be used. Until this happens, sites in the Amazon basin will be exploited only when industries can be located near to them, e.g. the aluminium industry which uses vast amounts of power.

4 To meet the rapidly growing demand for power in the large cities, a number of nuclear power stations have been planned. These will be located near to the cities and the first, at Dos Reis near Rio de Janeiro, has already been built. This development has been accompanied by the discovery of large reserves of uranium which will supply the needs of Brazil's nuclear power stations.

Few developing countries have such large power resources available. For Brazil the major limits on development are lack of money and inadequate technology. Lack of money is now a serious problem since Brazil is heavily in debt and is unable to raise loans for further development projects. In fact the recent world recession has made it impossible for Brazil to repay the interest on existing debts. In these circumstances it is unlikely that the country's energy resources will be developed in the foreseeable future. This is the situation in many other developing countries.

In the Developed World, on the other hand, the search continues for alternative sources of energy. These include wind and wave power, solar and geothermal power, and energy from the waste products of the countryside and city. See Fig. 5.39.

6 Industry

INDUSTRIAL EMPLOYMENT AND STAGE OF DEVELOPMENT

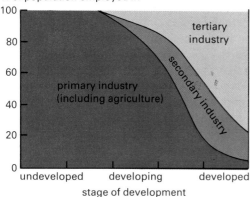

% of population employed in

Primary Industries – those concerned with the winning of goods and materials from nature, e.g. agriculture, mining, forestry.

Secondary Industries – those concerned with changing those materials, i.e. all *manufacturing industries.*

Tertiary Industries – those which neither produce nor process goods or materials, e.g. transport, banking, insurance, i.e. *service industries.*

Fig. 6.1

Most of the world's industries are located in the developed countries. In fact, the nature and extent of industrialisation is often used as a measure of development as a means of distinguishing between the Developed and Developing Worlds (see Fig. 6.1).

Using the information given in Fig. 6.1 and the associated table, complete the following exercise.

a   i   Describe the pattern of industry found in undeveloped countries.
    ii   Which type of industry is likely to dominate these economies?
b   How do the economies of the developing countries differ from this pattern?
c   Describe the pattern of industrial development found in the developed countries.
d   Using the statistics in the table:
    i   Draw a graph showing GNP on the vertical axis and percentage of the GNP obtained from agriculture on the horizontal axis.
    ii   Describe the relationship which exists.
    iii   Draw a second graph showing GNP and the proportion of the GNP obtained from tertiary industries.
    iv   Describe the relationship and compare it with that shown on the previous graph.
e   For each country on the list, state whether it is likely to be undeveloped, developing or developed.

Such an exercise suggests that, as countries develop, manufacturing industry (secondary industry) tends to replace farming as the main source of employment. In addition, the highly developed countries can be identified by the large proportion of the labour force employed in service (tertiary) industries.

| Country | % of GNP obtained from | | | |
	agriculture	mining + manufacturing	tertiary industry	GNP
Gambia	56	3	41	370
Nigeria	23	37	40	870
Brazil	10	28	62	2220
Mexico	8	37	55	2250
USA	2.7	30.3	67	12820
China	8	45	47	300
India	32	23	45	260
Bangladesh	48	14	38	140
Japan	3.5	52.5	44	10080
Spain	7	27	66	5640
United Kingdom	2	31	67	9110
USSR	16	52	32	4750

Primary industry

Primary industries are those which are concerned with the winning of goods and materials from nature. The most important primary industries are farming, fishing, mining and forestry.

As we have seen, in many less developed countries dependence on agriculture is almost complete. In Mali, for example, the proportion of the working population employed in farming is 83% and industrialisation is obviously at a very low level. Furthermore, the industries which have been established tend to be other primary industries – in particular, forestry and mining.

WORLD FOREST RESERVES (MILLION HECTARES)

	Coniferous	Non-coniferous	Total
Developed Countries	1109	563	1672
Less developed countries	115	1925	2040
World	1224	2488	3712

TIMBER PRODUCTION (MILLION CUBIC METRES)

	1961	1982		
Type of timber	World total	DCs	LDCs	Total
Fuel wood	1030	250	1350	1600
Industrial timber	1019	1050	308	1358
Sawn wood	–	590	192	782
Pulp wood	–	328	40	368
Total	2049	2218	1890	4108

MAJOR FOREST REGIONS OF THE WORLD

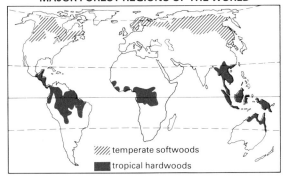

temperate softwoods

tropical hardwoods

DEFINITIONS

1 Coniferous trees – trees which bear their seeds in or on cones. Usually evergreen and softwoods.
2 Deciduous trees – trees which shed their leaves during one season of the year. Usually hardwoods.
3 Hardwoods and softwoods. Refers to the structure of the timber, not its hardness. Hardwoods have rings of large cells separated by rings of small cells. Sap passes through these 'pores' from the roots to the branches. Softwoods have a simpler, more uniform structure.

Fig. 6.2

Forest industries

At the present time the world's forests are disappearing at the rate of many thousands of hectares a year. To a large extent this is simply a reflection of the rapid increase in population which has taken place during this period. In the developing countries, for example, where population growth has been most rapid, the pressure on land has been enormous. Here large areas of forest have been cleared for agriculture (see page 99) and the cutting of trees for firewood has increased to such an extent that the existence of large areas of forest is now threatened. At the same time demand for industrial timber has also increased rapidly and this has placed an additional strain on the world's forest reserves. It is the commercial felling of timber which will be examined in this section.

The differences between the developed and the developing countries are very large. Some of these differences can be attributed to the differing levels of technology available. Equally important, however, are the physical and environmental conditions which have contributed greatly to the growth of what are, in fact, two totally different industries.

In terms of volume, it is the production of softwoods which is most important. These are obtained from coniferous forests, most of which are located in the temperate latitudes of the northern hemisphere (Fig. 6.2), i.e. in the Developed World. In the coniferous forests the number of different species is small and most are worth cutting. As a result an industry has grown up which is based on wholesale clearance followed by replanting.

The remainder of the industry depends upon hardwoods. Some of these are still cut in the remaining deciduous forests of the temperate latitudes. The area available is now very small, however, largely because of clearance for agriculture. As a result it is the hardwood forests of the tropics which now meet most of the world's demand. These are found mainly in less developed countries. In these forests the number of species is enormous and not all of them are worth cutting. In addition, there are serious problems of transport and often a lack of capital to establish pulping mills which can use poor quality timber. It is not surprising, therefore, that in many areas a very different industry has grown up, based on the selective felling of the most valuable trees.

Softwood industries: Irkutsk Oblast (USSR)

Irkutsk Oblast (Fig. 6.3) is an administrative district of the Soviet Union. It is situated on the northern shores of Lake Baikal in Southern Siberia. The south eastern part of the district covers an area of 750 000 square kilometres. Within this area, the timber industry is in the hands of the Irkutsk Forest Industry Administration, a government controlled agency which oversees the work of 14 logging corporations. In 1980 this single agency produced no less than 8% of the timber cut in the Soviet Union.

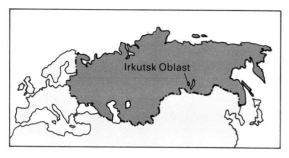

Location: Belaya Valley, Irkutsk Oblast, USSR
Climate: Cool temperate, continental
January temperature −6°C
July temperature 18°C
Rainfall 375 mm
Vegetation: Coniferous forest (Taiga)
(pine and larch)
Products: Commercial softwoods

Fig. 6.3

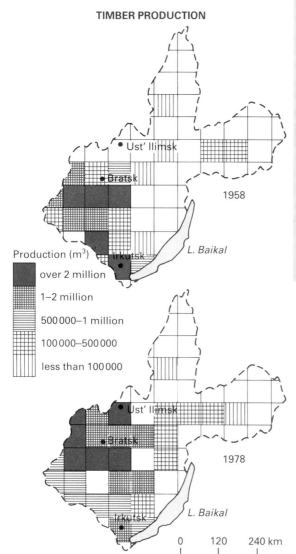

Fig. 6.4

The region is situated near the southern margin of the great coniferous forest zone (or taiga) which covers large areas of northern Europe and Asia. It is a forest dominated by two species – pine and larch, both of which provide good commercial softwood. Large scale forestry became possible when the Trans-Siberian Railway reached the region (see Fig. 6.10), giving access to markets in European Russia. By 1938 output exceeded three million cubic metres of sawn wood. Since that time production has increased rapidly and today 35 million cubic metres of timber are cut each year. This growth has been achieved by opening up new areas of forest and by increasing production in the areas already worked (Fig. 6.4). In both cases development depends upon gaining and improving access to the forests.

Study the two maps in Fig. 6.4 showing timber production in 1958 and 1978.

a i In which area was the timber industry located in 1958?
 ii Two major forms of transport were available to the industry at that time. Name them.
 iii What was the main link with the markets in European Russia to the west?
b Compare this pattern with that shown on the map of production in 1978.
 i In which squares has production declined?
 ii Why are these areas likely to have been among the earliest to be developed?
 iii In which squares has production increased?
 iv Two major production centres have been built at Bratsk and Ust'-Ilimsk. What are the advantages of these locations?
c Study the information given in Figs 6.6 and 6.7.
 i During which season of the year is production of timber greatest?
 ii This pattern of production is strongly influenced by problems of transport. What are these problems likely to be? (Study the climatic statistics.)

A similar pattern of development is to be seen in all the main logging areas. The Belaya Corporation, for example, works an area of 4000 square kilometres in the Belaya Valley (Fig. 6.5) to the north west of Irkutsk. It is one of the oldest areas of production and output is now declining. The development of the industry has been typical:

1 The building of the Trans-Siberian Railway gave access to the forests of the Belaya Valley.

2 Felling started on the lowlands near the Belaya River (one of the headwater streams of the Lena River) and the logs were floated downstream to sawmills near the railway.

3 These accessible areas were cleared and some of the lowland was brought under cultivation.

FELLING OPERATION: BELAYA VALLEY

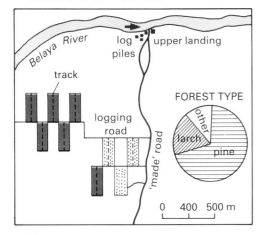

Fig. 6.5

THE BELAYA CORPORATION

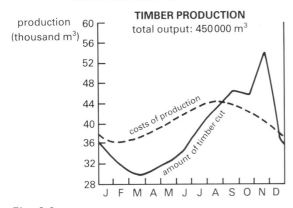

Fig. 6.6

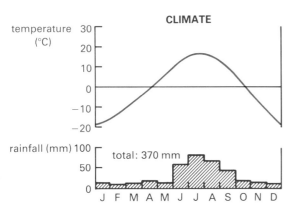

Fig. 6.7

4 Gradually less accessible areas of forest were developed. These were either along the upper reaches of the rivers or on the lower slopes of the mountains.

5 Development became possible in these areas only when roads could be built to gain access to the forest. Where possible rivers are still used to float timber down to the sawmills but logs are often hauled by road from the forests to the 'landings' on the rivers. In fact, in some of the new logging districts, water transport is no longer available and all timber is moved by lorry.

Logging is now being carried out at distances of almost 100 kilometres from the nearest sawmilling centre and the problems of transport strongly influence the way in which activities are organised. This is particularly true where the Belaya River is still the main link between cutting areas and the mills.

From a point on the river known as an upper landing an access road is driven deep into the forest. This is an all-weather road designed to carry lorries throughout the year. Felling takes place along this road and logging roads are built to give access to the planned cutting areas. These are dirt roads which become almost impassable during the spring and early summer when the deeply frozen earth thaws. During this period the logging roads are

Fig. 6.8 *Softwood forest on the shores of Lake Baikal, USSR*

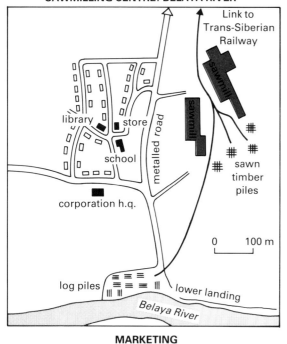

SAWMILLING CENTRE: BELAYA RIVER

MARKETING

Fig. 6.9

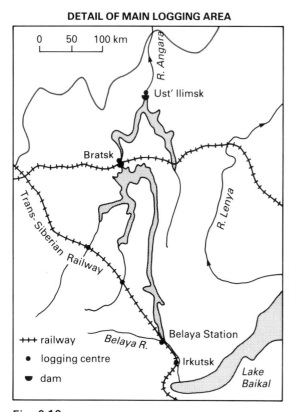

DETAIL OF MAIN LOGGING AREA

+++ railway
● logging centre
▬ dam

Fig. 6.10

reduced to mud and the transport of timber becomes difficult and expensive. For this reason most timber is felled during the winter when logs can be dragged from the forest and loaded onto trucks more easily. They are then carried to the upper landing where they are stacked until the river thaws and transport to the mills becomes possible.

At the same time, work in the felling areas is not completely seasonal. Stands of timber near to the main road are set aside for summer work and here logging is possible on a reduced scale. It has also proved possible to keep the main mills open during the winter when the rivers are ice-bound. Once again this depends upon the availability of timber served directly by all-weather roads.

Throughout the district the method of working is the same. Each of the felling areas is a large rectangle. Within this rectangle all trees are cleared. The next rectangular working area is some distance away and the forest between is left undisturbed. This reduces the risk of soil erosion and gives protection to the young trees which will be planted on the cleared land. When these young trees have grown sufficiently to protect the land the intervening forest is then cut. In this way the entire area is cleared and yet new forest is being planted for the future. (In the Belaya Valley it will be 100 years before these new trees will be large enough to cut).

The main sawmilling centre (Fig. 6.9) is located downstream at the lower landing. This location reflects the dependence of the industry on the river for transport. It is, however, a location pattern which is changing as water transport is replaced by road and railways and as local sources of energy (traditionally water power or hydro-electricity from the river) are replaced by an electricity grid system. At the mill the logs are cut into manageable lengths so that they can be shipped out as round-wood for further processing elsewhere. The main markets for this timber are the industrial areas of European Russia and the new timber processing plant at Bratsk.

The location of the processing plants is also strongly influenced by geographical factors. At Bratsk, for example, the mills depended upon:

1   The building of the rail link with the Trans-Siberian Railway. This gave access to large areas of forest.

2   The damming of the Lena River to form the upper Bratsk reservoir which provided both power and a second method of transporting logs. (Large rafts of logs can be floated on a lake of this size.) The main products of this plant are pulp, chipboard and plywood.

Hardwood lumbering in the tropics: Urubamba Valley, Eastern Peru

In the tropics the pattern of logging varies enormously. In some areas large scale lumbering operations, similar in scale to those seen in the temperate latitudes, have grown up. Often, however, the resources available for development are limited and operations remain on a comparatively small scale. This can be seen quite clearly in the valley of Urubamba River (Fig. 6.11), a tributary of the Amazon on the eastern slopes of the Andes in

LOCATION: URUBAMBA VALLEY, PERU

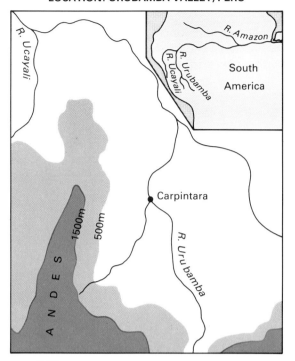

Fig. 6.11

Fig. 6.12 *A clearing in the Amazon rainforest.*

TYPICAL SECTION THROUGH THE AMAZONIAN RAINFOREST

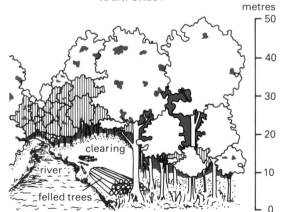

Fig. 6.13

Peru. Here, as in many developing countries in the tropics, the growth of the lumbering industry has depended upon the accessibility of the forests. Transport is very poor – railways and all-weather roads are non-existent – and the industry is completely dependent upon the rivers.

The forest is undisturbed tropical rainforest (Fig. 6.13). Trees generally grow to heights of 30 metres and the leaf canopy of the forest is at this level. Beneath the canopy there is little light and not much plant growth can take place on the forest floor.

Two features of this forest have strongly influenced the pattern of development:

1   The forest comprises more than 100 species of large trees. Not all of these are worth felling and this has encouraged selective felling rather than wholesale clearance. This is in contrast to the coniferous regions where the forest is made up of few species and where single species are often grouped to form large stands.

2   Many trees have large buttresses (the tree trunk thickens at ground level, providing support for trees which are usually shallow rooted). This makes felling more difficult and hinders the movement of logs down to the river.

The pattern of work reflects these difficulties and it is very different from that seen in the coniferous forests:

1   Logging is restricted to areas within easy reach of rivers.

2   Groups of valuable trees are located.

3   A temporary camp is established and an upper landing is cleared on the river bank nearby.

4   A narrow road is cleared through the forest towards the proposed logging area. This too is temporary and can be used only during dry weather.

5   Felling is possible only during the dry season.

6   Cutting is selective and only valuable trees (in this case mahogany and cedar) are felled.

7   Tools are comparatively simple (e.g. small power saws) and this limits the number of trees which can be felled. Because the trees are generally shallow rooted, falling trees often knock down other trees to form a small clearing.

8   Even when this happens not all logs are transported to the upper landing. There are several reasons for this:

a   Methods of transport are poor. Large logs are winched out of the forest, smaller logs are dragged by animals or men.

b   Such methods are time consuming and expensive so that only the most valuable logs are moved.

c   Some logs are so heavy that they will not float. These logs are not moved.

d   There are no pulping mills to make use of poor quality timber.

9   Branches and buttress roots are removed and the logs are stacked at the upper landing.

10   The logs are floated downstream to mills during the wet season when the river is in flood. The men follow the logs to ensure that they are not caught up in the piles of debris which clog the river.

11   The logging site is then abandoned and the forest is allowed to recover. Growth is rapid and trees large enough to cut again will have grown within 60 years. Using these methods little

damage is done to the forest and large scale replanting is not necessary.

This type of logging is widespread in the rain forests of the less developed countries. However, improvements in transport have given rise to very different methods in some areas of rain forest.

Commercial logging in the Amazon forests of Brazil

1   Aeroplanes are used to locate stands of valuable timber.

2   Roads are constructed to give access to them.

3   A camp is established.

4   Heavy machinery is moved in.

5   Wholesale clearance is practised.

6   Logs are dragged out of the forest by tractor.

7   Transport to the mills is by lorry.

8   Mills have been built to make chipboard, pulp and veneers (see Fig. 6.14).

9   Replanting is necessary. (Soils are poor and thin and the forest does not always recover. This can lead to soil erosion and the eventual destruction of the forest.)

Sometimes the land is left clear for agriculture.

Fig. 6.14 *Large scale logging in the tropics: a modern pulp mill in Brazil*

Mining industries

Energy shortages, especially dwindling reserves of oil, may impose limits on future industrial growth. Long before this happens, however, other equally serious problems may have arisen. For example, it is possible that the reserves of some minerals will be approaching exhaustion, with serious consequences for many major industries. In some cases mining will only continue if new methods are developed to extract metals from low grade ores (rocks containing very little of the metal which is being sought) and to obtain minerals from difficult environments or in forms which at present cannot be used (e.g. oil from oil sands and shales). This is a trend which has been apparent since mining began and fortunately the mining industry has so far been able to cope with the exhaustion of the richest and most accessible mineral deposits. It is a trend which has had a striking effect on the nature of the mining industry itself (Fig. 6.15):

1   Until the late eighteenth century mining was generally restricted to rich deposits which either outcropped or were near enough to the surface to be mined in shallow pits. Such deposits were quickly worked out and this type of mining is rarely found today.

THE CHANGING PATTERN OF MINING

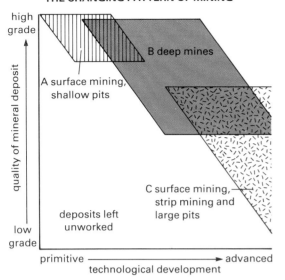

Fig. **6.15**

2   The development of new techniques of ventilating and draining pits allowed minerals to be worked at considerable depths. This type of mining is very expensive and it is now practised only if the mineral deposits are rich or if the mineral extracted is very rare and therefore very valuable.

3   As the richest deposits were worked out interest shifted to reserves which were of much poorer quality. The working of these deposits became possible only when machines were developed which allowed large scale open pit mining. This is the cheapest method of mining and it dominates the mining industry today.

The result of this pattern of development is that all mining operations, whether they are in developed or less developed countries, are on a vast scale and are expensive to undertake. This can be seen by looking at two case studies – the deep mining of gold in South Africa and the surface mining of copper in the United States.

Gold mining: Klerksdorp, South Africa

South Africa produces nearly 50% of the gold mined in the world each year (Fig. 6.22). Most of this gold is mined in the Witwatersrand Basin near Johannesburg (Fig. 6.16). It is thought that the gold bearing rocks of the region were laid down in a large lake which occupied the area some 500 million years ago. Rivers flowing into the lake carried pebbles and coarse sand which built up fan shaped deltas. During periods of low flow the rivers carried finer materials, including tiny particles of gold. These sands and silts were deposited in the lake to form the gold bearing reefs which make up a very small part of the sedimentary rocks laid down during the period. Later sediments covered the area and earth movements folded and faulted the gold bearing rocks. Eventually the Witwatersrand System was left like a giant saucer, tilted so that one edge is deeply buried while the opposite (northern) rim is exposed or very near to the surface. It is on this northern edge that present gold mining started and is still concentrated.

The development of the mines at Klerksdorp is typical of the development of mining in the area as a whole. Gold was discovered on the surface in 1886 – the same year that the first deposits were found at Johannesburg. The discovery led to a gold rush and the tiny town of Klerksdorp became a major mining centre. Within a few years, however, the surface reefs had been worked out and mining virtually ceased in the area. Forty years later the area was surveyed again and drilling revealed the first of the deep reefs. Mining began again in 1942 and further discoveries were made at even greater depths. It is these reefs which are being worked today (see Figs 6.16–21).

Using information given in Figs 6.16–22, complete the following exercise.

a   i   How many men work at the mine?
   ii   How many members of the labour force are black?

THE SOUTH AFRICAN GOLDFIELDS

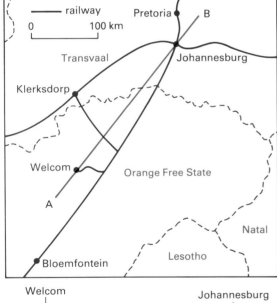

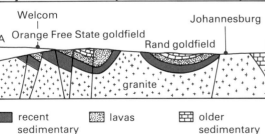

Fig. **6.16**

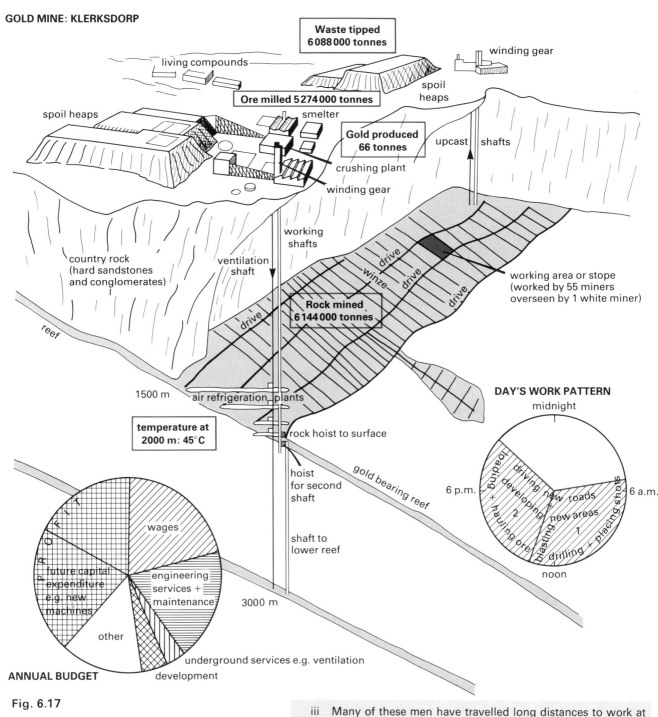

GOLD MINE: KLERKSDORP

Waste tipped 6 088 000 tonnes

living compounds

winding gear

Ore milled 5 274 000 tonnes

spoil heaps

spoil heaps

smelter

Gold produced 66 tonnes

upcast   shafts

crushing plant

winding gear

working shafts

country rock (hard sandstones and conglomerates)

ventilation shaft

drive   winze   drive   drive   drive

working area or stope (worked by 55 miners overseen by 1 white miner)

Rock mined 6 144 000 tonnes

reef

1500 m   air refrigeration plants

DAY'S WORK PATTERN

midnight

temperature at 2000 m: 45°C

rock hoist to surface

hoist for second shaft

gold bearing reef

6 p.m.   driving developing new areas   loading + hauling ore 2   blasting   drilling + placing shots 1   6 a.m.

shaft to lower reef

noon

3000 m

ANNUAL BUDGET

P R O F I T

wages

future capital expenditure e.g. new machines

engineering services + maintenance

other

development

underground services e.g. ventilation

Fig. 6.17

iii Many of these men have travelled long distances to work at the mine. Name four important source areas of labour, arranging them in order of importance.

iv Where do they live while they are employed at the mine?

v Describe how the work force is organised.

b i What is the depth of the upper reef and the lower reef?

ii Both reefs dip (slope) steeply. Describe how methods of mining have been adapted to make use of this feature.

iii Why is it necessary to refrigerate the air which is pumped around the mine?

c i Approximately how much rock is mined during the year (i.e. how much waste is tipped)?

ii How much of this rock is ore?

iii How much gold is obtained from this ore?

iv What does this represent as a yield per tonne of ore?

d Outline the problems of deep mining of this kind. Why do you think it is worth continuing with this type of mining here?

150

SECTION THROUGH THE WORKINGS

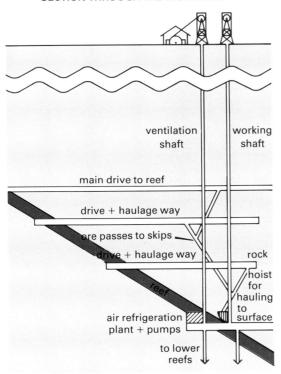

Fig. 6.18

APARTHEID IN SOUTH AFRICA

Apartheid – an Afrikaans word meaning 'separate'. Now applied to the official government policy which has, since 1948, sought to separate the four main racial groups (the Africans, the Asians, the Coloureds and the Whites), both socially and in terms of where they can live.

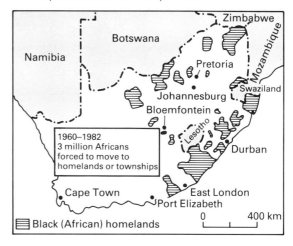

1960–1982
3 million Africans forced to move to homelands or townships

☷ Black (African) homelands

AFRICAN HOMELANDS IN SOUTH AFRICA

'Homelands' are areas set aside for the African population. They have a degree of self government and should eventually become independent. Not all Africans live in the homelands, and Black 'townships' are found in every major city.

THE STATISTICS OF APARTHEID

Population: total 20.8 million, of which 15.6% are White, 72.5% African, 9.0% Coloured and 2.9% Asian

	White	African
Land area	87%	13%
Infant mortality (per 1000)	13	+100
Cases of tuberculosis (per 1000)	0.12	7.8
Spending on schooling (per pupil)	913 rand	140 rand

APARTHEID AND INDUSTRY

Population in African homelands	10750000
Non-agricultural jobs available in homelands	95000
Workers migrating to White areas (for long periods)	1329000
Workers commuting (daily) to White areas	745000

Average wages: Africans 2728 Rand, Whites 11232 Rand

DIFFERING VIEWS OF APARTHEID

1 A policy designed to give political freedom to all groups in the country and to develop economic cooperation between Blacks and Whites. (The South African Government)
2 A policy designed to deprive the Africans of any say in the government of South Africa (they have no vote) and to ensure White supremacy.
3 A policy designed to ensure a continuing supply of cheap labour.

Fig. 6.20

SOURCES OF LABOUR FOR THE MINE

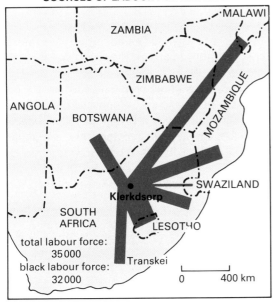

total labour force:
35000
black labour force:
32000

Fig. 6.19

This type of mining is made possible by two factors:

1 There is a plentiful supply of cheap labour both in neighbouring countries and in the 'black homelands' of South Africa (see Figs 6.19 and 6.20). In these areas the population is growing rapidly and unemployment is high. This has forced large numbers of men to leave their homes to work in South Africa. The Vaal Reef Mine at Klerksdorp, for example, employs 33000 black workers, many of them attracted from distant areas and most of them living in compounds near the mine for the entire period of

Fig. 6.21 *Underground workings*

employment (each contract can be for up to 18 months). Three quarters of this labour force is employed underground during the first shift of the day; most of them drilling holes into the working faces and placing explosives. At the end of the shift the explosives are fired and a smaller afternoon shift moves in to clear the ore produced by the blast. This operation is highly mechanised, although manual labour is used to pick up the small rock fragments and dust which often contain a high proportion of gold. The ore is transported to hoppers at the bottom of the workshafts and is hauled to the surface.

2   Work at such depths and on such a scale is possible only because of the advances which have taken place in mining technology. At depths of 3000 metres, for example, temperatures exceed 45°C, making work impossible. To overcome this the entire air supply of the mine is refrigerated. In addition, an underground transport system had to be developed to transport men and carry ore back to the shafts. Continuous hoists are needed to lift rock such long distances to the surface.

On average every tonne of ore raised to the surface yields about twelve grammes of gold. It is important, therefore, that the gold should be extracted from the ore as near to the pit head as possible. Three extraction plants have been built and here the ore is crushed and ground to a fine powder. This powder is mixed in a solution of potassium cyanide which takes up the metal content of the ore. The gold (often containing silver and other metals) can be precipitated from the solution. It is then refined by melting it in crucibles and removing the other metals as slag. A large amount of waste is produced by this method and, to keep transport costs to a minimum, this is tipped nearby.

This type of mining is very expensive and it is used only when the returns are likely to be very high, i.e. when the mineral deposits are very rich or the mineral produced is very valuable. It is not surprising, therefore, that most of the minerals used in the world today are obtained from mines which employ less expensive methods. Indeed most of these mines are open pits of various kinds.

WORLD PRODUCTION OF GOLD IN 1981 (BY COUNTRY)

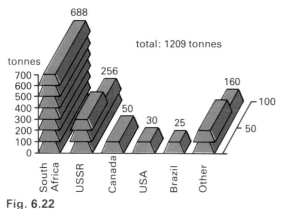

Fig. 6.22

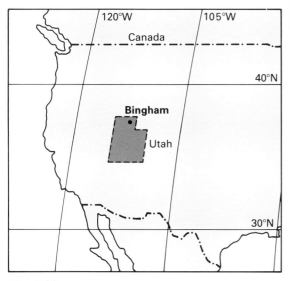

Fig. 6.23

Copper mining: Bingham, Utah, USA

For a long time copper ranked second only to steel as the most widely used metal in the world. In recent years it has lost this position to aluminium but it remains one of the most useful metals available and in 1982 more than 7.8 million tonnes of copper were used.

Copper occurs as an ore, in a variety of forms in the rocks of the earth's crust. Deposits are widely scattered in a large number of countries but in almost every case the metal content of the ore is very low (an ore containing 2% copper would be regarded as rich and even ores containing less than 0.5% copper would probably be mined). This, more than anything else, has determined both the methods of mining used (open pit) and the location of the primary processing industries (as near to the mine as possible). This can be clearly seen at Bingham (Fig. 6.23), the oldest and one of the largest open pit copper mines in the world.

The Bingham ore deposit, which also contains important deposits of silver, is located at the head of the Bingham Canyon. This is a narrow steep sided valley in the mountains 40 kilometres to the south west of Salt Lake City (see Fig. 6.24). Copper occurs in small quantities in rocks throughout the district. In the Bingham area, however, the rocks were shattered by the intrusion of molten igneous rock. This caused the copper bearing rocks to melt and during the cooling which followed copper was deposited in cracks and fissures in the shattered rocks. Furthermore the copper was deposited in a form which allowed it to be dissolved in weak acid solutions. As a result rainwater has washed the copper out of the surface layers of the rock and redeposited it in the lower layers. This zone of enrichment has given the richest ores with a copper content of more than 2%.

The Bingham ore deposit was discovered in 1863 by prospectors looking for gold, but copper mining did not begin until 1906. There were several reasons for this delay:

1   Transport was so poor that only precious metals or very rich ore deposits could be economically worked. The arrival of the transcontinental railway at Salt Lake City changed this and during the late nineteenth century a rail network was built to serve the mining towns of the area. Bingham was linked to that network.

2   Water was needed to process the ore (see Fig. 6.24e). This presented serious problems in an area of low rainfall. Fortunately, however, the only permanent river in the area – the Jordan River – flowed to the east of Bingham and this was eventually used.

3   Open pit mining was the only economic method of mining ores of such low metal content and this became possible only with the development of steam powered mechanical diggers at the end of the nineteenth century. In fact mining started in 1906 and within ten years Bingham was the largest copper mine in the world.

As we have seen, open pit mining is very simple. The problems usually stem from the vast amount of rock which has to be moved.

153

BINGHAM: LOCATION

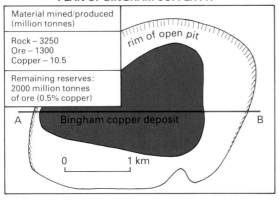

Great Salt Lake

R. Jordan

Salt Lake City

Bingham •

Wasatch Mountains

Utah Lake

⊡ volcanic intrusion

0   30 km

Fig. 6.24 (a)

PLAN OF BINGHAM COPPER PIT

Material mined/produced (million tonnes)

Rock – 3250
Ore – 1300
Copper – 10.5

Remaining reserves: 2000 million tonnes of ore (0.5% copper)

rim of open pit

A   B
Bingham copper deposit

0   1 km

Fig. 6.24 (b)

Using information given in this section, complete the following exercise.

a i Calculate the dimensions of the mine.
   ii How much ore has been extracted from the mine?
   iii How much overburden and waste has been produced? Why has it been necessary to excavate so much waste rock?
   iv Describe the methods of mining used here. Compare them with those shown on page 150.
   v What are the main problems caused by the depth of the mine? How have they been overcome?
b i Describe the processes necessary to obtain copper from ore.
   ii At which stage does the greatest weight loss occur?
   iii What effect is this likely to have on the location of the different branches of the copper industry?

At Bingham it has been necessary to mine deeply into the copper bearing rock. This has had two important results. In the first place the pit has been extended far beyond the boundaries of the ore deposit and in the process a vast amount of waste rock has been removed. Second, and even more important, the increased depth made the removal of the ore from the pit very difficult and expensive. This problem was eventually solved by driving a tunnel through the side of the pit to the processing plant in the canyon.

Because the metal content of the ore is so low most copper ores are processed as near to the mine as possible. This is particularly true of the milling operations during which the greatest loss of bulk takes place. Any industry which produces a reduction of bulk on this scale (it can be greater than 95%) is likely to be located near to the source of its raw materials (see page 158).

SECTION
2400 m
2200
A poor ores
2000 enriched ores (zone of redeposition)   0.4%
1800 outline of pit   2% copper
                                                       0.6%
B

Fig. 6.24 (c)

MINING STATISTICS: AVERAGE ANNUAL AMOUNTS

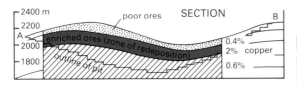

Rock mined (90 million tonnes)

Ore mined (35 million tonnes)

Copper produced (200 000 tonnes)

Fig. 6.24 (d)

PROCESSING THE ORE

Mining	Milling	Smelting	Refining

open pit mine

+ water

concentrating

+limestone

1 tonne copper (99.9% pure)

ore 150 tonnes

crushing   grinding

3 tonnes ore concentrate

roasting   reverberatory furnace   converter   refining furnace   electrolitic refining

overburden 350 tonnes

settling pond 145 tonnes

slag 1.8 tonnes

gold silver

Fig. 6.24 (e)

Fig. 6.24 (f) *Bingham copper mine*

Both of these problems (deep mining and low quality ores) are likely to become worse at Bingham – and at many other copper mines – as the best ores are worked out. Bingham does in fact have vast reserves of ore but the copper content may be less than 0.5%. Such ores are so expensive to mine that attempts are being made to extract the metals by dissolving them in acids, leaving the parent rock relatively undisturbed.

These problems are not confined to the copper mining industry. Demand for almost all minerals has been so great that the richest deposits have been worked out and the future seems very uncertain.

Mining: the future

Life in the Developed World depends upon the availability of a large number of minerals. The economic growth and prosperity which followed the Second World War caused the demand for these minerals to increase rapidly. Production was increased to meet this demand and the effects of increased production are now being felt.

All the minerals which make up the earth occur in limited quantities. For a long time this presented few problems since increased production was more than matched by the discovery of new reserves. Recently, however, the situation has changed dramatically and in some cases production has far outstripped the discovery of new deposits.

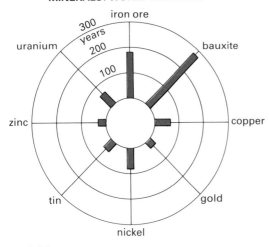

MINERALS: WORLD RESERVES

Fig. 6.25

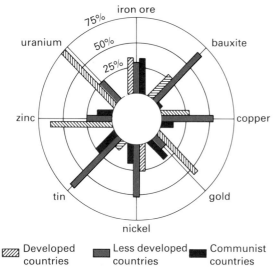

MINERALS: DISTRIBUTION OF KNOWN RESERVES (%)

▨ Developed countries ▬ Less developed countries ▬ Communist countries

Fig. 6.26

The situation for several of the developed countries is even more serious since the mineral reserves of the Developed World were the first to be exploited and are now even nearer to exhaustion (Fig. 6.26). This has meant that the richer industrialised nations have become increasingly dependent upon the countries of the Developing World for supplies of vital minerals.

Attempts are being made to adjust to these changes.

1   Demand for minerals has been reduced. In part this has been the result of deliberate policies on the part of the developed countries but even more important has been the slowing down in economic growth which followed the oil price rises of the 1970s.

2   Great interest has been shown in the recycling, i.e. the re-use, of minerals. For a long time the more valuable scrap metals have been recycled but during the 1970s attempts were made to re-use less valuable metals and products which use other minerals such as oil.

3   Attempts have been made to use more common minerals in place of those which are becoming increasingly rare. Aluminium in particular has been used to replace a range of other metals.

4   Most important of all, in the short term efforts have been made to develop new supplies of major minerals. These attempts have taken two forms:

a   The search for new methods of extracting useful minerals from deposits which are either of very poor quality or which present serious problems when mining is attempted. We have already seen that attempts to extract oil from shales and tar sands have met with some success and that by using modern methods the rate of extraction from oil fields has been considerably increased (see page 126). Equally important efforts are now being made to extract metals from ores which are of such low grade that traditional mining is unlikely ever to be economic. This has been done by dissolving the metals in situ, i.e. in the ground.

b   Even more exciting, new mineral deposits have been discovered in unlikely places. Off some coasts, for example, metal ores occur on the sea bed in the form of small nodules. These are very rich and offer an abundant supply of metals such as manganese. The major problem is of course the extraction of the nodules from what is often deep water.

Whatever steps have been taken the basic problem remains. The world's supply of minerals is finite, i.e. it is limited and at some stage in the future the total reserves of those minerals which are of value will be exhausted (Fig. 6.26). In some cases this stage appears almost to have been reached and, within a comparatively short time, the situation will be much more serious.

Manufacturing industry (secondary industry)

MANUFACTURING INDUSTRY: A SIMPLE MODEL

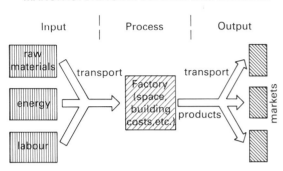

Fig. 6.27

Manufacturing industry is concerned with changing the materials produced by primary industries to create goods which are both more valuable and more useful (see Fig. 6.27). As we have seen, the importance of manufacturing industry varies from country to country. In some of the least developed countries manufacturing industries are virtually non-existent, while in the most highly developed countries there are signs that they are being replaced by other forms of industry as the main source of wealth. In spite of this, manufacturing industry is still the most important element in the pattern of industrial development throughout the world.

In fact manufacturing industries are so numerous and so varied that any study of world industrial patterns is bound to be difficult. By concentrating on the location of industries, however, it is possible to gain an understanding both of the workings of industry in general and of the distribution of industrial activity on the earth's surface.

Every industrial establishment has a location, i.e. it occupies a part of the earth's surface. There are reasons for the choice of that location – reasons which may to a greater or lesser degree be shared by similar industries in different parts of the world (see Fig. 6.28).

FACTORS INFLUENCING THE LOCATION OF FACTORIES (ALL INDUSTRIES)

	%
Access to markets	21
Size of market	14
Labour supply	7
Wage costs	2
Access to raw materials	4
Freight costs to raw materials	6
to markets	11
Living conditions	4

Fig. 6.28 (a)

Using information given in Figs 6.27 and 6.28, complete the following exercise.

a   Study the simple model of manufacturing industry.
   i   Name four general factors which are likely to influence industrial location.
   ii Which aspects of the actual site of the factory are likely to influence industrial location?
b   Study the data extracted from a survey completed by businessmen in the United States. List the factors mentioned by them when considering the location of a new factory. Arrange the list in order of importance.
c   Although the same factors were mentioned regardless of the industry concerned, they do tend to vary in relative importance from industry to industry.
   i   Describe the differences between the replies for the three industries illustrated – oil refining, metal smelting and engineering.
   ii Which of the industries is most strongly influenced by access to raw materials, including fuel?
   iii Which of the industries is most strongly influenced by access to markets?
   iv Which industry is most dependent upon the availability of skilled labour?

FACTORS INFLUENCING THE LOCATION OF FACTORIES (BY INDUSTRY)

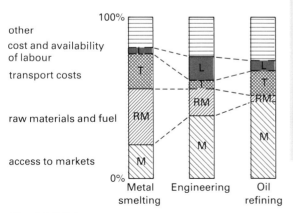

Fig. 6.28 (b)

The most important factors influencing the location of a modern industry include:

1   Access to raw materials and markets which, in turn, implies the existence of an efficient transport system.

157

2 The availability of a supply of suitable labour.

3 Space to construct the necessary buildings.

It is probable that these necessities will be available at many places on the earth's surface and this can make the choice of the best location for a factory extremely difficult. Since most industries are planned with the intention of making a profit, however, factories will tend to be located where the costs of production are as low as possible, the least cost location. This will of course vary according to the type of industry but it will also be affected by other influences, such as government policies and the choices made by individual businessmen. It is the combination of these factors which helps produce the different patterns of industrial location seen in the world today.

Raw material based industries

The location of any major industry is complicated. In certain cases, however, a single factor may be of great importance in determining the location chosen. Some industries, for example, use large amounts of a bulky raw material and, in the manufacturing process, greatly reduce that bulk (Fig. 6.29). This means that the transport costs of raw materials will be greater than the costs of transporting the finished products to the markets. As a result, many of these 'bulk reducing' industries are located either near to the source of the major raw materials or at a point where an efficient transport system allows the raw materials to be assembled cheaply.

Examples of such industries occur throughout the world. However, a closer examination of any of these industries suggests that an apparently simple pattern can in fact be much more complex.

Wood pulp and paper making

Most of the paper manufactured in the world today is made from wood pulp – usually pulp produced from the softwoods obtained from coniferous forests. On average three tonnes of timber are needed to make one tonne of paper (see Fig. 6.32). Given this large reduction in bulk during the manufacturing process, it is likely that the industry will be located near to major forest areas.

BULK REDUCING INDUSTRIES

e.g. mineral processing, metal smelting, timber processing

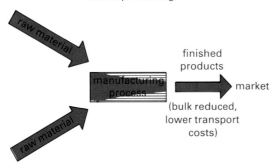

Fig. 6.29

FOREST INDUSTRIES (BY COUNTRY)

	Production			Consumption	
	Timber (million m³)	Pulp wood (million tonnes)	Paper (million tonnes)	Paper (million tonnes)	per capita GNP ($)
USA	322	45	59	55	12820
Canada	161	19	13	4.1	11400
Brazil	217	33	3	3.2	2220
China	224	2.3	8.8	6.3	300
India	214	0.5	0.7	1.2	260
Japan		0.9	17.8	17.3	10080
Sweden	53	8.7	6.1	5.5	14870
UK	4.7	0.15	3.8	3.1	9110
USSR	356	8.7	8.7	9.1	4750
DCs	810	105	138	146.2	–
LDCs	1467	6.6	12.7	19.1	–
World	3020	120	174	173	–

Study the information given in this section and complete the following exercise.

a Describe the relationship between paper production and (i) timber production (ii) paper consumption in the countries listed in the table. (It may help to draw a simple scattergraph or to calculate the correlation coefficient.)

iii Which is the stronger relationship?

iv What effect is this likely to have on the location of the paper industry in the world? Does the actual distribution shown in the map, Fig. 6.33, confirm this?

b Sweden is an important producer of wood pulp and paper.

i Using an atlas list four important paper making centres.

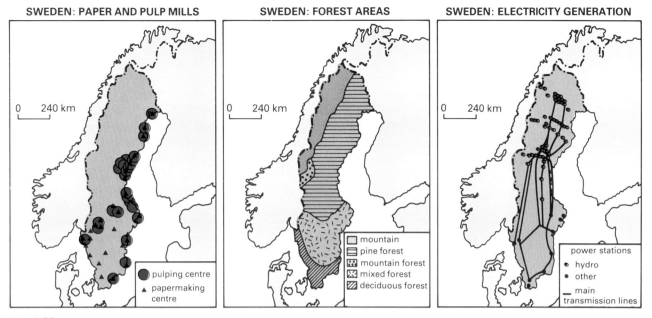

SWEDEN: PAPER AND PULP MILLS

SWEDEN: FOREST AREAS

SWEDEN: ELECTRICITY GENERATION

0   240 km

pulping centre

▲ papermaking centre

mountain
pine forest
mountain forest
mixed forest
deciduous forest

power stations
hydro
other
main transmission lines

Fig. 6.30

Fig. 6.31 *Sawmill in Sweden*

THE STAGES IN PAPERMAKING

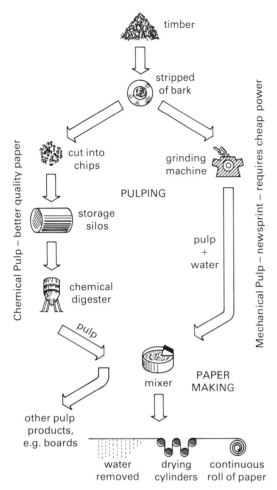

Fig. 6.32

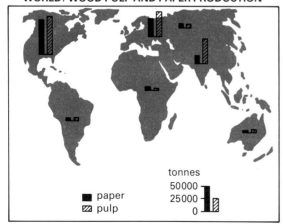

Fig. 6.33

ii Describe the pattern of location and relate it to major influences such as materials and markets.
iii Other raw materials (and inputs such as power) are needed in the making of pulp and paper. What effect are they likely to have on the location of individual mills in Sweden?

Sweden is a major producer of wood pulp and paper. No less than 57% of the country is forested, so the basic raw material, timber, is widely available. Given these circumstances it is interesting to examine the distribution of the industry and of individual mills (Fig. 6.30).

1 Most of the large modern mills are, as might be expected, located in the central and northern provinces where the largest areas of commercial forest are found. In the south much of the forest has been cleared for agriculture, and the paper industry, which grew up there in the nineteenth century, has declined.

2 The northern forests are remote from the main centres of population and industry in Sweden. Most of the pulp and paper mills are located on the lowlands on the edge of the forests. Here rivers, roads and railways are available to transport both raw materials and finished products.

3 Because a large proportion of the output of pulp and paper is exported, many mills are located on the coast.

There are, however, many exceptions to this comparatively simple location pattern. The move to locations near to the northern forests is far from complete and traces of an earlier industry remain. During the nineteenth and early twentieth century most of the paper and pulp produced in Sweden was made using mechanical methods, i.e. the timber was broken down by passing it through huge grinding machines. Large amounts of electricity were needed to drive these machines and the best locations for the mills were near waterfalls where direct water power was available and hydro-electricity could be generated. Such locations were almost always inland and often in remote mountain areas.

During the twentieth century this pattern of location began to change. Timber production generally was increasing and new areas of forest were being developed in the north. At the same time an electricity grid system was being constructed and this reduced the need for the industry to locate near to hydro-electric plants. Most important of all, however, a new method of making pulp and paper was introduced. Instead of grinding the timber to form a fine paste, chemicals were used to break down the structure of the wood. This not only produced pulp which could be used to make better quality paper, it greatly reduced the amount of electricity used. This influenced the pattern of location. The industry has tended to move to the coast or to other sites with efficient communications. Here access to timber produced in the northern forests and to the other raw materials needed to make chemical wood pulp is both cheap and easy.

Movements of this kind are rarely complete and some of the old paper making centres remain. Some of these still use mechanical methods to produce pulp; others have changed their methods but not their locations. When this happens it is called industrial inertia. Examples of industrial inertia are found throughout the Developed World where industries often have a long history.

Iron and steel

Most metal extracting industries are bulk reducing industries. It is not surprising, therefore, that many of them tend to be located near to a source of the major raw material, usually the ore deposit. This is certainly true in the case of copper extraction (see page 153) and the production of alumina from bauxite (see page 167). In both cases the mineral content of the ores is often very low and the initial manufacturing process is comparatively simple. In other industries, however, the factors influencing location are more varied and the location pattern produced is not only more complex but has often changed dramatically within a comparatively short time. This is nowhere more apparent than in the production of iron and steel – an industry which was once located close to its raw materials but which in recent years has tended to move nearer to its markets.

Iron is the most widely used metal in the world today and in 1982, 750 million tonnes of steel (a form of iron) were produced. For almost 300 years the economic life in the developed countries has depended upon the mass production of iron, and since the middle of the nineteenth century, on the mass production of steel.

The metal occurs in rocks – iron ores – which also contain many impurities. The iron can be extracted simply by heating the ore but it will still contain carbon. As a result, it will be of very poor quality. To overcome this problem, and to control the amount of carbon in the iron, a complex method of production is used (Fig. 6.34).

Using information given in this section, answer the following.

a   Write a brief description of large scale steel production.
b   i   Describe the main characteristics of pig iron.
     ii   Describe the main characteristics of steel. Why is it more useful than pig iron?

STEELMAKING

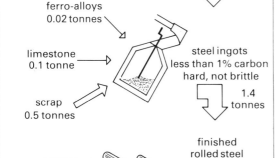

Fig. 6.34

The amount of carbon contained in the iron largely determines its quality. In pig iron the carbon content can reach 4% and this renders it too brittle to use. The amount of carbon is reduced by reheating the metal in a steel furnace. Pure oxygen is passed over the molten metal and this burns off the carbon. Other impurities are removed by adding a flux to both the blast furnace and the steel converter. Reactions take place which cause the impurities to rise to the surface as a slag which can be drained off before the metal is tapped. These processes use up vast amounts of raw materials.

It is not surprising, therefore, that the availability of the major raw materials strongly influences the location of the industry.

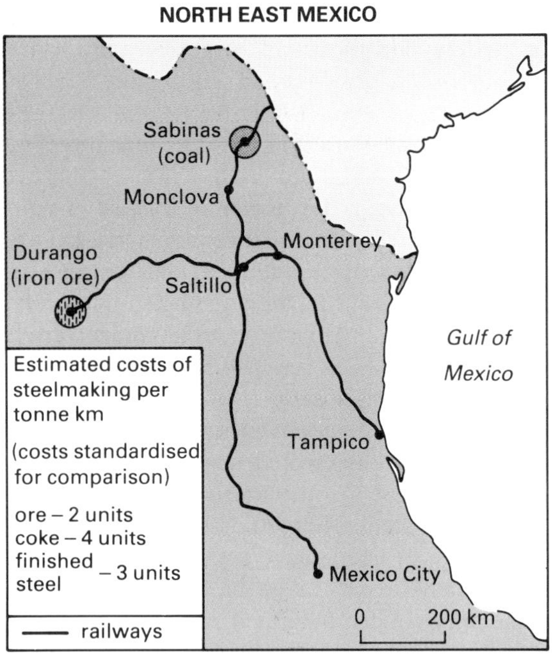

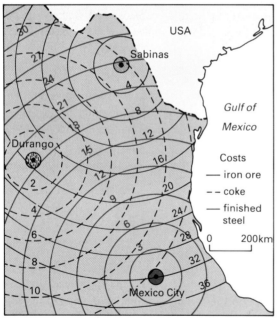

NORTH EAST MEXICO

Estimated costs of steelmaking per tonne km

(costs standardised for comparison)

ore – 2 units
coke – 4 units
finished steel – 3 units

—— railways

0   200 km

Fig. 6.35

NORTH EAST MEXICO: COST GRADIENTS FOR STEEL PRODUCTION

Costs
—— iron ore
- - - coke
—— finished steel

0   200km

Fig. 6.36

The location of a steelworks

Because so many factors are involved, the choice of the best site for a new steelworks is very complicated. This can be seen in a study of alternative sites in Mexico. Details of the three most important locational factors – supplies of coke and iron ore and access to the major market, Mexico City – are given in Fig. 6.35. In each case the cost per tonne kilometre has been calculated and the results have been standardised to make comparisons easy. This information has then been shown in Fig. 6.36 in the form of cost gradients from the sources of the main raw materials at Sabinas and Durango and from the main market, Mexico City.

Using information given in Figs 6.35 and 6.36, complete the following exercise.

a i   Trace Fig. 6.35. Locate on it a point which is equi-distant from Durango, Sabinas and Mexico City.
   ii Calculate the costs of steel production if a plant was built at this location (use the cost gradients in Fig. 6.36).
b   Calculate the cost of steel production at works located at:
   i   Sabinas, the main source of coking coal.
   ii Durango, the main source of iron ore.
   iii Mexico City, the main market for finished steel.
c   Which, if any, of these locations would have lower costs than those for a plant which is equi-distant from the three centres?
d i   Study the cost contours and work out the location where the combined costs are lowest (the least cost location).
   ii Locate this point on your map.
   iii How does this least cost location differ from the location which is equi-distant from the three centres?
   iv At which town would this plant be located? What are the advantages of this location?

Because many other factors (e.g. markets other than Mexico City, alternative sources of raw materials, sources of oil, gas and scrap metal, and the actual transport) have been excluded such an exercise can only give an approximate idea of the true situation. It is significant, however, that the two major steelmaking plants in the region are located at Monterrey and Monclova – the first near to the least cost location, the second near to the coalfield at Sabinas.

A further complication is the fact that the least cost location is affected by technological change:

1   In the early days of large scale iron smelting, blast furnaces were very inefficient and large amounts of coke were needed to melt the ore. It was usual, therefore, to locate furnaces on coalfields where coke was readily and cheaply available.

WORLD STEEL PRODUCTION (MILLION TONNES)

	1955	1965	1975	1981
Japan	9.4	41.1	107.3	101
USSR	45.6	71.2	144.8	149
USA	106.1	119.0	116.1	108
West Germany	21.3	36.8	42.4	41
China	2.8	12.0	26	35
Italy	5.3	12.6	23.4	24
France	12.5	19.6	23.2	21
United Kingdom	20.1	27.4	22.3	15.0
World	270.4	455.0	680.0	706.6

2 Improvements in blast furnace technology reduced the amount of coke needed and by the end of the nineteenth century locations on iron ore deposits were becoming attractive. This was particularly true in countries like the UK where the iron ores were of poor quality and the costs of transporting ore were therefore very high.

3 The period since 1950 has seen even more rapid changes in steelmaking. Coke consumption has been reduced even further and the preparation of iron ore by crushing, pelleting or by pre-heating with coke to form sinter has reduced the amount of ore fed into the furnaces. As a result, dependence upon raw materials has been reduced and there has been a tendency for new works to be located nearer to the main markets.

Because modern steelworks are large and expensive to build, the industry has often been slow to respond to such changes. As a result many locations are still used in spite of the fact that they are no longer efficient, i.e. there are many examples of industrial inertia. This is particularly true in the old established industrial nations such as the United States, the United Kingdom and many other European countries. It can also be seen in more recently industrialised countries such as Japan.

Fig. 6.37 *Inside a steelworks in Jamshedpur, India*

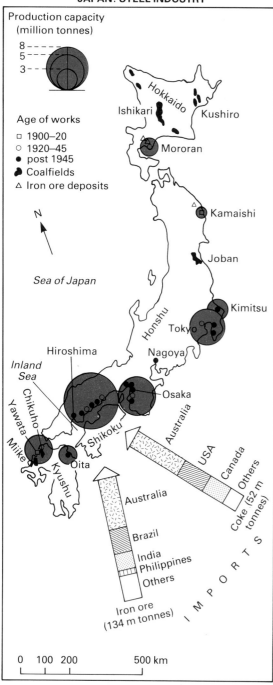

JAPAN: STEEL INDUSTRY

Production capacity
(million tonnes)

8
5
3

Age of works

□ 1900–20
○ 1920–45
● post 1945
🌰 Coalfields
△ Iron ore deposits

N

Hokkaido

Ishikari   Kushiro

Mororan

Kamaishi

Joban

Sea of Japan

Kimitsu

Honshu   Tokyo

Hiroshima   Nagoya

Inland
Sea

Chikuho   Osaka

Yawata   Shikoku

Miike   Australia

Oita   USA   Canada   Others

Kyushu   Coke (52 m tonnes)

Australia

Brazil

India
Philippines

Others

Iron ore
(134 m tonnes)   I M P O R T S

0 100 200   500 km

Fig. 6.38

The Japanese steel industry

Japan is one of the largest steel producers in the Free World. The Japanese steel industry produces steel so cheaply that it can undercut most other steel industries in their home markets. As this suggests, the Japanese industry is one of the most modern and efficient in the world. In spite of this, the pattern of location (Fig. 6.38) reflects the changes in technology which have affected almost all steel industries and examples of industrial inertia can be found even in this most up to date industry.

Study the map in Fig. 6.38.

a i Name two of the oldest steel making centres shown on the map.
   ii Suggest reasons for the development of each of the centres.
b After 1920 the steel industry changed location.
   i Where were the main new plants built?
   ii What were the advantages of such locations?
c Describe the pattern of location since 1945 and, referring to the photograph, Fig. 6.40, list the advantages of the sites available at the new locations.

At the beginning of the twentieth century the Japanese steel industry was very small and it was completely overshadowed by the industries in Europe and the United States. The industry depended very heavily on local supplies of ore and coking coal. As a result the major steelworks were located near the iron ore deposits at Kamaishi or near the coalfields on Kyushu and Hokkaido.

During the 1920s and 1930s Japan emerged as a major industrial nation and this, combined with the growth of the armed forces, led to a rapid increase in the demand for steel. Existing supplies of coal and ore could not meet these new requirements and the industry began to depend upon imported raw materials. This led to the location of new steelworks on the coast, near to the main markets, e.g. near the industrial areas around Tokyo and Osaka.

Much of this industry was destroyed by bombing during the Second World War but when the industry was re-established after 1945 similar locations were chosen:

1 On the coast so that imported ore and coking coal could be unloaded directly at the works.

2 Near to the main industrial areas so that transport to markets could be kept to a minimum.

Once again sites along the shores of Toyko Bay and Osaka Bay were developed. By the 1960s, however, the best of these sites had been used and the Japanese steel industry – by then the fastest growing steel industry in the world – was forced to look for new locations. This was not easy in a country which was not only mountainous but also so densely populated that few areas of lowland were available for large scale industrial development. In fact the only large areas of lowland remaining were situated in the salt marshes which border the Inland Sea. Drainage began immediately and within a few years construction had begun on some of the largest steelworks in the world. All of these plants had easy access to markets in Japan and, through the nearby ports, to export markets which were now becoming more important than the home market. Ore terminals could be built to serve each major steel producing complex. These were necessary because the industry was now importing 98% of its iron ore and 90% of its coking coal.

In spite of this dependence upon imported raw materials – most of them carried more than 7000 kilometres from Australia – Japan is still able to produce steel more cheaply than any other country in the world (see Fig. 6.39). There are several possible reasons for this.

1   The Japanese industry is newer than most of its competitors. As a result:

a   The furnaces and other plant tend to be more efficient. For example, steel furnaces in Britain and the United States use 50% more coke than those in Japan.

b   Locations have been carefully chosen to keep costs to a minimum and there are few works remaining in the older and more expensive producing areas (i.e. there are fewer cases of industrial inertia in Japan than in most other steel producing countries).

2   Labour costs are considerably lower in the Japanese industry when compared with its competitors. This is partly due to the fact that wage levels in Japan are lower than in some other countries (e.g. the USA). More often, however, it is due to the fact that labour is used more efficiently in the Japanese steel industry and the number of people employed to produce each tonne of steel is considerably lower.

3   The Japanese government has helped the industry by providing capital and by protecting the industry against overseas competition in the early days.

COMPARATIVE COSTS OF PRODUCING ONE TONNE OF STEEL

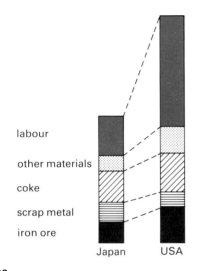

Fig. 6.39

Fig. 6.40 *Kimitsu steelworks, Japan*

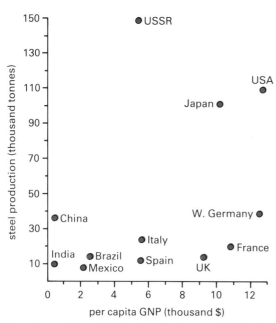

STEEL PRODUCTION AND GNP

Note the positions of China, USSR, Japan and USA. Try to explain them.

Fig. 6.41

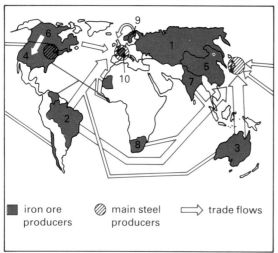

WORLD IRON ORE: PRODUCTION AND TRADE

■ iron ore producers   ⊘ main steel producers   ⟹ trade flows

Iron ore producer	Production (m tonnes)
1 USSR	243.5
2 Brazil	105.2
3 Australia	94.5
4 USA	78.8
5 China	72.0
6 Canada	50.4
7 India	40.0
8 South Africa	25.5
9 Sweden	22.3
10 France	22.2
World	874

Fig. 6.42

4   Japan has also become the world's largest producer of ships and motor cars (see pages 175 and 181). Both of these industries use large amounts of steel and this has given a large and expanding home market for the industry. As a result works could be planned on a scale seen nowhere else in the world. This is known as 'economy of scale', i.e. the more units (tonnes of steel, motor cars, washing machines etc.) produced on a given site the cheaper each unit is likely to be.

World patterns

Economic activity in the modern world depends upon a number of important factors. As we have already seen, one of these factors is access to one or more of the major sources of energy. Another is the availability of steel, the metal which is the basis of so much modern technology. There is a close relationship between steel consumption and the wealth of individual countries and steel consumption appears to be a good indicator of economic development.

It is not surprising that most of the major consumers are also major producers of steel. Almost without exception these countries are the most highly developed and the most heavily industrialised in the world (see Fig. 6.41); and in most cases a strong steel industry has been the basis of that industrial development. Furthermore, for a long time many of the developed countries have produced more steel than they can consume and this is exported, often to countries in the Developing World.

Since the Second World War, however, this pattern has tended to break down. The rapid growth of world steel production meant that many of the major producers were forced to look for new sources of iron ore. These were often found in countries which produced little or no steel. As a result, an enormous trade in iron ore developed (Fig. 6.42) with bulk ore carriers converging on Europe, North America and Japan from all parts of the world. Trade on this scale became possible only because:

1   The ores were so rich that they were more economic to use than the poorer quality ores which were available in the major steel producing countries.

2   The availability of bulk ore carriers, most of which exceed 100 000 tonnes in size, meant that transport costs remained small even when long voyages were involved.

The effects of this can be seen by comparing the cost of iron ore in Japan, which imports 98% of its requirements, with that in the United States, which imports less than 40%. (See Fig. 6.39.)

At first the less developed countries benefited from the opening up of new mines and the building of a transport system to serve them. In recent years, however, some of the developing countries have tried to establish steel industries of their own to make use of the raw materials which are often available. Because a large amount of capital is needed to establish a modern steelworks only the largest or richest of the developing countries, e.g. Brazil, Mexico and India, have managed to establish important steel industries. However, if recent trends continue, the pattern of steel production in the world could change dramatically.

Energy based industries

Since the oil price rises of the 1970s energy costs have played an increasingly important part in the location of industry. Even so, there are few cases of energy costs playing the major role in determining the location of an individual industry. The likelihood of this has, if anything, tended to decrease with the introduction of modern forms of energy. Electricity, oil and gas are now extremely flexible and in most developed countries nationwide grid systems have been built to carry the energy to the consumer. There are exceptions to this general rule, however. Of these, the aluminium industry is by far the most important.

Aluminium

After iron and steel, aluminium is the most widely used metal in the world today. It is usually obtained from the mineral bauxite. There are two stages in its production, each of which shows a different pattern of location.

a Bauxite→Alumina

Aluminium is one of the most common elements in the rocks of the earth's crust. Unfortunately it occurs only as a compound and in most of its forms it is difficult to extract. It is most accessible when it is found in a hydrated form known as bauxite.

Bauxite is formed when rocks which are rich in aluminium are weathered very rapidly. This causes them to decompose, forming a soft claylike deposit in which the aluminium is concentrated. Weathering on this scale occurs mainly in the tropics and it is here that most of the major deposits are found (Fig. 6.43).

WORLD BAUXITE RESERVES (Total 25 billion tonnes)

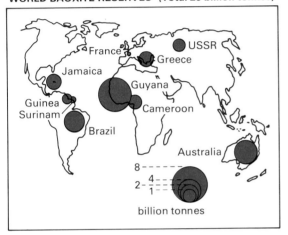

Fig. 6.43

Fig. 6.44 *Bauxite mine, Jamaica*

JAMAICA: BAUXITE MINING

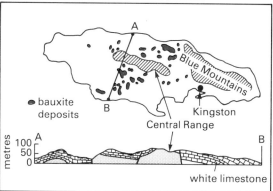

Fig. 6.45

BAUXITE: WORLD PRODUCTION
(total: 76 million tonnes)

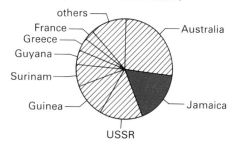

Fig. 6.46

Using the information given in this section, answer the following.

a i List the countries with large reserves of bauxite, arranging them in order of importance.
 ii List the leading producers of bauxite, arranging them in order of importance.
 iii Refer to the diagram, Fig. 6.25, and estimate the 'life' of the known reserves of bauxite.
 iv Which of the present leading producers of bauxite are likely to exhaust their reserves most rapidly?
 v Which countries are likely to be the leading producers of bauxite in the future?
b i Jamaica (Fig. 6.45) is the *first/second/fifth* largest producer in the world.
 ii What is Jamaica's position in terms of reserves?
 iii Jamaica will remain a major producer of bauxite for *less than 25 years/25–50 years/50–100 years/more than 100 years*.
 iv The bauxite in Jamaica was formed by the weathering of which rock?
 v It occurs *over large areas/in small pockets*.
 vi What methods are used to mine the bauxite?

Because bauxite is a soft rock, mining is comparatively easy and large open pits have been dug. The aluminium content of the ore is rarely more than 50% and, to save transport costs, the initial processing is carried out near to the pits. The simple process of crushing and washing the rock removes a large proportion of the clay content. The remaining purified bauxite is then dried and pulverised before it is treated with a hot caustic soda solution. This causes the alumina in the rock to dissolve, leaving behind impurities as a red mud. Pure alumina can then be obtained from the solution. On average, 4–5 tonnes of bauxite are needed to produce 2 tonnes of alumina, the raw material from which aluminium is made. In other words the industry is a 'bulk reducing industry' and this explains the pattern of its location (which is, of course, characteristic of some of the industries already described).

b   Alumina→Aluminium

Aluminium is obtained by melting alumina (Fig. 6.47b) and the location of this industry shows a very different pattern from that described above.

Compare the list of the world's leading aluminium producers with the map of world bauxite reserves, Fig. 6.43, on page 167.

a i Which major aluminium producers also have reserves of bauxite?
 ii Which aluminium producing countries will depend upon imported alumina?
 iii Why is alumina imported rather than bauxite?

WORLD ALUMINIUM PRODUCTION

	Aluminium production ('000 tonnes)	Per capita GNP ($)	Per capita energy consumption (kg coal equivalent)
USA	3925	12820	10204
USSR	1267	4750	5738
Japan	1015	10080	3575
Canada	816	11400	10070
W. Germany	698	12419	5450
France	395	10720	5110
UK	312	9110	4641
World	12657	–	–

It is obvious that aluminium production is concentrated among the richest countries of the Developed World. These countries are the largest consumers of the metal and, even more important, they have the largest electricity supply industries in the world. This is the major influence on the location of the aluminium smelting industry. Unlike most other metals, aluminium cannot be obtained directly from its basic raw material, alumina – even when that raw material has already been purified and concentrated. Instead the alumina has to be melted in a small electric furnace which has a thick lining of carbon. A carbon anode is dipped into the furnace and a heavy charge of electricity is then passed through the molten solution. This causes the main impurity (oxygen) to be attracted to the anode where it

Fig. 6.47 (a) *Aluminium works, UK*

ALUMINIUM: PRODUCTION AND USES

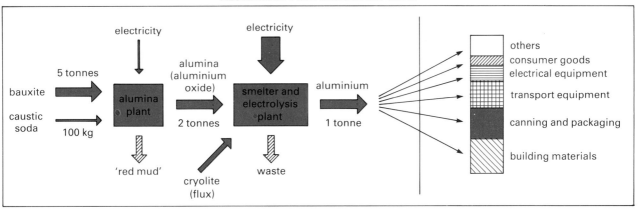

Fig. 6.47 (b)

USA: ALUMINIUM INDUSTRY

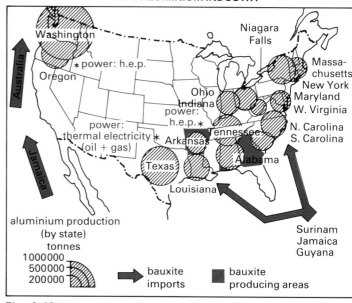

Fig. 6.48

USA ALUMINIUM INDUSTRY: COMPARATIVE COSTS

	Washington	Texas	Tennessee
Alumina	113	100	103
Electricity	100	158	176
Labour	141	138	100
Carbon	117	100	104
Transport (to markets)	137	136	100
Total	100	101	107
Electricity as a percentage of total cost	22	35	39

Note: each cost is expressed as a percentage of that found in the cheapest area

is burnt off while the pure metal settles to the bottom of the furnace. The use of electrolysis to purify the metal means that electricity costs are very high and it is not surprising that the industry tends to be located in countries which produce large amounts of electricity.

Even more striking is the influence that the availability of electricity has on the location of the aluminium industry within these countries. In almost every case smelting takes place in areas which produce a surplus of electricity. This can be seen most clearly in the United States (Fig. 6.48), where the centres of production have changed with the changing pattern of electricity supply.

Refer to Fig. 6.48 which gives information about the aluminium smelting industry in the United States.

a The first major centre of production was at Niagara. Give one reason for the choice of this location.

b In the 1930s new smelters were built in the Tennessee Valley. What were the advantages of this location?

c i Both these early locations depended upon the same source of energy. Name it.

 ii The Tennessee Valley is still important even though the costs of energy today are much higher. What are the other advantages of this area?

d i Name the source of energy available in the North West.

 ii What are the disadvantages of the region when compared with the other areas shown on the map?

e Why has the area near the coast of the Gulf of Mexico emerged as a major producing area since 1945?

Since the industry was established in the United States it has relocated several times. In each case it has moved to areas producing cheap electricity – usually hydro-electricity. This single requirement has overshadowed all other locational factors, including access to raw materials or nearness to markets. In fact the aluminium is moved great distances to the main industrial centres where it is made into finished products.

Market based industries

In recent years there has been a strong tendency for industries to locate near to markets. Such locations usually guarantee certain basic requirements such as labour, energy, water supply and the easy distribution of finished products. This is particularly important for industries which produce a range of products or which supply semi-finished goods to a wide range of industries.

Petro-chemicals

The petro-chemical industry is one of the most complex in the world (see Fig. 6.49) and the pattern of location of both individual factories and of the industry as a whole is difficult to understand.

The basic raw material of the industry is oil. However, the main centres of production are often located at great distances from the major oil producing regions. This is mainly because the industry depends not upon crude oil but upon naphtha, one of the products of the oil refining process. As we have already seen, it is usual for oil refineries to be located near to the major markets and for the oil to be transported to them in a crude form. It is not surprising, therefore, that the petro-chemical industry tends to follow a similar pattern of location, or that factories are often built near to the refineries. In addition, the petro-chemical industry produces materials such as nylon and plastics which are used in a variety of other industries. Locations within easy reach of these industries will be preferred.

Such factors combine to make the petro-chemical industry a good example of an industry which, in its location, has been strongly influenced by access to markets. This emerges quite clearly from a more detailed study of a single petro-chemical complex – the ICI plant at Rozenburg in the Netherlands.

ICI is a British-based multi-national company. It was formed in 1926 when four major chemical manufacturing companies joined together. Since then it has developed its interests to cover the full range of chemical products including petro-chemical feedstocks, fertilisers, artificial fibres, paints, plastics and pharmaceuticals. In 1961 the decision was taken to build a new plant in Europe, and a site at Rozenburg, near the recently established Europoort, was chosen. There were many reasons for making this choice:

1   At the time Britain was not a member of the EEC and by building a manufacturing plant in the Netherlands products could be sold in Europe without paying high import duties.

2   The site chosen was in one of the most densely populated parts of Europe with many industries which would provide markets for the products of the new plant.

3   Transport links between Rozenburg and the rest of Western Europe were good, both along the Rhine Waterway (see page 209) and via the road and rail networks.

4   A deep water harbour could be built to serve the plant and to allow raw materials to be imported from oil refineries in Britain (Fig. 6.50). The sand excavated to form the dock was used to raise the site of the factory above the level of flood waters.

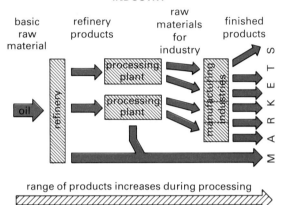

BASIC PROCESSES IN THE PETROCHEMICAL INDUSTRY

Fig. 6.49

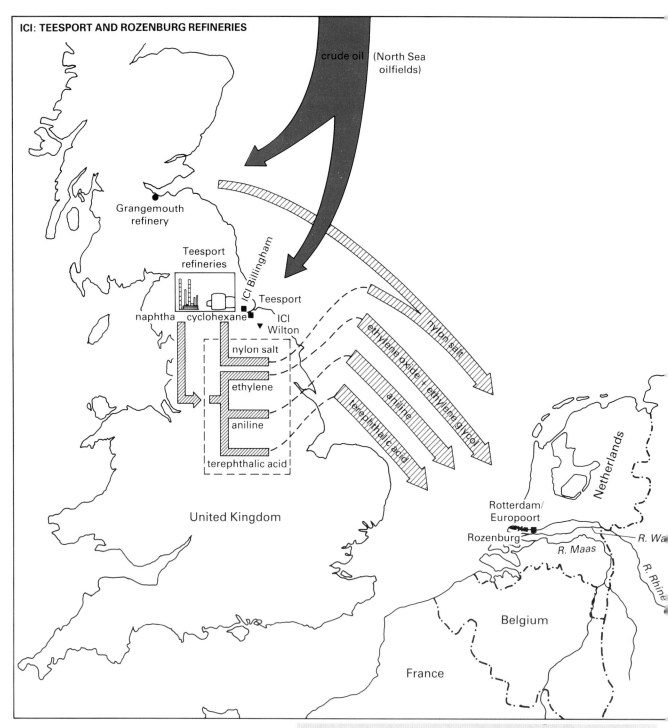

ICI: TEESPORT AND ROZENBURG REFINERIES

crude oil (North Sea oilfields)

Grangemouth refinery

Teesport refineries

ICI Billingham

Teesport

naphtha   cyclohexane

ICI Wilton

nylon salt

ethylene

aniline

terephthalic acid

nylon salt

ethylene oxide + ethylene glycol

aniline

terephthalic acid

United Kingdom

Netherlands

Rotterdam/ Europoort

Rozenburg

R. Wa

R. Maas

R. Rhine

Belgium

France

Fig. 6.50 (a)

Using information given in this section, complete the following exercise.

a   Name the dock which was built to serve the Rozenburg plant.

b i   Name the four major raw materials used at the works and in each case state where they are obtained from.

    ii   Each of these materials is obtained from a basic raw material. Name it and explain how it is produced (see page 124).

c i   What are the main products of the Rozenburg works?

    ii   In which industries are they used?

    iii   Where are these industries located?

West Germany

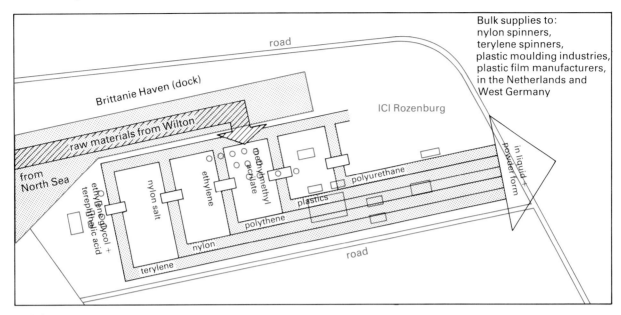

Bulk supplies to:
nylon spinners,
terylene spinners,
plastic moulding industries,
plastic film manufacturers,
in the Netherlands and
West Germany

Brittanie Haven (dock)

raw materials from Wilton

ICI Rozenburg

road

road

from
North Sea

in liquid +
powder form

nylon salt

ethylene

(dimethyl
terephthalate)

ethylene
glycol +
terephthalic acid

polythene

plastics

polyurethane

nylon

terylene

Fig. 6.50 (b)

Fig. 6.51 *ICI, Rozenburg chemical plant*

The Rozenburg chemical plant (Fig. 6.51) offers a classic example of a location strongly influenced by access to markets. A single basic raw material – naphtha – is gradually broken down into a large number of semi-processed raw materials, each of which requires special handling and is destined for a particular market for further processing or manufacture. Given these circumstances it is not surprising that, as in the oil refining industry itself, materials are transported over long distances before processing (e.g. as crude oil, naphtha or ethylene) or that the major processing plants have been established at locations which give easy access to markets. This reduces the expense of transporting each of the many products from the works to their markets.

A similar pattern can be seen in the worldwide distribution of the petro-chemical industry. This is clear even from the activities of a single large company like ICI. A vast range of products is manufactured, many of them based on oil. These are sold throughout the world but the main markets are still in the highly developed industrialised countries and it is here that the largest manufacturing plants are located.

Factors other than access to markets have influenced this pattern of location:

1 A large amount of capital is needed to build a modern petro-chemical plant. This is most readily available in the Developed World.

2 The labour force employed at such a works is very small. As a result little advantage can be taken of the low wage rates paid in most of the less developed countries.

3 The petro-chemical industry was one of the first high technology industries of the twentieth century. The skills required to establish such an industry were only available in the industrialised countries.

In recent years this pattern has started to break down. Demand for petro-chemical products – particularly fertilisers and fibres – has increased in the developing countries, thus producing a larger market there. Even more important, some of the oil producing countries have decided to use part of their oil revenues to establish new industries, including large oil refineries and petro-chemical plants.

FLOW DIAGRAM: ASSEMBLY INDUSTRY

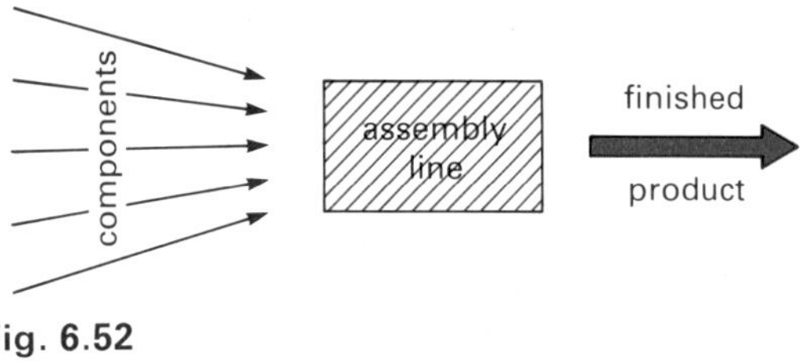

Fig. 6.52

Assembly industries

Many modern industries depend upon a large number of raw materials and components. These are brought to a single location for assembly (Fig. 6.52). The location of such industries – often called assembly industries – can be extremely complicated. This emerges from a study of two industries – shipbuilding and the motor car industry.

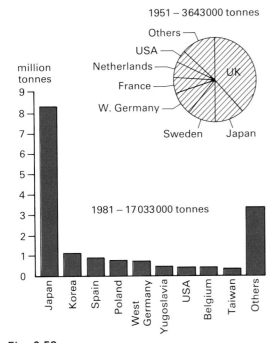

WORLD SHIPBUILDING OUTPUT, 1951 AND 1981 (BY COUNTRY)

Fig. 6.53

Shipbuilding

One of the oldest assembly industries, the shipbuilding industry clearly illustrates the changes in location which have taken place over a period of more than 300 years. In the days of wooden ships the location of the industry was comparatively simple. Because ships were very small they could be built at any location which possessed sheltered waters and easy access to suitable timber. Such locations were plentiful and the industry became widespread.

With the introduction of iron ships during the second half of the nineteenth century a dramatic change in the pattern of location took place. The industry was still tied to coastal sites but it was now attracted to locations near to major iron producing regions. It was during this period that the River Clyde in Scotland and the rivers of North Eastern England began to dominate the world's shipbuilding industry. At the same time the industry became a true assembly industry with a large number of small industries supplying parts which were assembled at the main shipyard.

This type of location and this pattern of production remained virtually unchanged until the 1950s when a new type of industry appeared – an industry which was the product of a rapidly changing world situation.

1   The volume of world trade increased enormously after the Second World War and demand for new ships was high.

2   New types of ships had been designed to carry special rather than general cargoes, e.g. oil tankers and bulk ore and grain carriers.

3   New methods of construction had been developed which allowed much bigger ships to be built. In 1950 most general cargo vessels were under 20 000 tonnes. By the early 1970s there were oil tankers which were approaching 500 000 tonnes. The basis of this change was the introduction of pre-fabrication techniques, i.e. the building of large sections which could be assembled at a later date and in a different part of the yard.

The leading shipbuilding countries were slow to respond to these changes and they were faced by a growing challenge from other countries (Fig. 6.53). The most important of these challengers was Japan.

The shipbuilding industry in Japan

By 1980 the Japanese shipbuilding industry completely overshadowed those of other countries. Of the orders placed in that year no less than 49% (in terms of tonnage) were placed with Japanese yards, and shipyards in other countries struggled to find work.

This successful modern industry is based on an earlier industry which was similar to those found in Western Europe and the United States. Its pattern of location (Fig. 6.54) was also very similar, with the major shipyards located near to the steel producing regions. A large part of this industry was destroyed during the Second World War but, as with steelmaking, when the industry was rebuilt similar locations were chosen. The rapid growth of the industry, together with the need to build larger

SHIPBUILDING IN JAPAN

		Number	Employees
1	Companies producing ships of over 10 000 tonnes	42	184 000
2	Component supplies	4000	137 000
3	Steel makes up 25% of the industry's total cost		
4	The industry uses 35% of the heavy steel produced in Japan		

175

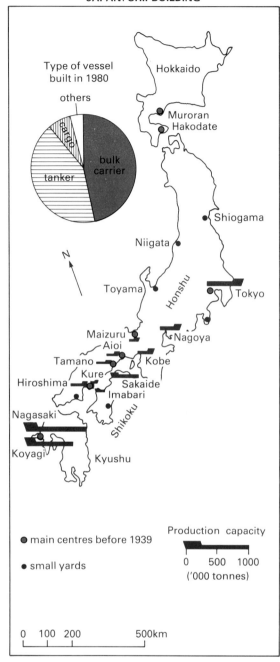

JAPAN: SHIPBUILDING

Type of vessel built in 1980

- bulk carrier
- tanker
- cargo
- others

Hokkaido

Muroran
Hakodate

Shiogama

Niigata

Toyama

Tokyo

Maizuru
Aioi
Tamano
Kure
Hiroshima
Sakaide
Imabari
Kobe
Nagoya

Honshu

Shikoku

Nagasaki

Koyagi

Kyushu

- ● main centres before 1939
- ● small yards

Production capacity

0   500   1000
('000 tonnes)

0   100   200   500km

Fig. 6.54

ships, led to a search for new sites and after 1950 a new pattern of location began to emerge.

Using information given in this section, answer the following.

a   i   Name two early centres of shipbuilding which are no longer of major importance.
    ii   Why did the industry develop at such locations?
    iii   Name two early centres which are still important.
b   i   Where are the largest shipbuilding centres located today?
    ii   Study the photograph, Fig. 6.56, and describe the type of site needed for a modern shipyard.
    iii   Why are such sites unlikely to be found near to the early shipbuilding centres?
    iv   What are the disadvantages of these new locations?

Competition for land was intense around Tokyo Bay and on the mainland coast of the Inland Sea. The shipbuilding industry was forced to look for sites in less accessible areas. Two areas in particular became important – the islands of Shikoku and Kyushu. Both offered the space needed for modern shipyards and had the additional advantages of a position in the south of Japan. Here the climate was warm enough to allow a large proportion of the assembly work to take place out of doors. This reduced the need for expensive buildings and helped to keep down the costs of establishing the industry. At the same time the new locations were far from both the suppliers of steel and the existing shipbuilding areas. As a result the industry faced relatively high costs in transporting steel and in encouraging the movement of skilled labour to the new yards. Even more important, the shipbuilding industry, being an assembly industry, depends upon a large number of subsidiary industries which supply components to the yards. At first these industries were located far from the new yards and components were transported from the older industrial areas. Eventually, however, some of these industries moved to locations near to the new yards and this reduced costs.

The shipbuilding industry is a comparatively simple assembly industry (Fig. 6.55) and its pattern of location is easier to understand than that of most modern industries. It is, for example, heavily dependent upon a single raw material – steel, and it is tied to coastal or riverside locations. As a result the choice of location for a modern shipyard would appear to be very simple. In fact, as the Japanese industry clearly shows, the most obvious locations are not always available and the most modern ship-

MATERIALS FLOW IN A MODERN SHIPYARD

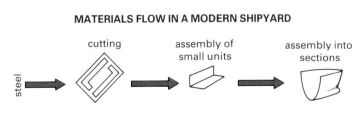

steel → cutting → assembly of small units → assembly into sections

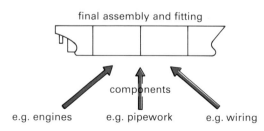

final assembly and fitting

components

e.g. engines   e.g. pipework   e.g. wiring

Fig. 6.55

Fig. 6.56 *Shipyard in Japan*

yards have been built in comparatively remote areas where transport costs for raw materials are high but where there is space for building and water deep enough to launch the largest modern vessels.

Because shipbuilding is a comparatively simple industry which requires a large labour force and makes use of little advanced technology, it has attracted the interest of countries in the Developing World. Here labour costs are low and if there is a local steel industry ships can be produced as cheaply as in Japan. Less developed countries such as Korea and Brazil are emerging as major shipbuilding nations. The highly industrialised countries outside Japan can compete only in the building of warships with complex weapons systems.

The motor industry

The motor industry is the largest single industry in the world today apart from basic industries such as iron and steel and oil production. It consumes a greater proportion of the world's resources such as metals and oil based products than any other industry. It is of course a twentieth century industry – large scale production of motor vehicles did not begin until just before the outbreak of the First World War in 1914 – and it became established in the highly developed industrialised countries. These countries still dominate the industry (Fig. 6.57) although in recent years, as with shipbuilding, there has been a tendency for factories to be built in less developed countries where production costs are lower.

The industry started as a branch of the engineering industry in Britain, Europe and the United States. As such it showed a similar pattern of location. For example, it was found:

WORLD MOTOR VEHICLE PRODUCTION IN 1982

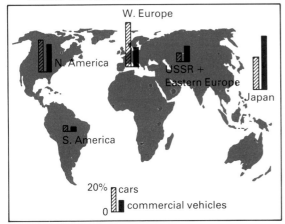

Fig. 6.57

MOTOR MANUFACTURING: AN ASSEMBLY INDUSTRY

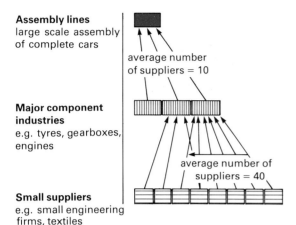

Assembly lines
large scale assembly of complete cars

average number of suppliers = 10

Major component industries
e.g. tyres, gearboxes, engines

average number of suppliers = 40

Small suppliers
e.g. small engineering firms, textiles

Fig. 6.58

1 In existing industrial areas which provided a skilled labour force.

2 Near to major centres of population which were to be the main markets for cars.

3 Near to major steel producing centres.

It was during this period that many of the present centres of production emerged, e.g. the Great Lakes region of the United States, the lower Rhine Valley in Germany, the Midlands of England and, at a slightly later date, the Tokyo region of Japan.

This simple pattern of location quickly began to break down. In the first instance this was because the industry itself changed from a skilled engineering industry producing individual cars to an assembly line industry (Fig. 6.58) using methods of mass production. Such an industry, depending as it did upon a large number of component industries and needing to maintain access to mass markets, began to display a much more complicated pattern of location. This in turn became even more difficult to understand when the industry was taken over by a small number of giant companies such as General Motors, Ford, Toyota and Volkswagon. Most of these companies became multi-nationals, i.e. they operated in many different countries throughout the world and this has had a strong influence on the development of the motor industry.

This is best understood by looking at one of these companies – General Motors, the largest producer of motor vehicles in the world.

General Motors

In 1981 General Motors produced nearly five million motor vehicles. It employed more than half a million people in 24 different countries and had interests which extended far beyond the motor industry. This makes General Motors one of the largest companies in the world.

General Motors started as a small car producing company in the United States before the outbreak of the First World War. From 1916 onwards it began to acquire other motor manufacturing companies including Oldsmobile, Cadillac, Buick and Chevrolet. Within ten years it had taken control of overseas factories in Denmark, the United Kingdom and Germany.

In spite of this rapid expansion the company remained firmly based in Detroit, the motor manufacturing centre of the United States. Here it competed with the other giant American motor manufacturers, Ford and Chrysler, who also owned numerous factories in the area.

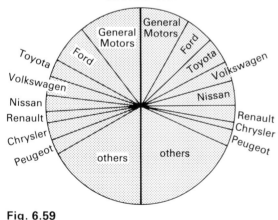

WORLD MOTOR INDUSTRY OUTPUT BY FIRM, 1973 AND 1981

Toyota
Ford
General Motors
General Motors
Ford
Toyota
Volkswagen
Volkswagen
Nissan
Nissan
Renault
Renault
Chrysler
Chrysler
Peugeot
Peugeot
others
others

Fig. 6.59

Using the information in this section, answer the following exercise.

a Give the advantages of the Detroit area as a motor manufacturing centre: (i) in relation to basic raw materials (ii) in terms of access to the American market.

b What is meant by an assembly industry?

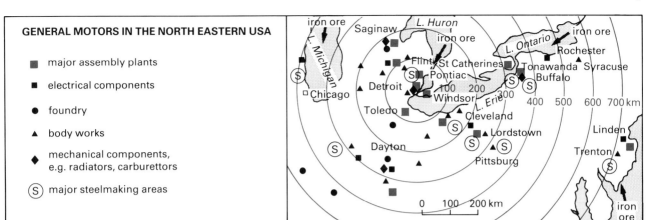

Fig. 6.60

c i Using the assembly plants at Flint and Buffalo, work out the minimum distance which the following materials are likely to be transported: radiators, car bodies, electrical equipment. (If they are produced in the area state that they are local.)

ii Which location is most efficient in terms of access to these materials?

iii Give advantages possessed by the other location.

Some impression of the complexity of the modern motor industry in the United States can be obtained from the map, Fig. 6.60. This shows that the old established car producing centres have remained important, particularly those near to the Great Lakes. At the same time new plants have been built, often at considerable distances from Detroit. In every case, however, communications with component suppliers are good.

This pattern became even more complicated when component factories were reorganised to produce a limited range of products. As a result, old established assembly plants often found themselves dependent upon new component industries, many of them a great distance away. Such a development was made possible only by an improvement in transport. This allowed the large scale movement of components both within the Detroit region and to assembly plants in other parts of the United States.

The oil price rises of the 1970s caused great changes in the motor manufacturing industry. This was particularly true in the United States where cars were large and tended to use large amounts of fuel. The American manufacturers lost a large proportion of the market to smaller cars from Japan and Europe (see Fig. 6.59). The industry was forced to develop cars which could compete with the Japanese models both in price and in fuel consumption. As part of this campaign General Motors planned a 'world car' which would be built by its subsidiary companies throughout the world.

As we have seen, General Motors had been a multi-national company for more than 50 years. For the greater part of this period, however, subsidiary companies were allowed to operate independently, producing their own models often for a compara-

GENERAL MOTORS: WORLDWIDE OPERATIONS

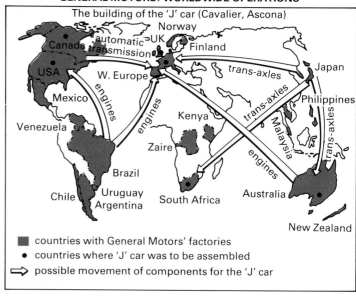

Fig. 6.61

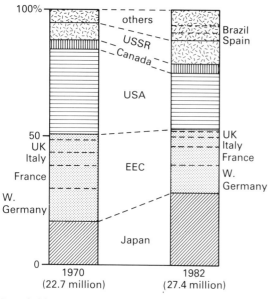

Fig. 6.62

tively small market. This policy was changed in response to the changes which were taking place in the world's motor manufacturing industry:

1　Petrol prices had risen enormously and this had caused the growth in car sales in the world to slow down.

2　The Japanese motor industry proved to be highly efficient and it continued to grow. As a result Japanese companies were taking an ever increasing share of the world market (including the vast USA market which had been the basis of General Motors' prosperity).

3　To compete with the Japanese, General Motors decided to produce a single type of car at its factories throughout the world. This car was to be suitable for distribution in different forms. Assembly of completed cars would take place in many countries but individual plants would be expected to concentrate on the production of a small range of parts. This specialisation was designed to give production on a scale large enough to reduce the cost of components to the levels found in Japan.

4　The plan required the large scale transport of materials over great distances (Fig. 6.61). This had become possible only with the development of new forms of freight transport, particularly container trains and ships.

The costs of such a development were enormous (estimated at five billion dollars) but the car quickly won an increased share of the world market for General Motors. It is possible, therefore, that more worldwide projects will be planned by multi-national companies. If this happens it is probable that our ideas about the location of industry will have to change.

At the same time, it is important to remember that the most successful motor manufacturing industry in the world today is in Japan and that its pattern of location is very much simpler.

JAPAN: MOTOR VEHICLE INDUSTRY

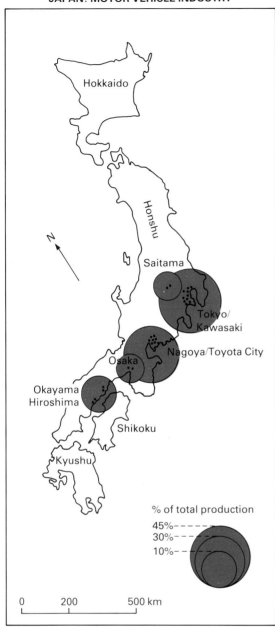

Fig. 6.63

Motor manufacturing in Japan

Refer to the map of the motor vehicle industry in Japan.

a i Name four of the major motor vehicle manufacturing centres in Japan.
  ii Arrange them in order of output.
b Compare the pattern of distribution with that shown for steel and for shipbuilding (pages 164 and 176).

Two regions do in fact dominate the Japanese motor industry – the Keihin region (around Tokyo) and Chukyo (around Nagoya). Together these two regions produce three quarters of the motor vehicles made in Japan (see Fig. 6.63). They are the oldest motor manufacturing centres in the country, the original factories dating back to the 1930s. Since the establishment of the first works, however, the location of the industry within the regions has shown a marked change.

1 Keihin – Nissan built the first assembly plant here and the industry became located on the southern outskirts of Tokyo. It remained here until the early 1960s when the rapid expansion of the industry led to the building of vast new factories. These required so much room that they had to be built in the countryside outside the city. The component industries were slower to respond to these changes and the majority are still located in south Tokyo.

2 Chukyo – the industry here is dominated by a single company, Toyota. A large works was built in 1938 in what is now called Toyota City and even today the company employs 90% of the working population of the town. Other manufacturers were attracted to the area at a later date and Nagoya has become a major centre of the motor vehicle industry. Once again, however, modern factories have been built on the outskirts of the large cities while the smaller component industries have often remained in their original locations.

This pattern of location reflects that of Japanese industry as a whole. In Japan, as in most other countries, there is a strong tendency for industry to become concentrated in certain well defined regions, e.g. the shores of Tokyo Bay, Nagoya and the coastlands bordering the Inland sea. The motor industry was attracted to these regions because there was a large population, a strong industrial base and a coastal situation which gave easy access to the export markets (upon which the industry came to depend).

Industrial regions

The concentration and dispersal of industry

In most developed countries industries show a marked tendency to group together to form distinct industrial regions. This was first seen on a large scale on the coalfields of Britain and is now to be seen in places as far apart as the New York region of the United States, Tokyo Bay in Japan and the lower Rhine Valley in West Germany and the Netherlands. Here the scale of concentration of industry is enormous and it raises the question of why so many industries choose to be so close together.

The early concentration of industries on coalfields can easily be explained in terms of access to fuel and basic raw materials such as iron ore. Later growth is more difficult to explain, particularly when some of the modern industrial regions (Fig. 6.64) are far from coalfields and when the variety of industries is so great. This suggests that the advantages of different industries locating close together extend far beyond the availability of raw materials.

The advantages of industrial concentration include:

1   The fact that industries already exist in an area means that there is likely to be a relatively skilled labour force available.

2   The existence of this labour force means that there may be a market for the products of a new factory.

3   Any industry has certain basic requirements, e.g. communications, finance etc. These are more likely to be available in an existing industrial area.

4   Existing industries may also provide components for a new industry.

While forces such as these are working to draw new industries into existing industrial regions, equally strong forces are making other industries move away from these areas.

Part of the West Midlands industrial conurbation

The disadvantages of industrial concentration include:

1   Congestion is a serious problem in most industrial areas. This reduces the efficiency with which products and materials can be moved which, in turn, increases the costs of production.

2   Space for development also tends to be limited. This is important at a time when many industries are trying to achieve economies of scale by building large factories. As a result many major industries have been forced to locate outside existing industrial regions.

3   Even when land is available it tends to be very expensive.

4   Because so many industries are located so close together living conditions for the workforce are often poor. This has encouraged companies to look for locations outside the existing industrial areas.

5   Governments sometimes encourage companies to build factories outside existing industrial areas.

The locations of many of the traditional industries can be explained in terms of combinations of various locational factors. The most important factors appear to be the costs of gaining access to raw materials and to markets, the availability of labour, the availability and cost of power and the cost of land. Given these factors, the ideal location for any industry should be at a place where costs are lowest. This is known as a 'least cost location' and it is this type of location which was taken up by many of the old established industries in the world. But, as we have seen, such simple patterns have tended to break down. For example, some industries have been slow to respond to changes in the pattern of costs and have remained on sites which are no longer ideal. Such cases of 'industrial inertia' are particularly common in countries like the United Kingdom which have a long history of industrial development.

Another development which has distorted patterns of industrial location is the tendency for governments to try to influence the decisions taken by industrial companies. In the Developed World this has been seen largely in attempts to support declining industries such as steelmaking and shipbuilding or to offer incentives to companies to locate factories in areas of declining industries and high unemployment. In less developed countries governments have encouraged the establishment of industries which are felt to be important, almost regardless of cost.

There is also strong evidence that the location of modern industries, particularly high technology industries, cannot be explained in simple terms. The electronics industry of the United States is a case in point.

WORLD INDUSTRIAL REGIONS

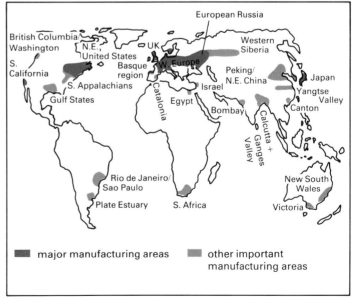

Fig. 6.64

The location of a high technology industry: the electronics industry in the USA

FACTORS INFLUENCING THE LOCATION OF THE ELECTRONICS INDUSTRY IN THE USA

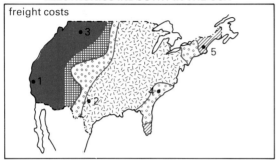

freight costs

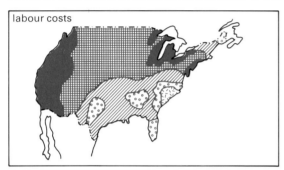

labour costs

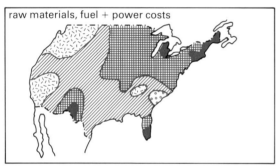

raw materials, fuel + power costs

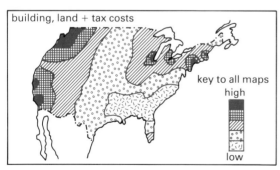

building, land + tax costs

key to all maps
high
low

Fig. 6.65

Imagine that you are about to locate an electronics factory somewhere in the United States. Five possible locations (1–5 on the maps in Fig. 6.65) have been suggested.

a Using information in Fig. 6.65, select the best location and (i) explain why you have chosen this location (ii) describe the advantages and disadvantages of the locations you have rejected.

b The following is a breakdown of the estimated production costs at the factory when it is built: labour 90%; raw materials, fuel and power 5%; freight (transport) 3%; land and taxes 1%.
  i Given this information, now select the best location for the factory.
  ii Explain why you have made this choice.

c Compare each of your choices (or the single choice if you did not change location) with the map, Fig. 6.67, which shows the distribution of the electronics industry in the United States. Can you give any reasons for the pattern of location shown here?

It is obvious that the locations favoured by the electronics industry in the United States are not least cost locations. In fact the two major centres, in California and on the North Eastern Seaboard around New York (Fig. 6.67), are among the most expensive possible locations (the true least cost location would be in the South East, probably in South Carolina). This suggests that other factors have influenced the location of the industry. For example:

1 The amounts of raw material used (silicon chips, wire cables, metal parts) are small and can be easily transported.

2 The finished products are very valuable and are of little bulk. They can be transported long distances to the markets.

3 Labour supply is obviously the most important single factor but the electronics industry is not simply concerned with the cost of labour. Of more importance is its quality and the industry requires a highly skilled labour force. This is available from universities and research centres, most of which are located in the existing centres of population. It is this more than anything else which encouraged the development of the industry in its present high cost locations.

Under these circumstances the influence of traditional location factors is comparatively small and industries like the electronics industry can be established at almost any location. For this reason they are known as 'footloose' industries. In recent years,

184

Fig. 6.66 *Silicon Valley, California, USA*

LOCATIONS OF THE ELECTRONICS INDUSTRY IN THE USA

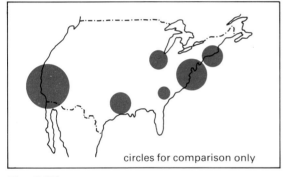

circles for comparison only

Fig. 6.67

as the problems of the great cities have increased, there has been a tendency for such industries to find locations in small towns and even rural areas which offer a pleasanter life style for the employees. In the United States one such location has been in the south eastern states – the area which was, and still is, the ideal least cost location for the industry. There has also been a tendency for manufacturing plants to be established abroad in areas of low labour costs (e.g. Taiwan), while research and development continues in the United States.

Industry in the less developed countries

One of the most obvious and important facts to emerge from any study of world industry is the enormous contrast in industrialisation between the developed and the less developed countries. In fact one of the features which most clearly identifies the less developed countries is their low level of industrial development and therefore low levels of employment in industry. This division remains, in spite of attempts by the developing countries to establish new industries.

Many of the less developed countries were once colonies. They were developed to supply raw materials to the colonising countries, most of which were in Western Europe. At the same time the colonies were expected to provide markets for manufactured goods produced by the colonising countries. This pattern of trade tended to undermine industries in the colonies which could not compete with the larger and more efficient producers in the Developed World. These colonial industries were mostly very

185

Fig. 6.68 *Footwear factories in Cawnpore, India: typical of industrial development during colonial times (Photograph by Deane Dickason from Ewing Galloway, NY)*

small, serving only local areas, but some, e.g. the textile industry in India, were large enough to export goods to other countries.

By 1850, however, some businessmen were finding it more profitable to set up factories in the colonies so that raw materials could be processed before they were exported to Europe and the United States. Once again it was the textile industry which led in this development, and cotton and jute mills were established throughout the Indian sub-continent. Other industries quickly followed and this type of industrial development continued throughout the colonial period. In almost every case large scale methods of production were used, similar to those used in developed countries. This meant that machines and the skilled labour to use them had to be imported. The sugar refining industry is typical of these colonial industries.

Fig. 6.69 *Small scale sugar refining, India*

Early industries in the Developing World

Sugar refining: Lucknow, India

Sugar cane was one of the first crops introduced by Europeans to their colonies in the tropics. It was grown on large plantations in colonies as far apart as Brazil and the East Indies (see page 69). Because the cane has to be processed within 24 hours of cutting (otherwise the sugar content is greatly reduced), simple refineries were built on the plantations.

In India sugar cane was grown in many areas, usually on small farms. Processing was very simple:

1 The cane was chopped and crushed to produce juice.

2 The juice was then heated in an open pan (Fig. 6.69) so that the liquid was evaporated, leaving behind sugar. The sugar produced by this method bears little resemblance to the sugar used in most parts of the Developed World today.

The first modern sugar mills were built in India during the 1920s. A decision by the government to protect the industry led to more mills being opened. This growth continued when India became independent in 1947 and today there are more than 220 mills, producing four and a quarter million tonnes of sugar per year.

Whenever a new mill was built the most up to date technology was used. At first this involved importing most of the equipment needed. Later most of this equipment was made in India. These mills were as large as those in developed countries and a large amount of sugar cane was needed to keep them going.

The Lucknow mill is typical of these large modern refineries.

SUGAR PRODUCTION

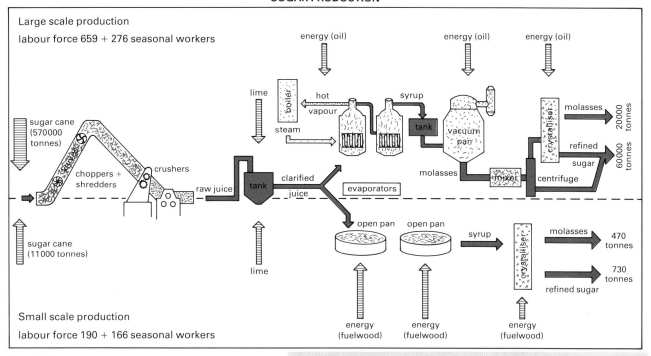

Fig. 6.70

Using information given in this section, complete the following exercise.

a i Name three major raw materials, other than sugar cane, used in the refinery.
  ii In each case explain what they are used for.
b i How much sugar cane is processed at the mill?
  ii Why does the mill have to be located in an area which produces large amounts of sugar cane?
c Describe the main processes carried out at the mill.
d i How much refined white sugar is produced?
  ii List the other products of the refinery and for each give one important use.

The basic methods used in the mill are similar to those used in the most primitive refinery plant – only the scale and the detail of the operations are different (see Fig. 6.70).

Cane is crushed in large quantities – up to 4000 tonnes per day. Since this cane has to reach the mill within 24 hours of harvesting, a large proportion of the farmers within one day's journey of the mill have turned to sugar cane as a cash crop. This can cause problems since production tends to expand until there is a large surplus and the price of cane collapses. Farmers then suffer hardship and turn to other crops. Eventually the mill runs short of cane and the price once again increases. This causes production to increase and the problem repeats itself.

There are other problems which the mill owners have to cope with. Because all of the cane is grown within a short distance of the refinery, it is harvested within a comparatively short period of the year (December to June). This means that the mill is likely to stand idle for almost half the year – a serious problem when the cost of plant and machinery has been high.

187

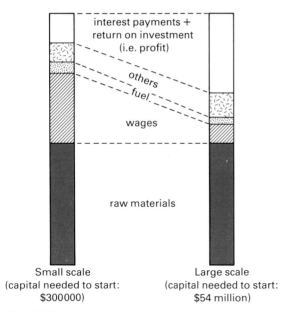

Fig. 6.71

Problems such as these have caused the Indian government to question the wisdom of building such large refineries and since 1960 a number of small sugar mills have been built. In these mills the crushing operation is the same as in the large refineries – only the scale is different (see Fig. 6.71). Once the juice has been produced, however, the methods used to produce refined sugar are very different. Instead of boiling the juice in large vats and separating the sugar crystals by means of expensive centrifuges, a simple system of open pans and filters is used. These can be manufactured locally and they can be used to process relatively small amounts of cane. This has many advantages over the large scale system:

1   A typical mill would operate on about 80 tonnes of cane per day. This can be obtained from the small farms in the surrounding area without dramatically changing the overall pattern of farming. As a result, food production increases and farmers do not become dependent upon a single cash crop.

2   Because the plant is cheaper to build and equip, it can work for a shorter period each year and still make a profit. This means that the seasonal labour supply is easier to organise and workers can even return to their farms at planting and harvesting time when labour is needed.

3   The mill uses more labour to produce a given amount of sugar. This is important in a country where unemployment is high and it does not harm the plant since wages are comparatively low.

4   The machinery is easier to operate and maintain. As a result breakdowns occur less frequently and the refinery is shut down for shorter periods.

There are also certain disadvantages:

1   The quality of the sugar produced is not as high.

2   More important, less sugar is obtained from the cane.

3   Because open pans are used, fuel costs are higher than in the large refinery.

These problems are typical of those faced by governments throughout the Developing World and the choice between plants using modern technology and those depending upon simpler, more labour intensive methods is far from easy, particularly if the industry is expected to make a profit.

Large scale industrial development in the Developing World

The sugar refining industry at Lucknow depends to a great extent upon locally produced raw materials. Such industries are called 'resource based' industries and it was industries of this type which were the first to be established in the developing countries.

Later a new type of industrial development was undertaken and the reasons for encouraging this were almost always the same. Most less developed countries, whether they were colonies or not, became dependent upon manufactured goods, most of which were imported from the Developed World. To reduce this dependence many less developed countries tended to establish industries which produced similar goods. This became particularly important after 1945 when former colonies began to achieve independence and when the cost of manufactured goods began to increase much more rapidly than the prices obtained for the food and raw materials upon which the developing countries depended.

In many cases industrial development was only possible if investment or even aid was made available by the countries of the Developed World (see page 217). This was to have important effects on the types of industry established. For example, most aid and investment was granted for large scale projects. As a result the governments of less developed countries were encouraged to establish the industries upon which the wealth of the developed nations appeared to be based, e.g. steel making and oil refining. Not only this, they were encouraged to build plants which were among the largest in the world and which often depended upon the most up to date technologies available (both of which brought great prestige to the governments concerned).

At first this approach appeared to have been successful. Within the space of 20 years Brazil, Mexico and India became major steel producers; in each case making use of raw materials produced within the country (see page 162). During the same period oil refining also became widespread, not only in oil producing countries but also in countries where oil imports were growing rapidly. Home refining industries, using bulk supplies of imported crude oil, could greatly reduce the cost of oil products. All too often, however, these industries did not provide the basis for further large scale industrial growth and most developing countries remained dependent upon a small number of resource based primary industries. An exception to this is the Chotanagpur district of Bihar state in North East India (Fig. 6.72). Here industrial development has taken place on a scale similar to that found in developed countries.

Chotanagpur: an industrial region in a developing country

During the period of British rule in India industrial development was slight. Railways had been built to give access to the coalfield at Jharia and to allow the working of other minerals such as copper at Ghatsila and bauxite at Muri. All of these developments were on a small scale and within the limits set by a relatively simple transport system.

In 1947 India became independent and the drive to develop new industries began. Chotanagpur was an obvious centre for such development. It possessed most of India's reserves of copper and uranium together with large deposits of coal, iron ore, bauxite, pyrites and industrial clays. There was also an existing railway system (Fig. 6.73) which could be extended to enable these minerals to be worked and to service any industries which might be established. This made the region an ideal location both for resource based industries and for modern heavy industries. It was a combination to be found in few developing countries and it encouraged the rapid growth of industry.

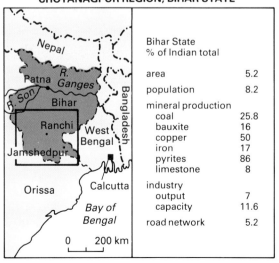

CHOTANAGPUR REGION, BIHAR STATE

Bihar State % of Indian total	
area	5.2
population	8.2
mineral production	
coal	25.8
bauxite	16
copper	50
iron	17
pyrites	86
limestone	8
industry	
output	7
capacity	11.6
road network	5.2

0   200 km

Fig. 6.72

BIHAR: INDUSTRIAL BASE

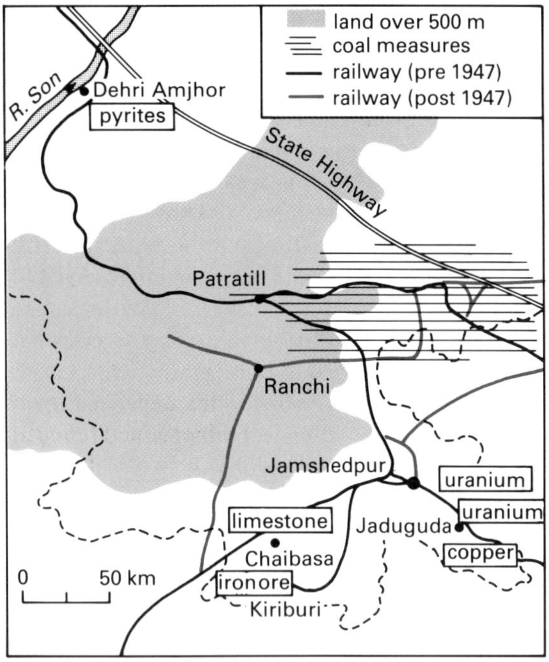

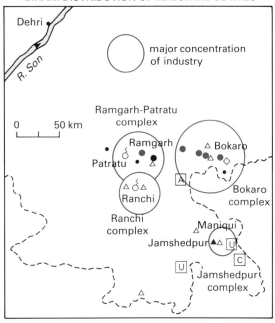

Fig. 6.73

BIHAR: DISTRIBUTION OF MAJOR INDUSTRIES

Industries (black – pre 1947) (brown – post 1947)

● coal + coke   A = aluminium   ◇ chemicals

▲ iron + steel   C = copper   △ engineering

□ non-ferrous   U = uranium   ♂ power station
   metals

                                   • other centres

Fig. 6.74

Using information given in Figs. 6.72–6.74, complete the following exercise.

a   Locate and name the main mineral deposits of the region.
b   Locate and name the main industrial complexes in the region.
   i   For each complex name the main industries located there.
   ii   For each industry state whether or not it is resource based.
   iii   In the case of the resource based industries state whether the raw materials are close at hand.
   iv   Give one other reason for the location of the main industrial centres.

Most of these developments have taken place on a large scale and it is obvious that several industries serve markets far beyond the boundaries of the state. As a result uranium, steel, cement and coal products are sent to other industrial areas in India and even exported, particularly to countries in the Far East and Middle East.

The effects of industrialisation have been considerable. Where groups of industries have developed to form industrial complexes (Fig. 6.74) the built-up areas have increased enormously. Living conditions in these industrial towns are poor, with severe overcrowding and serious pollution of the environment. Furthermore, this process of urbanisation is tending to spread to the more remote industrial centres, producing similar problems.

Fig. 6.75 *Steelworks at Jamshedpur, Bihar State, India*

Small scale industrial development in the Developing World

It has already been suggested that one of the main factors limiting the scale of industry in developing countries is the lack of an efficient system of transport. Large industrial plants usually serve large areas and this is not possible in many of the less developed countries. In recent years, however, other reasons have been put forward for questioning the widespread introduction of large scale modern industries into the Developing World. For example:

1   The cost of building is usually high.

2   Aid and investment is diverted from other worthwhile projects, particularly those concerned with the improvement of agriculture.

3   Modern production plants make use of expensive, complicated machines. These can only be obtained from countries in the Developed World and they need trained technicians to run them, most of whom will not be available in a developing country.

4   Maintenance is often difficult and many plants are closed down for long periods. This is important in view of the size and cost of the plant.

5   Even more important, modern machinery tends to reduce the number of workers needed in any factory. In most of the less developed countries unemployment is high and industries are needed which create jobs as well as wealth.

6   Many modern industrial plants produce goods of a quality not needed in most developing countries. A cheaper product of lower quality would often be more suitable.

For all of these reasons technology of this kind has been called 'inappropriate technology'.

In recent years many developing countries have tried to find industries which are better suited to their needs. On occasions this has simply involved investing in existing industries, particularly those serving relatively small rural areas. When it has been found necessary to establish new industries, however, every effort has been made to introduce smaller, less complicated plants which can be built in the country concerned and which are easy to maintain.

Small scale rural industries in China

One of the first of the less developed countries to adopt this approach was the People's Republic of China. There were many reasons why this alternative appeared attractive.

After the Communist take-over in 1949 China found it difficult to raise money for development projects. As a result there was an early interest in schemes which depended upon simple, easy-to-introduce technologies.

The 'Great Leap Forward', which started in 1958, was designed to transform China into a modern industrial power within the space of 20 years. Money was found to fund large scale industrial projects and, where necessary, technology was

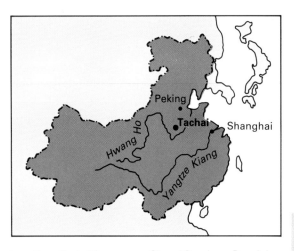

Location: Tachai Commune, Shansi Province, People's
Republic of China
Plant: Small scale cement works
Product: Portland cement
Works built: 1968
Raw materials: Coal, limestone, clay, iron ore
Output: 45000 tonnes

Fig. 6.76

imported. At the same time the entire country was organised into communes (see page 90) and encouragement was given to small self-help schemes including the establishment of local industries. Particular interest was taken in industries which helped to increase agricultural production, e.g. the production of fertilisers and agricultural machinery.

Ten years later this policy had changed. During the Cultural Revolution links with other countries were reduced and China increased its dependence on small scale industries. The Tachai cement factory is typical of the small industries established at that time.

Tachai cement plant: Hsi-Yang County, Shansi Province, China

The Tachai cement works (Fig. 6.76) was opened in 1968 and in its first year it produced 7000 tonnes of cement. Twelve years later production had reached 40 000 tonnes – still a small output by modern standards. During the same period the number of small cement works in China increased enormously and today more than half of the country's cement production comes from such works. One reason for this was the political decisions taken during the Cultural Revolution. Another reason was that most of the demand for cement is from rural communities, particularly those which are undertaking large scale flood control or irrigation projects. Such a demand is best met from small rural cement works like the Tachai plant.

Throughout this period of development four basic ideas were followed:

1 The technology used must be simple.
2 As much equipment as possible must be made locally.

TACHAI CEMENT PLANT

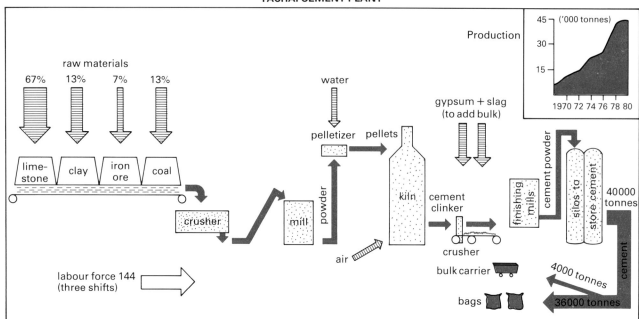

Fig. 6.77

Fig. 6.78 *Stacking bags of cement for shipment: cement works, China*

3 Local raw materials must be used.

4 Money for building and development must be raised locally.

It was these factors which determined the nature of the Tachai cement works.

Using information given in this section, complete the following exercise.

a List the raw materials used in the making of cement, arranging them in order of importance.

b i Describe the main processes used in the manufacture of cement.

   ii For which operations has it been necessary to buy in machinery?

c Why are gypsum and slag added to the cement?

d How is the cement transported to the markets?

e To what extent does the Tachai plant meet the requirements established by the government for small local industries?

Portland cement is made by fusing together, under heat, minerals containing calcium, silica, alumina and iron. In developed countries this is done on a vast scale and the industry is highly mechanised so that productivity per worker is very high. At Tachai (Fig. 6.77) two very simple kilns have been built and manual labour is still used in work which could be mechanised. This is particularly true in the handling of raw materials and in the distribution of the finished product. The simple forms of transport used – ranging from tractor powered trailers to hand carts – means that loading and unloading still has to be carried out by hand.

In spite of such limitations the Tachai plant is comparatively efficient and productivity is only slightly less than at some of the largest cement works in China. This is largely because breakdowns are rare, little maintenance is needed and a three shift system can be worked with little interruption. Furthermore, the size of the labour force is most important in a commune which has a surplus of labour except during times of planting and harvesting. Workers are encouraged to move from farm to factory and to return if necessary.

The development of small scale industry in China is strongly controlled by the government and is often heavily subsidised. In some cases this is carried to extremes and the industry is not even expected to show a profit. Such a pattern of development is rarely found in non-Communist developing countries.

Small scale rural industries in Kenya: metal working, Kiambu District

In Kenya, as in most developing countries, the influence of markets on industry is much greater than in Communist countries such as China. Government aid is available but industrial development generally depends much more upon

Location: Kiambu, nr. Nairobi, Kenya
Industry: Small scale metal working
Area: 582 646 sq km
Population: 17 million
GNP (per capita): $420
% of GNP from agriculture: 30
          from manufacturing: 13

Fig. 6.79

1947	Firm founded. Total capital $60	One temporary hut. Simple hearth. Homemade fan to blow hearth	Products: buckets Total sales: $700 Profit: $160	Workforce: 1
1958		Same premises	Similar products, plus cooking pots & road rollers Sales: $3400 Profit: $250	Workforce: 3
1969	Government aid: plot of land in village Loan: $13 000	Large new shed. Improved hearths	Increased range of products: simple tools and simple farm equipment	Workforce: 2 craftsmen 5 apprentices
1979	Application for more aid	Larger premises planned	Addition of welding equipment Sales: $56 000 Profit: $6800	Workforce: 4 craftsmen 8 apprentices

BUDGET: 1947

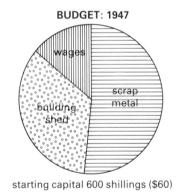

starting capital 600 shillings ($60)

BUDGET: 1980

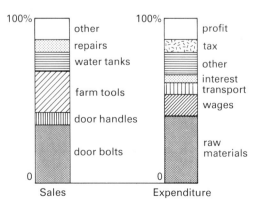

Fig. 6.80

private funds. The industry is expected to show a profit within a comparatively short time. If this does not happen the business will become bankrupt.

The development of a small metal working industry at Kiambu (Fig. 6.79) is typical.

This is an industry which buys in its major raw materials, iron and charcoal. Processing takes place using very simple equipment (hearths, bellows, anvils etc.), much of it home made. The products are very simple but they find a ready market in the surrounding area because they are strong and are easy to repair. The industry serves a comparatively small area around the village and its growth has been limited as much by difficulties of transport as by lack of capital. In spite of such problems growth has been steady and over a period of 30 years the firm has been successful (Fig. 6.80).

It is obvious why many governments in the Developing World prefer to support large scale industrial projects. How many small industries of the kind described above are required to provide both a strong industrial base and employment for a large number of people? If this question is asked, a single large industrial plant often appears very attractive.

This is a problem facing almost all less developed countries and the way in which it is resolved is most important since it will determine the use of very scarce resources. It also has implications for the countries of the Developed World, particularly with regard to the way in which aid is given.

7 World links

It can be dangerous and misleading to concentrate on the differences which exist in the world. The contrasts between different places on the earth's surface and between the activities which exist in those places are undoubtedly great, but equally strong are the links which bind all parts of the world together. These links are most obvious in the communications networks which exist over land and sea and in the air between the countries of the world. Equally important, however, is the use which is made of these lines of communications to move not only goods but also money, people and even ideas from one place to another.

As soon as people appeared on the face of the earth they began to establish lines of communication. At first these were nothing more than pathways used in the never ending search for food, but when the first regular settlements were formed some of these pathways became enlarged by frequent use until they formed wider tracks. In many countries these early routeways were to form the basis of the present road network.

Internal routes

Roads
In the Developed World road systems can be extremely complicated and traffic is dominated by vehicles driven by oil powered internal combustion engines. In the less developed countries the situation is very different, with largely unmade roads and traffic dominated by pedestrians and vehicles drawn by animals. In both cases, however, the underlying principles are the same:

1 The road system has developed to meet the needs of the people.

2 A hierarchy of roads is likely to exist in any given area, i.e. there will be a framework of major roads; secondary roads will feed into this framework; and these, in turn, will be served by a network of minor roads and tracks. Together these roads form a network.

3 The purpose of any road network is to allow people and goods to move from place to place with the greatest possible ease. Some networks are more successful in achieving this than others. The degree of success is known as the 'efficiency' of the network and it is important to be able to measure this so that communications networks in different parts of the world can be compared. Many different methods have been used to measure the efficiency of communications networks.

One of the simplest is to measure the 'connectivity' of the network, i.e. the ease of moving from place to place within the network. This can be done simply by counting the links which exist between settlements in any given area. A second measure is the 'directness' of those links. Because road systems have developed slowly over a long period of time they rarely provide direct links between major settlements. Instead roads tend to wind from village to village, often avoiding areas of difficult terrain. This reduces their efficiency as lines of communication. Directness can be measured by comparing the actual length of such links with the shortest possible distance between the settlements in the network.

Each of these measures emphasises the distance between places. This is not necessarily the best indicator of efficiency. In many developing countries, for example, roads are so bad that even comparatively short journeys can take a long time. In the industrialised world, on the other hand, the sheer number of vehicles on the roads can greatly increase travel time. In these circumstances journey time rather than distance travelled may give a better indication of the efficiency of the network.

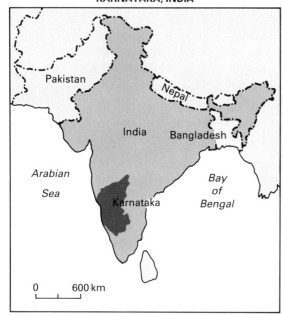

KARNATAKA, INDIA

Area: 192000 sq km

Population: 29300000

Road system: 64000 km
surfaced: 15000 km
unsurfaced: 49000 km

Number of vehicles: 340000
trucks: 30000
cars: 60000
two wheelers: 176000
buses: 11000

Fig. 7.1

Road networks: Karnataka, India

Karnataka is situated on the west coast of India (Fig. 7.1). It covers an area of 192 000 square kilometres and has a population of 29 million. This population is housed in 216 towns and more than 25 000 villages.

The settlements are served by a road system over 64 000 kilometres in length. Half of the system is made up of village roads, most of which are little more than dirt tracks, impassable during bad weather to all but pedestrian traffic. District roads vary enormously. Some are metalled all-weather roads while others are simply larger versions of the village roads. The latter are most numerous in the western part of the state which is mountainous. Only the highways provide reliable all-weather routes for motor vehicles and they make up less than a quarter of the entire system.

Taken together these roads form a very complex network. The map, Fig. 7.2, shows only a part of that network. It excludes the village roads but it gives some impression of its complexity. What it does not show is the efficiency of the network.

One simple measure of the efficiency of routeways is the 'index of directness' or 'detour index'. Because the present road network has developed over a long period of time and to serve a large number of settlements it is probable that roads linking major settlements will not be direct. This can be seen when the roads between the state capital, Bangalore, and five of the district centres are examined.

Using the information given in Fig. 7.2 and the associated tables complete the following exercise.

a   Calculate the index of directness for each of the routes on the list.
b   i   List the routes in order of directness (the smallest number will be first on the list).
    ii List the routes in order of length (the shortest will be first on the list).

KARNATAKA: MAJOR ROAD NETWORK

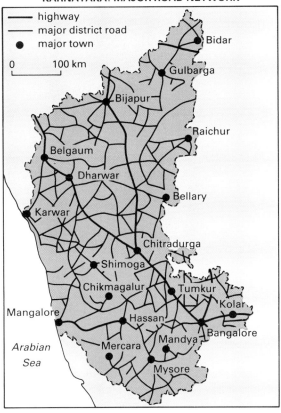

— highway
— major district road
● major town

0   100 km

TYPE OF ROAD
(total length 64000 km)

0   100%

| village roads | district roads | high ways | |
— major highways

INDEX OF DIRECTNESS OF LINKS BETWEEN BANGALORE AND FIVE MAJOR CENTRES

| | Distance from Bangalore (km) | |
	(a) In a straight line	(b) By shortest road link
Mangalore	297	399
Mysore	120	135
Kolar	72	102
Dharwar	384	415
Bijapur	472	505

Index of directness $= \dfrac{\text{shortest distance by road}}{\text{straight line distance}} \times 100$

(the smaller the number the more direct the route)

Mean index for the routes listed $= \dfrac{\text{Sum b}}{\text{Sum a}} \times 100 = \dfrac{1556}{1345} \times 100 = 115.7$

Fig. 7.2

c Compare the two lists and:
  i Describe the relationship between the index of directness and the length of route.
  ii Explain why this relationship is likely to be found in many parts of the world.
  iii Name one route which does not conform to this relationship.
  iv Give one possible reason why the index for this route is so low.

It is obvious from the exercise that relief has a strong influence on the efficiency of a route network. In Karnataka, for example, the detour indices for north–south routes are considerably lower than for east–west routes, suggesting that travel from Bangalore northwards is comparably easy. This pattern is caused by the high relief in the western part of the state which has produced lower population densities and made road building much more difficult and expensive.

A second simple measure is the degree of 'connectivity' between places in the network. To study this for all the district centres in Karnataka would take a long time. However, useful results can be obtained by examining the road network in a small part of the state.

A hill road in southern India

ROAD NETWORK: CENTRAL KARNATAKA

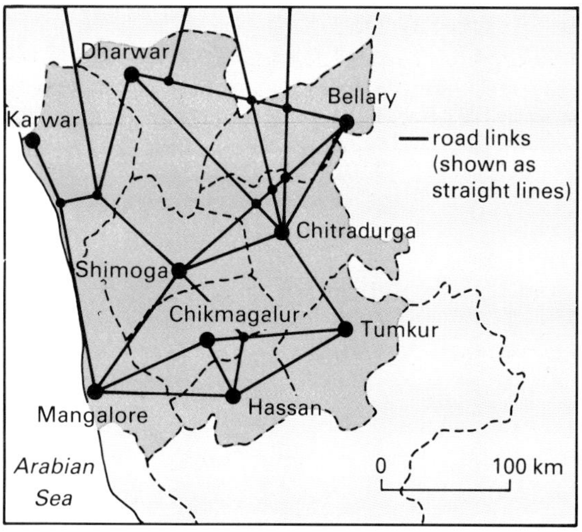

Fig. 7.3

MATRIX SHOWING CONNECTIVITY OF CITIES IN CENTRAL KARNATAKA

(cities arranged in rank order according to population)

Centre / Centre	1	2	3	4	5	6	7	8	9	Total
1 Dharwar	—	2	4	2	3	2	3	3	3	22
2 Mangalore		—								
3 Bellary			—							
4 Shimoga				—						
5 Tumkur					—					
6 Chitradurga						—				
7 Hassan							—			
8 Chikmagalur								—		
9 Karwar									—	

To complete the matrix:

1 Refer to the map above.
2 For each of the routes given in the matrix count the number of 'links' which make up the route (a link is a stretch of routeway between two dots). If alternative routes are available choose the one with the shortest number of links.
3 Calculate the total for each centre.
4 The centre with the lowest total is the best connected.

Refer to Fig. 7.3 and the matrix below.

a   Complete the matrix for the road system of Central Karnataka. Use the method described under the matrix itself.
b   i   Name the two centres which have the highest indices of connectivity.
     ii   Describe one locational feature which they have in common.
c   i   Name the two centres which have the lowest indices of connectivity.
     ii   Describe one locational feature which these centres have in common.
d   Draw up two lists – one showing the centres in rank order of population, the other showing them in rank order of connectivity.
     i   Calculate the correlation coefficient, using the two sets of statistics.
     ii   Describe the relationship, if any, which exists between population and connectivity.

Fig. 7.3 and the matrix below it (when completed) illustrate several features of road networks which may be found in other parts of the world. For example:

1   Because they have evolved over a long period of time roads rarely provide efficient links in terms of directness.

2   Roads, with the possible exception of modern highways, are strongly influenced by relief.

3   Of the centres served by the road network the best connected are likely to be located near the centre of the network and the worst connected are likely to be found towards the outer limits.

4   Most surprising of all perhaps, the relationship between the size of settlements and their degree of connectivity is often very weak.

Railways

All communications networks develop to serve people. Because most road networks have evolved slowly over a long period of time they often appear inefficient and, when examined on a national or international scale, unnecessarily complicated.

Railways, on the other hand, are a comparatively recent development. The first commercial railways were built in the United Kingdom during the first half of the nineteenth century and since then they have been introduced into most countries in the world. In almost every case they have been built with a specific purpose in mind – usually to provide an efficient means of moving bulk commodities overland.

Since most of these commodities are the products of agriculture, industry and mining, it usually means that railways will provide more obvious and direct links between the major centres of population in any given country. At the same time any rail network is likely to be strongly influenced by relief and this will affect the efficiency of the network.

Railways provided a cheap and efficient method of moving bulk commodities over land. In Britain the building of railways led to the introduction of freight rates which were less than 20% of those previously quoted by road carriers. Only water borne transport could compete and this was not always available or was expensive to provide where rivers were not navigable.

For railways the major problem has always been that of gradient. Engines, regardless of the power source used, cannot haul heavy loads up steep gradients. As a result, railway builders have always sought out lowland routes. Where this has proved impossible, tunnels, cuttings and bridges have had to be built (at high cost). Any rail network is likely, therefore, to be a compromise between the desire to provide the most direct and most efficient set of links between the major centres of population and the need to avoid areas of difficult terrain where building costs may be very high. This can be clearly seen in the railway network of Turkey.

Rail network: Turkey

Turkey is a land of rugged relief (Fig. 7.4). A large part of the country is above 1000 metres in height; most of it in the form of a high central plateau. In the east, however, particularly along the borders with the USSR, Iran and Syria, the land becomes very mountainous with the highest peaks reaching 5000 metres. These high mountain ranges extend westward along the Mediterranean and Black Sea coasts of Turkey where individual peaks approach 3000 metres in height. In both of these areas the mountains are very near to the sea and only in the far west of the country is there a large area of coastal lowland.

This pattern of high and often very rugged terrain has strongly influenced the development of the railway network. Firstly, and most obviously, it has made the building of railways in many parts of the country difficult, if not impossible, and almost everywhere it forced the engineers to make use of valley routes and low mountain passes. As a result, the routes are rarely direct and detour indices are often high. Secondly, and in the long term more important, has been the effect of relief on the distribution of population. Most of the high mountain areas are very sparsely populated and, since railways usually depend upon goods produced by people for most of their traffic, they tend to serve densely populated areas and to avoid areas of low population.

Most of the population of Turkey is concentrated in the west, particularly on the lowlands overlooking the Aegean Sea and the Sea of Marmara, but other centres of population are found along the shores of the Black Sea and on the lower parts of the plateau. In the interior most of the settlements are agricultural and most of the freight available to the railway system is farm produce. To the east farming is limited by both the height and ruggedness of the land and by a lack of rainfall. As a result freight movements have never been large enough to warrant the building of railways.

The first railway was built in 1860 and today the network is more than 8000 kilometres in length. How well does this network serve the population?

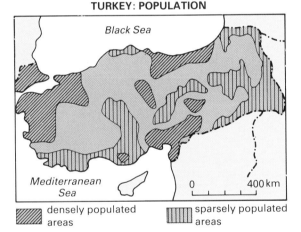

TURKEY: POPULATION

Black Sea

Mediterranean Sea

0   400 km

▨ densely populated areas   ▥ sparsely populated areas

Fig. 7.4 (a)

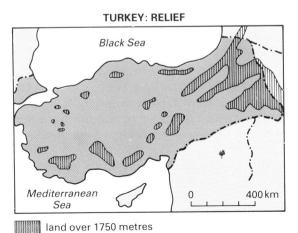

TURKEY: RELIEF

Black Sea

Mediterranean Sea

0   400 km

▥ land over 1750 metres

Fig. 7.4 (b)

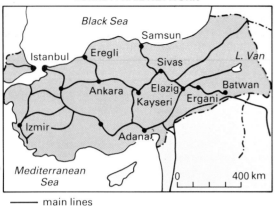

TURKEY: RAIL NETWORK

Black Sea

Samsun
Istanbul • Eregli •
Sivas
L. Van
Ankara • Elazig •
Kayseri • Ergani • Batwan
Izmir •
Adana •
Mediterranean Sea
0   400 km

—— main lines

Fig. 7.4 (c)

Study the maps in Fig. 7.4.

a Trace the outline of one of the maps.
b Using the tracing:
   i Draw lines to connect the main centres of population.
   ii Close the network, i.e. leave as few unconnected lines as possible. In each case keep the distances travelled across areas of low population to a minimum.
c Adjust the lines to miss the high mountain ranges.
d Compare your network (there are many possible networks and no correct answers) with the actual rail network in Turkey. Give any reasons you can think of for the differences which exist between the actual and the predicted networks.

Study Fig. 7.4 and complete the given exercise. An exercise such as this is likely to predict many of the lines which make up a rail network. At the same time there will be some lines which are predicted but which have never been built and there are others which actually exist but which would not be predicted using the simple information given above. It is these differences which give a greater understanding of the development of rail networks.

There can be many reasons for lines not being built when there appears to be a large enough population to support them. In the case of the Turkish network two reasons are particularly important:

1 The physical difficulty of building the lines. For example, the lack of a link between Istanbul and the Asiatic mainland of Turkey can be explained in terms of the difficulty of bridging the Dardanelles which is a major shipping lane. The failure to build a line linking the settlements along the Black Sea coast is partly a result of the high mountain ranges which border the coast. In both cases the technology exists to build the lines but the costs would be high and Turkey is a comparatively poor country. This is a problem which faces road and railway engineers in most developing countries.

2 Alternative forms of transport may exist. Most railways have been built in areas which have existing road networks. Only rarely, however, could these roads compete with railways either in the rapid movement of passengers or, even more important, in the movement of bulk freight. As a result, in most parts of the world, roads have tended to act as feeders for the railways. The exception to this is in the Developed World where modern highways can now compete with railways for long distance freight traffic. In Turkey, however, this is not the case and the only alternative to the railway is water borne traffic. Coastal shipping in particular is highly developed and the sea routes along the Black Sea coast have greatly reduced the need for a railway there.

Other reasons exist for building railways which run through sparsely populated areas and for which there is apparently no great demand:

1 The most obvious reason is the need to gain access to important resources. This could be a forest area or an area of rich farmland. In Turkey, as in most of the less developed countries, it

Fig. 7.5 *Railway in mountains, Turkey*

is usually a rich mineral deposit which makes the great expense worthwhile. Almost without exception the development of mineral deposits depends upon the availability of an efficient bulk transport system and this has led to the building of several railways in remote and underdeveloped parts of Turkey. An example is the line giving access to the copper deposit at Ergani and the oil fields at Batwan further to the east.

2   Because railways provided rapid communications at a time when alternative forms of travel by road or by sea were very slow, lines were often built to link remote parts of a country to the centres of government. It was this more than anything else which led to the building of the first transcontinental railways in America and the trans-Siberian railway in Russia.

In Turkey political considerations led to the building of railways to the remote eastern provinces which were under threat from Russia, Iraq and Iran.

3   Few communications networks develop in complete isolation. The Turkish railways are connected to the rail networks of all neighbouring countries. Some of these links pass through very sparsely populated areas.

Road v rail

Advantages of road transport
1   Flexible, i.e. not tied to a limited network of tracks.
2   Allows door to door delivery in a single vehicle.
3   It is generally quicker.
4   It requires a smaller labour force.
5   As a result, it is generally cheaper, particularly over short distances.

Disadvantages of road transport
1   More vehicles needed to move the same tonnage.
2   Can cause serious congestion.
3   Engines cause serious pollution.

Road and rail: changing patterns

For more than 100 years, up to the outbreak of the Second World War, the pattern of transport throughout the world was much the same.

Road transport was generally inefficient. Traffic could be heavy in and around major settlements and it was usually slow moving. In most of the less developed countries road transport was still largely pedestrian or dependent upon animals. Only in the industrialised world was motor transport important and even here it was on a comparatively small scale.

Freight, particularly bulk cargo, was carried along coastal shipping lines or on inland waterways. Where this was impossible railways were built. In fact there was a great dependence on railways for both freight haulage and the rapid movement of passengers. By 1945 only the most underdeveloped countries were without a rail network of some kind. In the Developed World these networks were often complex and dense, i.e. the length of the lines making up the network was very large compared with the area of the country. In the less developed countries the networks were usually sparse, with a few poorly connected lines, but they were of great importance to the economies of the countries concerned.

After 1945 this comparatively simple pattern changed dramatically, largely as a result of improvements in the efficiency of road transport. Lorries increased in size, roads were improved enormously and journey times were greatly reduced. As a result, for the first time road transport not only challenged the railways but had several important advantages over them. However, the investment needed to take advantage of these improvements was considerable and this has resulted in great variations in the pattern of transport throughout the world.

TRANSPORT AND ECONOMIC DEVELOPMENT IN EIGHT COUNTRIES

Country	Per capita GNP ($)	% total freight carried by	
		Road	Rail
West Germany	12 419	51	26
United Kingdom	9 110	84	15
Poland	2 512	24	74
Congo	879	18	28
Morocco	657	20	80
Brazil	2 220	79	21
Japan	10 080	40	10
USA	12 820	58	9

Using information given in this section, complete the following exercise.

a i Explain why traffic has tended to be diverted from the railways to the roads in the last 30 years.

ii What are the problems caused by such a change?

b Draw a scattergraph to show the relationship between Gross National Product and road transport (expressed as a percentage of total freight traffic). GNP should be represented on the vertical axis.

i Is the relationship positive or negative?

ii Is the relationship strong or weak?

iii Describe what this tells you about the pattern of road transport in the world.

c Draw a second scattergraph to show the relationship between GNP and rail transport.

i Is the relationship positive or negative?

ii Is the relationship strong or weak?

iii Describe what this tells you about the pattern of rail transport in the world.

d Describe the differences which are likely to exist between developed and developing countries.

It is clear from the table showing the relationship between transport and economic development that it has been the developed countries which have had the resources to develop an efficient system of road transport. Elsewhere the railways still dominate. The oil price rises of the 1970s which greatly increased the costs of motor transport are likely to ensure that this remains the same in the foreseeable future.

International links

As we have seen, the internal communications systems of most countries depend to a great extent upon road and rail networks – the actual balance between the two varying considerably from country to country. In contrast, international links (i.e. the links between countries) are dominated by traffic movements along the seaways and airways of the world. These movements show a much greater degree of specialisation than those along internal routes. Air transport is responsibe for the bulk of international passenger movements and sea transport accounts for most of the world's international trade.

Sea routes and world trade

The most obvious and important link binding together the different parts of the world is the movement of goods and raw materials from one country to another, i.e. the international trade of the world. Most of these goods and materials are transported by sea. Throughout history the great sea routes of the world have tended to reflect the changing patterns of world trade.

PATTERN OF WORLD TRADE: BEFORE 1945

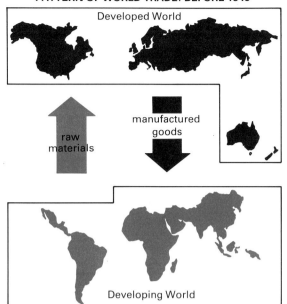

Fig. 7.6 (a)

PATTERN OF WORLD TRADE: AFTER 1960

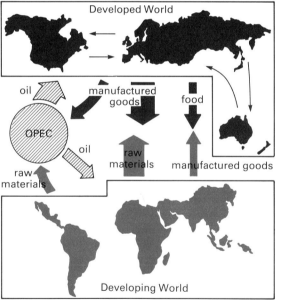

Fig. 7.6 (b)

Before the Second World War a comparatively simple pattern of world trade existed. This was based on two main traffic flows.

1 The industrialised countries of the world in Western Europe, North America and to a lesser extent Japan and the USSR imported food and basic raw materials for their industries from countries in the Developing World.

2 In return and to gain currency to pay for these materials the industrialised countries exported manufactured goods to the Developing World.

In general the balance of this trade, i.e. the difference in value between what was bought and sold, favoured the industrialised countries. It was the desire to increase this type of trade which had encouraged several of the industrialised countries to establish colonies in underdeveloped areas. These colonies had eventually formed the basis of large overseas empires which, by providing sources of raw materials and a protected market for manufactured goods, had greatly added to the prosperity of the colonising countries. Britain benefited most from these developments but France, Germany, Belgium and later Italy and Japan all tried to establish empires.

After 1945 this simple pattern began to break down and by the early 1960s a very different pattern of world trade had emerged (Figs 7.6 (a) and (b)).

1 The world had become increasingly dependent upon oil, and the major oil producing countries – many of them underdeveloped countries – found themselves in a position of great importance. Several of them joined together to form OPEC (see page 125) and used their power to raise the price of oil. This meant that these countries became so rich that they became a third force in the pattern of world trade. They exported oil and in turn were able to import manufactured goods from the developed countries and food and raw materials from the less developed countries.

2 The developing countries tried to correct the imbalance of trade between themselves and the industrialised world. They began to establish new industries such as textiles, clothing, iron and steel and shipbuilding. By doing so they hoped to export these products to the Developed World and, at the same time, to reduce their dependence on the industrialised countries.

3 Unfortunately these efforts coincided with a rapid increase in population in the developing countries. As a result, they became for the first time dependent upon foodstuffs imported from the industrialised countries where farming was becoming more efficient and where food surpluses were beginning to appear.

4 Trade in manufactured goods between the industrialised countries began to increase.

These factors have combined to produce the present complex pattern of world trade.

As we have seen, internal transport networks developed mainly to meet the immediate needs of the people living in a country or area. They clearly reflect the distribution of population within the area. In the case of international routeways, however, this relationship is much less marked and other factors are more important.

The Suez Canal

The great trade routes of the world have, throughout history, centred on the richest nations. In 1950 they converged on the industrialised regions of North America and Western Europe. These areas remain important today but new centres have emerged in the Far East and in the oil producing countries of the Middle East (Fig. 7.8).

These changes, which have largely taken place since 1960, coincided with major changes in shipping and this too has had an important effect on the pattern of trade routes. In particular:

1   Ships have increased enormously in size. Between 1960 and 1980 the size of the largest vessels increased ten times, and many today have tonnages of over 500 000. Such vessels were too large to pass through two of the great man-made routeways of the world – the Suez and Panama Canals. For most of the first half of this century these two canals provided passage for a large proportion of the world's shipping, saving the long voyages around the Cape of Good Hope and Cape Horn. With the introduction of large ships, however, it became more economic to make the longer voyage, and trade through the canals declined. (The Suez Canal was in any case closed to shipping throughout the 1970s by the Arab-Israeli hostilities.)

2   In 1960 most of the merchant ships afloat were general cargo vessels, i.e. on any given voyage a variety of cargoes would be carried. Since that time more and more ships have been built to handle special cargoes. The first, and best known, of the ships were the oil tankers but today vessels are built to carry ores, grain, other bulk dry cargoes, liquid cargoes other than oil and, of course, containers. The reduction in handling costs in the ports

WORLD TRADE ROUTES: 1960
(width of line indicates tonnage carried)

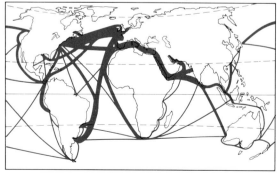

Fig. 7.7

WORLD TRADE ROUTES: 1982

(width of line indicates tonnage carried but scale is not comparable with the 1960 map)

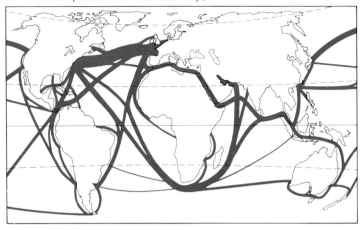

Fig. 7.8

and the rapid 'turn around' of the ships (which means that less time is spent unproductively in port) more than offset the cost of building specialised handling facilities in the ports.

All trade routes start and end at ports. These ports may differ greatly in location and appearance, ranging from the enclosed dock systems of old established ports such as London and Rotterdam to the oil terminals of the Gulf States which may be nothing more than an anchorage off an exposed coastline. Whatever their location or type all of these ports have certain features in common:

1 They offer access to the vessels which are likely to be used in any given type of trade. Today this usually involves deep water access.

METHODS OF HANDLING CARGO

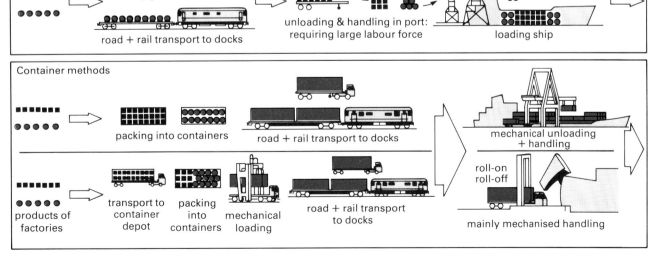

Traditional method

road + rail transport to docks — unloading & handling in port: requiring large labour force — loading ship

Container methods

packing into containers — road + rail transport to docks — mechanical unloading + handling

products of factories — transport to container depot — packing into containers — mechanical loading — road + rail transport to docks — roll-on roll-off — mainly mechanised handling

Fig. 7.9

1981	
Port	Tonnage handled (millions)
1 Rotterdam	268
2 Kobe	143
3 New York	118
4 Yokahama	115
5 Marseilles	93
6 Le Havre	76
7 Antwerp	72
8 Singapore	70
9 Hamburg	54
10 London	51

LOCATION OF ROTTERDAM/EUROPOORT

Fig. 7.10

2   They provide safe berths at which cargoes can be quickly and safely loaded or unloaded. In many cases this will involve the provision of a variety of highly specialised handling facilities.

3   They provide the facilities needed to assemble or to distribute cargoes. These are drawn from the area around the port. This area is known as the 'hinterland' of the port (i.e. the areas served by the port) and it can range in size from a few hundred square kilometres in the case of a small local port to many thousand square kilometres in the case of a major international port.

It is the large ports which have been most strongly influenced by recent changes in cargo handling (Fig. 7.9). This can be seen clearly in the case of the world's largest port complex – Rotterdam/Europoort.

Port study: Rotterdam/Europoort

Rotterdam (Fig. 7.10) first emerged as a port towards the end of the thirteenth century when a dam was built across the River Rotter, creating a stretch of deep sheltered water, suitable for loading and unloading ships. Because the river was a relatively small distributary of the Rhine Delta silting was a major problem. For the next 600 years the growth of the port was slow and it was overshadowed by neighbouring ports such as Antwerp and Amsterdam.

The nineteenth century saw the rapid industrial development of the regions bordering the Rhine Valley. This produced increased traffic on the river and a growing demand for direct access to the North Sea. Rotterdam was well situated to benefit from this development and attempts were made to improve the river link between the port and the sea. Initial attempts to build a canal link were only partially successful and it was not until 1872 that the New Waterway (Fig. 7.11) was opened, giving a deep water channel to the sea. The rise of Rotterdam to its present position as the world's largest port has been based on the building of this channel and of the improvements which have since been made to it.

Since 1870 the nature of the port has changed out of all recognition and the rate of change has been particularly rapid since the end of the Second World War. During this time the tonnage handled at the port has more than doubled and a range of specialised handling facilities have been built to enable ships of all types and sizes to be loaded and unloaded.

Using information given in Figs 7.11 and 7.12, complete the following exercise.

a   i   Rotterdam experienced a long period of steady growth. When did that period end?
    ii In the space of ten years (1963–73) the tonnage handled at the port *increased by 50%/doubled/trebled*.
    iii Most of this growth was the result of an increase in one branch

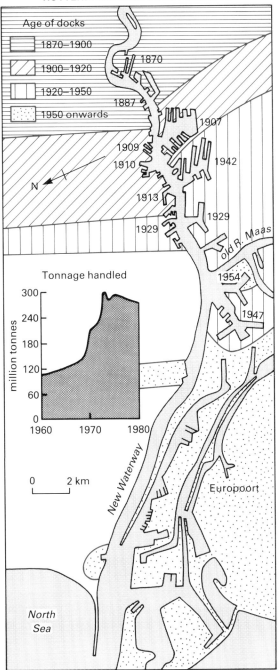

ROTTERDAM/EUROPOORT: GROWTH

Age of docks

- 1870–1900
- 1900–1920
- 1920–1950
- 1950 onwards

1870
1887
1907
1909
1910
1942
1913
1929
1929
old R. Maas
1954
1947

Tonnage handled

million tonnes

300
240
180
120
60
0

1960   1970   1980

0   2 km

New Waterway

Europoort

North Sea

Fig. 7.11

of trade. Name the commodity concerned.

iv   Since 1960 the tonnage of general cargo handled at the port has *greatly increased/greatly decreased/remained about the same*.

b   i   The oldest docks are located *at the river mouth/upstream above the entrance to the old river channel* (R. Maas).

ii   What is the depth of water in the main channel at this point?

iii   Name the type of cargo handled at these docks today.

c   i   The newer docks have been built *upstream/downstream* from the original port of Rotterdam.

ii   What is the name given to this new dock complex?

iii   What is the main advantage of developing this new site?

iv   Name the main cargo handled in this part of the port.

v   Give one reason why this cargo is handled at these docks.

It is clear from the maps, Figs 7.11 and 7.12, that the initial site of the docks at Rotterdam imposed serious restrictions on the growth of the port. The river channel itself was comparatively shallow and the early docks lacked the depth to allow the handling of many modern ships. As a result this area of the port still concentrates on the smaller general cargo vessels. More importantly, it provides facilities for the trans-shipment of cargoes to and from the barges which carry goods along the River Rhine.

From the early years of the twentieth century special handling facilities were built downstream where the channel was deep enough to provide access for larger ships. These docks – most of them constructed to handle dry cargoes such as grain and minerals – are now too small to cope with anything but general cargo ships and river barges. New specialised handling facilities have therefore been built near to the sea. This movement of the port downstream became more marked after 1950 when Rotterdam began to emerge as a major oil port. It was at this time that the complex which was to become Europoort was planned and during the 1960s oil terminals capable of handling tankers over 250 000 tonnes in size were built. Most of the port's trade is now concentrated in this area and additional deep water facilities have been developed to handle the trade in grain, coal and ores upon which Rotterdam has traditionally depended. The most recent development has been the provision of container handling facilities and roll on/roll off terminals. Once again the largest and most important of these have been located near to the deep water channel in the Europoort complex.

It has already been pointed out that a port depends for its prosperity upon the size and prosperity of its hinterland. Rotterdam is situated at the mouth of the Rhine, one of the largest navigable rivers in Europe. As a result, few ports have larger hinterlands and nowhere is there a hinterland which compares in terms of population, industrialisation and general prosperity. It stretches from the North Sea to the Swiss Alps and includes some of the major industrial regions of West Germany, France, Belgium and the Netherlands (see Fig. 7.15).

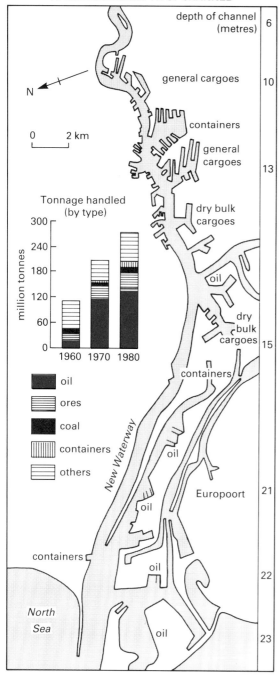

ROTTERDAM/EUROPOORT: TYPE OF TONNAGE HANDLED AND DEPTH OF CHANNEL

depth of channel (metres) 6

general cargoes 10

N

0   2 km

containers

general cargoes 13

Tonnage handled (by type)

dry bulk cargoes

300

240

180

120

60

0

million tonnes

1960 1970 1980

oil

dry bulk cargoes 15

oil

ores

coal

containers

containers

others

New Waterway

oil

oil

Europoort 21

containers

oil 22

North Sea

oil 23

Fig. 7.12

Fig. 7.13 *Older docks along the River Maas, Rotterdam*

Fig. 7.14 *Modern port facilities at Europoort*

ROTTERDAM AND ITS HINTERLAND

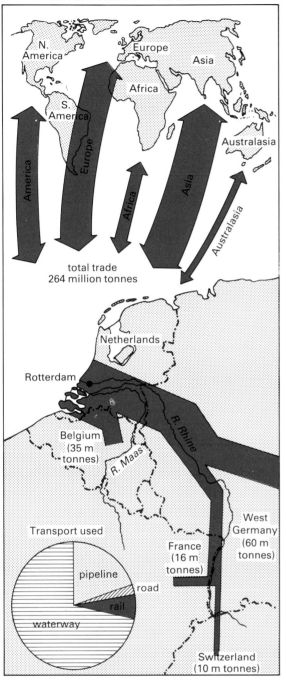

total trade
264 million tonnes

Fig. 7.15

The main link between the port and its hinterland is the River Rhine itself. Navigable from the Swiss border, the river carries more than two thirds of the goods and raw materials which pass through the port. Most of these commodities are transported on convoys of barges pushed by a single powered barge. Other forms of transport are less important but the growth of containerisation has led to increased traffic on the roads and railways. To provide efficient rail links with the hinterland large marshalling yards have been built. These allow the easy tranfser of goods from the port.

For most of this traffic, whether it is waterborne or on land, Rotterdam is the main trans-shipment point, i.e. it is the point at which goods are transferred from one form of transport to another. This means it is the major break of bulk point in North West Europe and this has had an important effect on the development of industrial and commercial activities in the port.

1 Because cargoes are trans-shipped large storage areas have been built around many of the docks. This can be seen most clearly in the vicinity of the oil terminals (see Fig. 7.14) since Rotterdam is today the centre of the north European oil trade.

2 Related to this has been the growth of commodity markets, i.e. markets for the buying and selling of bulk raw materials. Once again it is in the oil trade that Rotterdam is most important but similar markets exist for grain and minerals.

3 Of greater importance as far as employment is concerned has been the growth of industries based on the cargoes handled in the port. As we have already seen, industries tend to be attracted to break of bulk points and this makes Rotterdam one of the most attractive locations in North West Europe. The most important of these industries are based on the bulk commodities which are handled in the port, e.g. oil refining, the processing of vegetable oils, flour milling and the refining of metals.

These basic port activities support a large population which has in turn provided a market for the other manufacturing and service industries associated with a prosperous and highly developed region.

At the same time Rotterdam has not escaped the effects of the decline in oil consumption which followed the price rises of the 1970s. The volume of traffic through the port reached its peak in 1972 and total trade has since declined by about 10%. Most of this decline is the result of the reduced demand for oil in North West Europe although the recession has also affected shipments of other commodities such as ores, coal and manufactured goods. Compared with other ports, however, the effects have been slight. It is likely that, given the advantages of its position at the entrance to the Rhine and the massive improvements which are taking place downstream from Europoort, Rotterdam will remain the largest and most important port in the world.

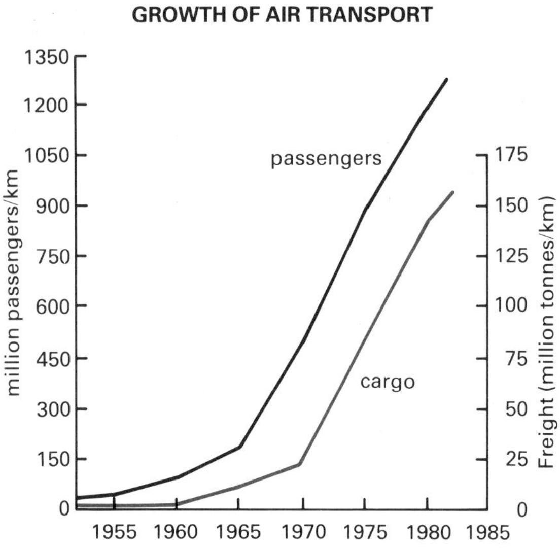

GROWTH OF AIR TRANSPORT

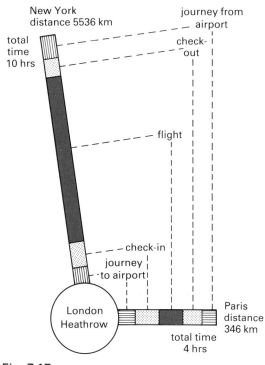

Fig. 7.16

Air traffic and air routes

The first successful flight in a motor powered aeroplane took place in 1903. Today the aeroplane is the major method of long distance passenger transport. Until the Second World War air travel was comparatively unimportant and most long distance passenger movements took place by rail or by ocean going liner. Since 1950, however, the situation has changed completely (Fig. 7.16). This can be seen most clearly in a highly developed country such as the United States where the number of passengers travelling by air has increased enormously. At the same time, regular liner services across the Atlantic and Pacific Oceans have disappeared and the long distance rail routes are struggling to survive. These trends are less apparent in the Developing World where both railways and coastal shipping routes carry a large number of passengers. Even here, however, international passenger transport is dominated by air travel.

The reasons for this rapid development of air transport are obvious. Most people undertaking long journeys – they are usually on business or travelling to and from holidays – want to arrive as quickly as possible. Air travel is faster than any of the alternatives at present available. This means that journey times generally tend to be shorter. When aircraft were first introduced on long distance routes the effects were dramatic. In 1950, for example, the fastest sea crossing of the Atlantic took almost four days; the equivalent crossing by air was less than 20 hours. Since that date the speed of aircraft has more than doubled and the journey time has been reduced to little more than seven hours. It is this development which led to the total dominance of air travel on long distance routes and saw the great liners of the world consigned to the scrapyard or relegated to the role of cruise ships.

The dramatic improvements in journey times achieved during the 1950s and 1960s are unlikely to be repeated even if the speed of aircraft continues to increase.

TYPICAL JOURNEYS BY AIR

(showing the time taken for different stages of the journey)

Refer to Fig. 7.17 and answer the following questions.

a   What is the total journey time (i) from London to New York (ii) from London to Paris?
b   i   For each journey work out the proportion of the journey spent in the air.
    ii   How is the rest of the journey time occupied?
c   If the speed of the aircraft was doubled what would the total journey time be in each case?

It is quite clear that air transport is most effective when the distance travelled is great and when the journey has to be completed as quickly as possible. A reduction in either of these requirements often results in other forms of transport being used. There are several reasons for this, all of them stemming from the basic problems of air transport:

1   A large amount of fuel is needed to lift an aircraft. Today this fuel (aviation spirit) is expensive and this helps to make air travel more expensive than many of its competitors.

Fig. 7.17

DON MUANG INTERNATIONAL AIRPORT

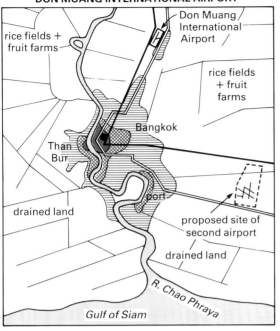

Land use

■ CBD

▦ industry + slum housing

▤ residential

═══ highway

━━━ railway

Location: Don Muang International Airport, Bangkok, Thailand

Situation: 22 km N.E. of city centre

Area: 8 sq km

Runways: two
(a) 3550 m × 60 m
(b) 3000 m × 45 m

Links with city: coach, bus, rail
(a) coach – every 30 minutes, journey time 30 minutes.
(b) bus – every 5 minutes, journey time 60 minutes.
(c) rail – journey time 30 minutes.

Airlines using airport: 39

Route network (direct or by connection): 198 cities

Flights into and out of airport: 52972

Passengers using airport: 5298000

Freight handled: 92000 tonnes

Fig. 7.18

2 The payload (i.e. the number of passengers or the amount of freight) carried by even the largest modern aircraft is comparatively small. This has had two important effects. First, very little freight is moved by air and when suitable cargoes can be found they tend to be commodities which are small, light and of high value. Second, costs per passenger are high.

3 The actual flight makes up only part of the journey. A considerable amount of time is spent either in the airport or travelling to and from the airport. It is this more than anything else which reduces the efficiency of air transport, ensuring that increases in aircraft speed are not fully reflected in improvements in overall journey times. In fact, on short journeys the amount of time spent on the ground can be much greater than the time spent in the air (Fig. 7.17). This greatly reduces the attractiveness of air transport and enables other forms of transport to compete over shorter distances.

Much of the inefficiency of air transport stems from the location of major airports, most of which have been built at considerable distances from the cities which they serve (see Fig. 7.18). There are of course very good reasons for choosing such sites.

Any modern airport requires a large area of relatively level land. Individual runways need to be very long to handle large modern aircraft. Furthermore, with aircraft landing or taking off in rapid succession, very large terminal buildings are needed to provide baggage handling facilities, waiting areas and services such as shops and restaurants. Large areas are also needed near to the terminal buildings to provide car parks and access to other forms of transport which will carry passengers to and from the city. Such large areas of land are unlikely to be available near to the city centre and if they were they would be too expensive to put to such use.

Using information given in Fig. 7.18, complete the following exercise.

a i Name the airport which serves the city.
   ii Calculate (a) its distance from the city centre (b) the area it occupies.
b The large area of land required is one reason for locating airports on the outskirts of cities.
   i Give two other reasons for choosing such locations.
   ii Why is the site shown a particularly suitable choice for a modern airport?
c i List the lines of communication linking the airport to the city centre.
   ii Name the quickest form of transport and state how long the journey is likely to take.
d What are the advantages of the proposed new airport site?

Fig. 7.19 *Bangkok airport*

AIR TRAFFIC AND OTHER DATA FOR SELECTED COUNTRIES

	Total air traffic (million passenger km) per month	Area ('000 sq km)	Population (millions)	GNP per capita ($)
USA	32 331	9 363	229	11 400
Japan	4 644	372	117	10 080
UK	3 663	244	55	9 110
Canada	2 453	9 976	24	12 820
India	1 105	3 287	683	260
Italy	1 048	301	57	6 480
S. Korea	1 009	98	38	1 520
Brazil	954	8 511	121	2 220
Rumania	95	237	22	2 340
Zaire	55	2 345	28	220

Air transport is one of the safest methods of travel but the periods of greatest risk are on take off and landing. It is not surprising, therefore, that people prefer flight paths to and from airports to be routed away from heavily built up areas. Furthermore, since there is a lot of noise, few people would want to live near a modern airport. This too has encouraged the choice of sites outside the city.

As we have seen, the volume of air traffic has increased enormously in recent years. This increase has taken place in almost all parts of the world but it has varied enormously in extent from country to country (see Fig. 7.20). Air transport is most important among the wealthy countries of the Developed World. Variations do occur within this group, according to the size of the country (large countries tend to make greater use of air transport for internal communications) and the size of the population (passenger movements will tend to be greater if the population is large). Reasons for air travel being more widely used in the Developed World are fairly obvious. They include the enormous costs of operating an air transport system and, in the case of less developed countries, the costs of importing the equipment and the trained workers needed to keep the system running.

AIR TRAFFIC IN FIVE COUNTRIES

CANADA

Area: 9976139 sq km
Population: 24.21 million
Per capita GNP: $12820

0   2000 km

Average air traffic per month: 2453 million passenger km
% of traffic internal: 51%
Longest internal flight: 4859 km

ITALY	UNITED KINGDOM
	Area: 244046 sq km Population: 55.83 million Per capita GNP: $9110
Area: 301225 sq km Population: 57.2 million Per capita GNP: $6480	0 1000 km
Average air traffic per month: 1048 million passenger km % of traffic internal: 12% Longest internal flight: 867 km	Average air traffic per month: 3663 million passenger km % of traffic internal: 6% Longest internal flight: 753 km
JAPAN Area: 372313 sq km Population: 117.64 million Per capita GNP: $10080	MALAGASY REPUBLIC Area: 587041 sq km Population: 8.96 million Per capita GNP: $350
0 1000 km	
Average air traffic per month: 4644 million passenger km % of traffic internal: 52% Longest internal flight: 1610 km	Average air traffic per month: 25 million passenger km % of traffic internal: 50% Longest internal flight: 373 km

Fig. 7.20

Study the information given in the table on page 212

a Describe any relationship which may appear to exist between total passenger/kilometres flown and (i) the area of the countries listed (ii) wealth (as measured by per capita GNP). It may be necessary to plot the data on scattergraphs or to calculate correlation coefficients.

b Describe how these patterns differ between internal and international air traffic.

c The maps in the adjoining column give details of air traffic in five countries. For each country:
 i Describe the pattern of air traffic.
 ii Describe the pattern which might be expected from the relationship described above.
 iii Explain any differences which occur.

In some cases the pattern of influences is comparatively clear. For example:

1 The United States is one of the richest countries in the world and one of the largest both in terms of size and population. It is not surprising, therefore, that air traffic is greater here than in any other country in the world. Neither is it surprising that internal traffic greatly exceeds international traffic. The distances between major cities are so great that the aeroplane is often the most effective form of passenger transport.

2 The United Kingdom is also rich but its area is less than 3% of the area of the United States and the distances between major centres of population are comparatively short. Air transport finds it difficult to compete with road and rail and longer distance international flights are much more important than internal flights. Once again, however, it is important to note that the system of air transport is highly developed.

3 Zaire is one of the poorest of the less developed countries and the situation here is typical of the Developing World as a whole. Air transport is poorly developed and, in spite of the vast size of the country, internal traffic is small. Such countries would probably benefit from the availability of an efficient system of long distance passenger transport but the costs of a modern airline system are too great. Furthermore, the economy is so small that the number of international flights is unlikely to be very large.

The same influences can be traced in the overall pattern of the world's major air routes (Fig. 7.21). It is obvious from the map that the concentration of routes is greatest among the wealthy countries of the Developed World and that elsewhere the network is thin and poorly developed. If the volume of traffic on the routes is taken into account the contrast becomes even more marked.

This also happens if charter flights are included. International tourism has grown rapidly since 1950 and much of this growth has been based on the availability of package holidays which, in turn, depend upon the availability of charter flights. These flights are generally much cheaper than the normal scheduled flights. In spite of this, few people in the less developed countries can afford them and most of the traffic originates in the Developed World.

213

MAJOR INTERNATIONAL AIR ROUTES

Note:
1 it is not possible to show internal routes on a map of this scale. These are particularly numerous in North America.
2 The fact that the map is centred on Western Europe has led to the concentration of routes in this area.

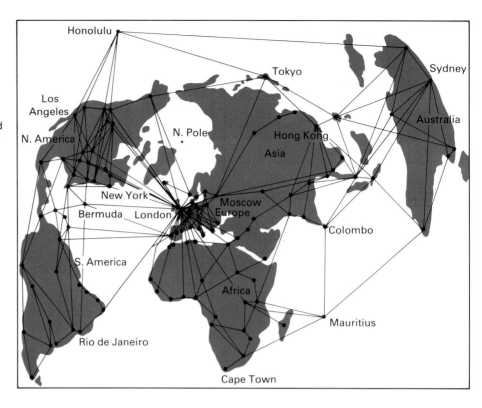

Fig. 7.21

Furthermore, at the moment most of the tourist destinations are in developed countries. There is, however, evidence that this pattern is beginning to change.

In recent years some of the less developed countries have tried to establish a tourist industry as a means of earning foreign currency. Often they are countries which have great natural advantages in terms of climate, beaches etc. However, there are many problems to be overcome before large numbers of tourists are likely to be attracted:

1   An airport will have to be built, capable of handling large modern jet aircraft.
2   Facilities at the airport have to compare with those at airports in the Developed World.
3   Transport to the resort areas has to be rapid and efficient.
4   Hotels and leisure facilities have to be built, to the standards expected in the Developed World.
5   Hygiene and medical services have to be provided at a level not likely to be found in the rest of the country, e.g. supplies of pure running water and efficient sewerage systems.

Developments of this kind are expensive and beyond the means of most of the less developed countries. As a result, tourism in the Developing World appears almost insignificant when compared with its scale in the Developed World. In spite of this, small scale developments are often very important to individual developing countries. In the Gambia, for example, the small tourist industry (Figs 7.22–4) is an important earner of foreign currency for a country which has few natural resources and which is heavily dependent upon agricultural products.

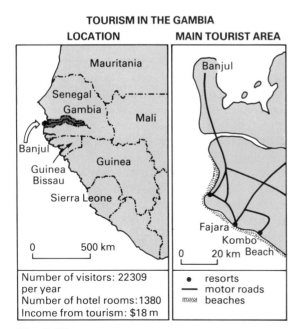

TOURISM IN THE GAMBIA

Number of visitors: 22309 per year
Number of hotel rooms: 1380
Income from tourism: $18 m

Fig. 7.22

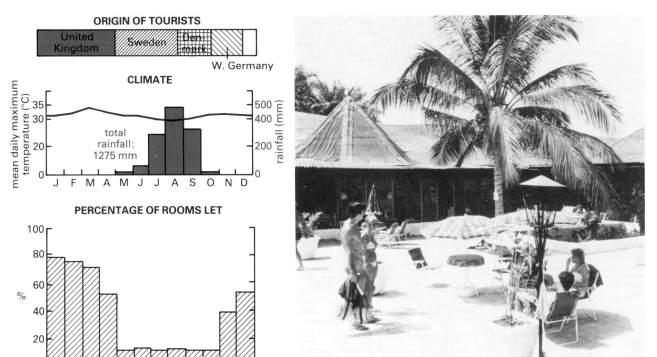

ORIGIN OF TOURISTS

United Kingdom | Sweden | Denmark | W. Germany

CLIMATE

total rainfall: 1275 mm

PERCENTAGE OF ROOMS LET

Fig. 7.23

Fig. 7.24 *Typical holiday complex: Wadua Beach, Gambia*

Trade between the Developed and Developing World

TERMS OF TRADE*

Year	Purchasing power of agricultural exports
1970	100
1977	96
1978	94
1979	86
1980	71
1981	69

* measured by the amount of manufactured goods and oil which can be bought by a given amount of agricultural exports from less developed countries. 1970 = 100.

The air, sea and land routes described in this chapter are the physical links which join together the many and varied countries of the world.

The traffic on these routes has produced a pattern of trade which greatly favours the industrialised nations of the Developed World. Furthermore, this imbalance in trade between the Developed and the Developing World is becoming more and more marked. One reason for this is recent changes in the terms of trade (see the adjacent table). The price of the raw materials (excluding oil) upon which the countries of the Developing World depend has risen less rapidly than the price of the manufactured goods produced by the developed nations. This means that poor countries have to export more and more raw materials and agricultural products simply to buy the same quantities of manufactured goods. This is a problem which has existed since the early days of colonialism; it has become much worse following the oil price rises of 1973.

Facing such problems, many developing countries have tried to increase the production of food and raw materials and to establish industries so as to reduce the need to import manufactured goods. In both cases large amounts of capital are needed and most of it has to be obtained from the Developed World (Fig. 7.25).

Investment by large companies

Many large multi-national companies have invested money in developing countries. They have built factories, opened mines and established farms to grow cash crops. The size of such investment is often large, particularly when compared with the wealth of the countries concerned. In spite of this, however, there are many doubts about the benefits gained from the investment.

1 The industries introduced are not always the industries which would most benefit a developing country. For example, too many make use of modern technology and employ few people in areas where unemployment and underemployment is widespread.

2 These industries also tend to attract local investment and this means that there is less money available to start more suitable industries or to improve farming. Furthermore, some of the profit will almost certainly be lost to the developing country.

3 The governments of the countries concerned may lose control over a large part of their economy and the multi-national company can play too great a part in the running of the country. These are serious problems but few of the less developed countries can afford to turn down the possibility of investment on such a scale.

Borrowing from banks

Less developed countries also obtain capital for development projects from banks. Sometimes these are normal commercial banks which charge normal rates of interest. Sometimes they are international institutions like the World Bank and the International Monetary Fund (IMF) which can offer lower rates of interest over a longer period of time. However, the IMF may impose conditions on the government of the country taking out the loan, forcing it to change some of its policies. This can cause resentment, particularly since the IMF is controlled by the rich countries of the Developed World.

There is also a danger that most loans will be made for large scale projects such as hydro-electric schemes, large manufacturing plants and the growing of cash crops. As we have seen, such schemes do not necessarily give the best returns to a developing country.

A more serious problem, however, is the amount of borrowing (and hence the size of the debt) and the effect it is likely to have on the future development of developing countries. In the early 1980s it was estimated that the less developed countries had borrowed more than $350 billion and that, with the worsening terms of trade, no less than one eighth of their total earnings from exports would be needed to pay the interest and to repay the debt. Even more disturbing, 20 of the developing countries accounted

TYPES OF AID + INVESTMENT IN LESS DEVELOPED COUNTRIES

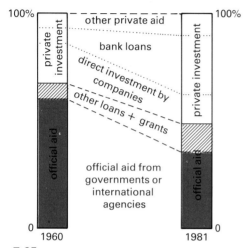

Fig. 7.25

WORLD DEBT: THE TEN LEADING DEBTOR NATIONS IN 1982

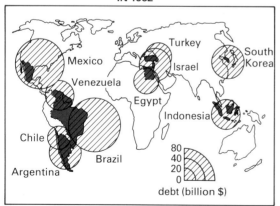

Fig. 7.26

DIFFICULTY OF REPAYING DEBTS

Country	Interest on debts as a % of yearly earnings from exports
Argentina	154
Israel	126
Mexico	126
Brazil	117
Chile	104
Venezuela	101
Turkey	65
S. Korea	49
Egypt	46
Indonesia	28

AID FOR DEVELOPING COUNTRIES

ONE VIEW

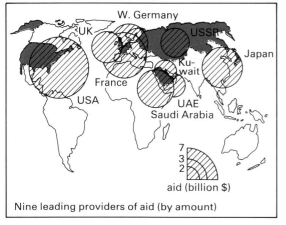

Nine leading providers of aid (by amount)

AN ALTERNATIVE VIEW

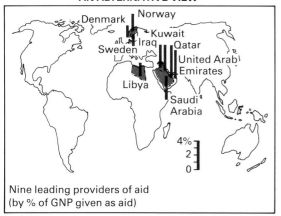

Nine leading providers of aid
(by % of GNP given as aid)

Fig. 7.27

for more than 80% of the total debt (Fig. 7.26). In these countries, which include Brazil, Mexico and Argentina, the burden of repaying the debts has become so great that the periods for repayment have been extended and in some cases new loans have been granted simply to repay the interest. Under these circumstances there is likely to be little money available for future development projects.

Foreign aid

Foreign aid became important after the end of the Second World War. Throughout this period it has been dominated by the flow of capital from the developed nations to the countries of the Developing World (Fig. 7.27). Since 1973, however, the OPEC countries have distributed some of the proceeds of oil sales as aid. The sums given are often large but they represent less than 1% of the GNP of the developed countries and in recent years this percentage has, if anything, tended to decline.

Aid is given in many different forms. For example, most aid is granted direct from one country to another. Conditions are often applied which benefit the country giving the aid. At its simplest this can mean nothing more than an agreement that any imported goods or materials required for the aid project will be bought from the country granting aid. At the other extreme aid can be used as a means of gaining influence over governments receiving help. A smaller amount is channelled through international agencies such as the World Bank. In this case the influence of individual countries is removed but there is still a tendency for aid to be given for projects which bring in imports from the Developed World, i.e. the countries giving the aid.

This problem is made worse by the fact that most aid is given to fund specific projects – usually large scale projects such as hydroelectric and irrigation schemes which require technologies available only in developed countries. Attempts to give aid which is not tied to specific projects have often simply encouraged the buying of more manufactured goods from developed countries, usually with little benefit to the country receiving the aid.

Other problems are equally serious.

1 Most aid is tied to specific projects which are usually large and are often unlikely to create many long term jobs. Not only this, they depend upon imported materials and this means that little encouragement is given to local industries. In recent years there has been increasing pressure to change this pattern by funding small scale projects which make use of local skills and encourage the development of local industries. Unfortunately such schemes are difficult to manage and the costs running them can be high.

2 In a world where a large proportion of the population in the less developed countries is on the verge of starvation, food aid is obviously needed. In spite of this, such aid makes up only 15% of the total aid given. To some extent this is the result of difficulties in distributing the aid in the areas of greatest need, where populations are often scattered and where transport is usually poor. In addition, it is known that such aid can be stolen by corrupt officials and in some countries it is feared that importing

217

food on such a large scale actually discourages farmers from trying to grow their own food under difficult conditions.

3   The most obvious response to this pressure has been the increased funding of schemes designed to improve food production in the less developed countries. Even here, however, there has been a tendency to concentrate on the large scale production of livestock and cash crops (often for export) rather than on improving the output of food on the small farms upon which most of the population depends.

4   Related to this there is a danger that it will be the better off who will benefit most from aid. For example, any improvements in farming, whether they are the introduction of irrigation or the provision of fertilisers, are likely to benefit those with the largest land holdings. These farmers will begin to earn more money and this may enable them to buy more land from the poorest members of the community. As a result the rich may become richer and the poor may become landless labourers. In short, aid can extend the division between rich and poor – the very division it is designed to reduce.

Given such problems, it is tempting to dismiss the aid given to developing countries as a pointless exercise designed to ease the consciences of the rich nations. This would, however, be a very dangerous conclusion to draw. The divide between the richest and the poorest nations in the world is already vast and it is growing. Aid is one method of trying to reduce this gap but it is not enough. Instead means must be found for establishing in developing countries economic activities which will provide long term employment and create new wealth. This involves not only more effort from the developed countries but also changes in the ways in which developing countries are governed. Unless such changes take place the problems of food supply and poverty will remain in a world which will become even more divided.

Fig. 7.28 *The start of an aid project in Ghana*

ne world?

The theme of this book has been the contrasts that exist in the world today. There is, as we have seen, much evidence to suggest that the world is deeply divided: between rich and poor; developed and less developed; and communist and capitalist. Such divisions or contrasts have been highlighted in the case studies relating to patterns of population growth and of settlement, to different systems of agriculture, and to the methods used for energy production and industry.

It is important, however, to recognise that in discussing these contrasts we are very often comparing other systems or patterns of development with our own and also drawing conclusions based on our own experience. In the last twenty years it has become apparent that models of development are all too often based on patterns of development in the Developed World. As we have seen, such models may be inappropriate both in terms of the technologies required and of the demands placed upon the developing countries. In many developing countries, particularly those with massive overseas debts, resources have been diverted into large scale production of cash crops and into the rapid exploitation of reserves of raw material. Such developments not only require large amounts of capital (which may have to be borrowed, thus adding to the debt problem) but have also often led to environmental problems, such as the destruction of the rain forests and the spread of deserts.

If the contrasts between the rich and poor and the Developing and Developed World are to be reduced, there are many basic assumptions of the development models that need to be questioned. We need to ask ourselves whether it is appropriate for the less developed countries to follow the example of development in the Developed World. Development in the advanced industrialised nations has brought with it many benefits but it has also created problems, such as pollution, unemployment, high crime rates and stress-related illnesses. Perhaps the developing countries can avoid these problems and reduce their debts to the Developed World by following plans for development that have been formulated to suit their own specific aims and needs. In Kenya, for example, much attention is given to conservation of the environment and management of wildlife; to the encouragement of small scale industries; to the use of appropriate technologies; and to education.

World Contrasts has set out to describe some of the contrasts between nations but it has also emphasised the links between them. This inter-relationship has been recognised as one of the most important factors for future development policies because we now know that an action taken in one part of the world is likely to affect other parts: despite the many contrasts we are, in fact, 'one world'.